I Eat Vegetarians

Cows are vegetarians, aren't they?

By

Mike Muth

2010

Mike's Books, Halstead, Kansas

Halstead, KS and Stadtlauringen-Fuchsstadt, Germany
June 17, 2009

This book is available in a variety of formats. If you don't see a format in which you would like to read this book, send an e-mail to publisher@unverbesserlich.org.

ISBN:
0-615-22203-X (ebook version)
0-9841042-0-8 (Print Version)

ISBN-13:
978-0-615-22203-5 (Kindle Version)
978-0-9841042-0-8 (Print Version)

Other books by Mike Muth:

The Speisekarte: Recipes from Mike's Place
Tag Lines: bumperstickers for your e-mail
Poor Michael's Almanac: for the month of October
Poor Michael's Almanac: for the month of November
Poor Michael's Almanac: for the month of December
Poor Michael's Almanac: for the month of January
Poor Michael's Almanac: for the month of February
Poor Michael's Almanac: for the month of March
Poor Michael's Almanac: for the month of April

Welcome stranger to this place,
Where joy doth sit on every bough,
Paleness flies from every face,
We reap not, what we do not sow.
-- William Blake, "Song 1st by a Shepherd"

Introduction

You hold in your hands a work of, if not love, at least pleasure. For over twelve years, I have enjoyed compiling this book. It is not a serious reference work; it is meant to be read. In places it will challenge and, perhaps, stretch your worldview. Most of all, though, the book should give you pleasure. This is a book which you can open to a random page and read for a bit. Some of these excerpts will puzzle you, some will leave you with a so-what feeling, some may even leave you wishing you had said that. And some may wake you up in the middle of the night.

I Eat Vegetarians is arranged alphabetically by name. I have made no attempt to group entries by subject and there is no index. Hey, you're supposed to read and enjoy this book, not use it as a reference. There is a hyperlinked table of contents to the alphabetic divisions.

You might ask, "Where did all this come from?" (Then again, you probably didn't.) A few items, like the Helmut Kohl quotation, came from television. Others came from contributions from friends. The Internet also provided more than a few pages. The vast majority of entries came from my reading (I read perhaps 100,000 pages a year.). Finally, I wrote some of the items. I've included stuff which struck my fancy or which just grabbed me by the ankles and yelled, "quote me!" My own section is limited to writings which other people have quoted or told me I should include. That's my story and I'm prepared to change it at need.

What you have has been revised dozens of times and bears little resemblance to the original work. I've pruned and grafted this creation (much as a farmer might care for his favorite fruit tree) - always seeking to keep within the de minimis* rules as applied to copyright law. There are some more twists and turns related to copyright law and you'll see some of that in the next section and in the appendices.

Since I work for Uncle Sam, I have to say: The viewpoints expressed in this book do not (and are not intended to) reflect the official (or unofficial) positions of the US Government, the US Army, or any government official. In fact, the views expressed herein are not necessarily mine. There's quite a bit in here with which I do not agree.

Most professional authors were kind enough to quickly grant permission. Some even provided additional material for potential inclusion. Many offered words of encouragement. There are literally hundreds of authors in this category, far too many to list. But they all deserve a big thanks. I got a bit of a kick from corresponding with these folks – people I otherwise would never have contacted.

Thanks to those who contributed in some way. Some encouraged the effort, some sent interesting items, and some critiqued my work. In alphabetical order: Allen Allison, Patti Avery-Bangert, Roger Brown, Linda Buix, Jeff Crabtree, "Heavy" Goodwin, Susan Keidan, Bob Knecht, Joel Knott, Gary Phelps, and Wayne Randall. Finally many thanks to my wife Ingeborg for putting up with me (and not just when I worked on this book).

I hope you enjoy reading this book as much as I enjoyed creating it.

* See Appendix 3

Table of contents

Note on Copyrights

This is a copyrighted work. Portions of this work may only be reproduced by the copyright owner with the following exceptions:

Some of the material is in the public domain. Generally speaking, material by an author who died more than 75 years ago is in the public domain – in the United States of America. Different countries have different rules about this. Since the extent of this material will change over time, I will leave this determination as an exercise for the reader.

You may freely quote anything which is attributed to me in the section which follows provided that you properly attribute the material with my name and the name of this document.

Some sections are included under the provisions of the GNU Free Documentation License. That work may be re-used under the terms of the license which can be found at Appendix 1. I have marked such sections with "(GFDL)" following the author's name. For example, you might see:

Harvey T. Hartsmoote (GFDL)

In this case, the material by Robert Heinlein which follows is subject to the terms of the GFDL. In those cases where some material is covered and some is not, I have segregated the quotations into two sections.

In other cases, I have obtained explicit authorization from the authors to quote them in this book. I have listed those authors in Appendix 2. If you wish to quote them in a manner which does not fall under Fair Use provisions, it is up to you to contact them and obtain permission. Even if Fair Use applies, it's still the right thing to contact them. Not one of the listed authors (or their agents) gave me any trouble and most responded very quickly. As I note elsewhere, I have removed dozens of pages of material because the authors did not grant permission.

~Anonymous or Unknown ~

A cat is always on the wrong side of the door.

A good sailor spits to leeward.

An injured Miami football player once said, "When you have two broken hands and go into the men's room, you find out who your real friends are."

Anarchy means having to put up with things that really tick you off.

Anyone who can't figure out that no company on the face of the earth is created to look out for his/her well-being, but rather to make money by any means legal or possible is far, far, away from reality.

Arguments with furniture are rarely productive.

Be kind to unkind people - they need it the most.

Casual sex is best because you don't have to wear a tie

Consensus does not equal right. It is possible for people to agree on something and for all of them to be wrong.

Did you ever get the idea that all of sports is chumps, druggies, or bozos?

Earn cash in your spare time, blackmail your friends.

Even the best of friends cannot attend each other's funeral.

Everyone has a sex life, it's just that some of them are livelier than others.

"Everyone knows" is not documentation.

Everyone's an idiot to someone else.

First law of Spam: SPAM expands to fill all space in your mailbox.

For a list of the ways technology has failed to improve the quality of life, please press two.

Human beings need limits and definition and parameters and borders to establish a sense of self, of being, of shape, of ability and that this sense is exactly what makes one truly free.

If there really is a pole at the North Pole, I'll bet there's some dead explorer guy with his tongue stuck to it.

If you voted for change, then you'd better start counting it.

Ignorance makes life easier.

It is a shame stupidity isn't painful.

Life is a rollercoaster. Try to eat a light lunch.

Miami, Florida is the most bizarre foreign country I have ever lived in.

Never call a man a fool. Borrow from him.

Nothing screams poor craftsmanship like wrinkly duct tape.

On the Internet, noone knows you're a dog, but they know instantly if you're an idiot.

Religion is not some kind of spiritual buffet table, where you pick and choose what you like, and leave the rest.

Remember: the average is as close to the bottom as it is to the top.

Security and freedom are like baseball and beer. They go well together, but are completely unrelated concepts.

Sex is like air: no big thing, unless you aren't getting any.

Slaves and captives are reusable if you don't break them :)

Some of the greatest pains in life can be contrived with marvelous ease.

The older you get, the easier it is to resist temptation but the harder it is to find.

The primary requisite for any new tax law is for it to exempt enough voters to win the next election.

The shortest distance between two points is under construction.

The surest sign that intelligent life exists elsewhere in the universe is that none of it has tried to contact us.

The thing I don't like about Wichita is the state symbol. It shouldn't be the sunflower, it should be the orange barrel.

The truth shall make you free, but first it shall make you angry.

There's no problem a high-powered rifle and a rooftop can't fix.

There is no snooze button on a cat who wants breakfast.

They don't have a problem with (repeat offenders) in the military because they kick them out.

Those who seek power are often those least suitable to wield it.

To make a bad day worse, spend it wishing for the impossible.

What is it exactly that surveyors do? One guy holds a stick. The other guy looks at it through a sight about thirty yards away. What do they learn from this? "I can see you you're holding a stick."

When all is said and done,
A battlefield is no fun.
"The Little Sergeant"

When shooting from the hip, people sometimes shoot themselves in the foot.

When subjected to extreme feminine heat and pressure, male hydrocarbons will produce a diamond.

When you go to court, you are putting your fate into the hands of twelve people who weren't smart enough to get out of jury duty.
[Although this is attributed to Norm Crosby, it's origin is unknown.]

Windows could be considered an exercise in sadomasochism. One must be a masochist to install the bloody thing.

You can get a lot more with a kind word and a gun than you can with a kind word alone.

Ancient computer saying

The three most dangerous things in the world are a programmer with a soldering iron, a hardware type with a program patch and a user with an idea.

Anonymous Indian chief, 1876

Tell your people that since the Great Father promised that we should never be removed we have been moved five times. I think you had better put the Indians on wheels so you can run them about wherever you wish.

Anonymous ISP executive

[Microsoft is] like an anthill, with all the ants moving in different directions. But when they leave the hill, that carcass is picked clean.

Anonymous West German artillery officer

We [the Bundeswehr] like this training area in Canada because, with its large open, flat areas, it is so much like the steppes of Russia.

Australian Aboriginal Elder

You white people are so strange. We think it is very primitive for a child to have only two parents.

English Professor

I am returning this otherwise good typing paper to you because someone has printed gibberish all over it and put your name at the top.

Epitaph for Leonidas and the 300

O Stranger! Go tell the Spartans that here we lie, obedient to their wishes.

Guard at the Grand Canyon

I guess people are basically stupid... you gotta hole in the ground, folks are gonna fall in the sucker.

Navy commander

As military officers and federal employees, one of the benefits we enjoy is the relative freedom from being sued personally as a result of job performance...In this litigious society, that is no small thing.

Not really Anonymous
[He just asked that I *not* use his name.]

Suffering is a necessary but not sufficient condition for true awareness. And sometimes it takes some help along the way to get there, more serious help than "smile...this is supposed to be a fun place."

Both offering and accepting that help are two of the more serious obligations we all have here, as sentient beings. If it were otherwise, God would have been better off giving us each a planet of our own.

~A~

Edward Abbey

Anarchism is founded on the observation that since few men are wise enough to rule themselves, even fewer are wise enough to rule others.

Power is always dangerous. Power attracts the worst and corrupts the best.

The patriot must always be prepared to defend his country from his government.

Paul Abrahams

A fool with a spreadsheet is still a fool.

First Baron John Emerich Edward Dalberg - Acton

Everything secret degenerates, even the administration of justice; nothing is safe that does not show how it can bear discussion and publicity.

Historic responsibility has to make up for the want of legal responsibility. Power tends to corrupt, and absolute power corrupts absolutely.

Ansel Adams

There is nothing worse than a sharp image of a fuzzy concept.

Cecil Adams

If hard data were the filtering criterion you could fit the entire contents of the Internet on a floppy disk.
- The Straight Dope Tells All

People nowadays have the historical awareness of squirrels

- http://www.straightdope.com/classics/a1_325.html

Douglas Adams

In the beginning, the universe was created. This made a lot of people very angry, and has been widely regarded as a bad idea.

Lot's of little synapses deep in his cerebral cortex all joined hands and started dancing around and singing nursery rhymes.

This, of course, is impossible...
- Hitchhiker's Guide to the Galaxy

What I love most about deadlines is the whooshing sound they make as they go by.

Henry Adams

No man means all he says, and yet very few say all they mean, for words are slippery and thought is viscous.

Practical politics consists in ignoring facts.

Joey Adams

Never let a fool kiss you, or a kiss fool you.

John Adams

It is not only [the trial juror's] right, but his duty to find the verdict according to his own best understanding, judgment and conscience, though in direct opposition to the direction of the court.

There is danger from all men. The only maxim of a free government ought to be to trust no man living with power to endanger the public liberty.

Mike Adams

Organic chemistry is the chemistry of carbon compounds. Biochemistry is the study of carbon compounds that crawl.

Samuel Adams

He who is void of virtuous attachments in private life is, or very soon will be, void of all regard for his country. There is seldom an instance of a man guilty of betraying his country, who had not before lost the feeling of moral obligations in his private connections.
-- Letter to James Warren, Nov. 4, 1775

Konrad Adenauer

An infallible method of conciliating a tiger is to allow oneself to be devoured.

History is the sum total of things that could have been avoided.

In view of the fact that God limited the intelligence of man, it seems unfair that He did not also limit his stupidity

The art of politics consists in knowing precisely when it is necessary to hit an opponent slightly below the belt.

The one sure way to conciliate a tiger is to allow oneself to be devoured.

Alfred Adler

It is easier to fight for one's principles than to live up to them.

Mortimer Adler

Friendship is a very taxing and arduous form of leisure activity.

Aeschylus

When a man's willing and eager, the gods join in.

Aesop

Any excuse will serve a tyrant.

Better beans and bacon in peace than cakes and ale in fear.

The fly sat on the axle tree of the chariot wheel and said, "What a dust do I raise!"

Agapet

When we associate with the virtuous we form ourselves in imitation of their virtues, or at least lose, every day, something of our faults.

Jean Louis Agassiz

Every great scientific truth goes through three stages: First, people say it conflicts with the Bible. Next they say it had been discovered before. Lastly, they say they always believed it.

Spiro Agnew

If you've seen one city slum, you've seen them all.

In the United States today, we have more than our share of the nattering nabobs of negativism. They have formed their own 4-H Club - the 'hopeless, hysterical hypochondriacs of history.

Howard Aiken

Don't worry about people stealing your ideas. If your ideas are any good, you'll have to ram them down people's throats.

Rabbi Akiva

True freedom is not the freedom to choose...it is the freedom from choosing.

Albanian Proverb

A woman must work harder than a donkey because a woman feeds on bread while a donkey feeds on grass.

Les Albert

Don't give up your day job, even if it is fraught with personal danger to you.

Forget about Help areas of the software. Real men just go into PLOK mode: Press Lots Of Keys.

If the bride is always beautiful then how come there are so many ugly wives?

It makes me think of Dorothy in 'The Wizard of Oz', but with lots of straps, zippers, and hooks-and-eyes.

Steam cars were smooth and silent until they exploded.

You are never too old to have a happy childhood.

Jim Albrecht

The great thing about living among freaks is that you have to do something really special to be shunned.

A.B. Alcott

To be ignorant of one's ignorance is the malady of the ignorant.
-- "Table Talk"

Sherri Alderson

If my husband looks at a pin-up and is so taken that he forgets his family, then he isn't the person I married and I am better off without him. On the flip side, I'm not going to poke his eyes out for looking at a pretty girl.

Aleksandr Aleksandrov (Soviet cosmonaut)

We were flying over America and suddenly I saw snow, the first snow we ever saw from orbit. I have never visited America, but I imagined that the arrival of autumn and winter is the same there as in other places, and the process of getting ready for them is the same. And then it struck me that we are all children of our Earth.

Ken Alibek

Smirnoff's product has done more than any foreign invader to undermine the health of Russian citizens.
- Biohazard

Cinan Alic

I believe it is good that the Americans are coming. But if the Russians come, that will not be good. You can buy a Russian general for 500 marks. There is not enough money in Tuzla to buy an American general.

Dante Alighieri

I am searching for that which every man seeks--peace and rest.

The hottest places in Hell are reserved for those who in time of great moral crises maintain their neutrality.

Saul Alinsky

Asking a sociologist to solve a problem is like prescribing an enema for diarrhea.

Once you accept your own death, all of a sudden you are free to live.

Power, or organized energy, may be a man-killing explosive or a life-saving drug. The power of a gun may be used to enforce slavery or to achieve freedom.

Ridicule is man's most potent weapon.

Herm Allbright

A positive attitude may not solve all your problems but it will annoy enough people to make it worth the effort.

Fred Allen

Hollywood is a place where people from Iowa mistake each other for movie stars.

I can't understand why a person will take a year to write a novel when he can easily buy one for a few dollars.

I have just returned from Boston. It is the only thing to do if you find yourself up there.

I like long walks, especially when they are taken by people who annoy me.

Steve Allen

Humor is a social lubricant that helps us get over some of the bad spots.

One of the nice things about problems is that a good many of them do not exist except in our imaginations.

The purpose of having an open mind is the same as having an open mouth, the object being eventually to close it on something solid. But one should never close either mind or mouth until the general circumstances of the moment make it reasonable to do so.

Tim Allen

Once you use a new paint tray, it's no good for serving snacks.

Tools are patient. Put 'em down in the middle of a job and they'll wait right there for you.

Margery Allingham

"Mourning is not forgetting," he said gently. "It is an undoing. Every minute tie has to be untied and something permanent and valuable recovered and assimilated from the dust."
-- The Tiger in the Smoke

Alan Allport

This is what I love about USENET. Whenever a potential flame-war is slowly simmering down, you can always rely on some berk to show up with a bottle of turpentine and a Zippo.

Guy Almes

There are three kinds of death in this world. There's heart death, there's brain death, and there's being off the network.

Robert Alston

But then anyone who shoots at anything against concrete or steel earns what they get.

Eric Alterman

My proudest achievement so far in life is managing to avoid law school.
- "Slacker Friday" Blog, July 20, 2005

Heinz Altmann

Loot is loot, and if the legal owner can be found, should be returned. Arguments that soldiers are entitled to booty (some call it souvenirs) are realistic, but they are not morally or legally sound.

The cardinal lesson to be learned from wars should be that enemies become friends, but only if both sides are willing, not to forget, but to forgive and move on.

The murder of a single human being is just as much of a crime, and is just as much to be mourned, as the annihilation of millions.

What is important today is that we do not use the past to give reason for misconduct now or in the future.

Barry Alvarez

When you think you've seen it all, you haven't seen it all.

Arnald Amaury, Papal Legate, at the surrender of Beziers

Kill them all, for God knows His own.

Bonzo Amin

Sometimes, all you can do is look at the smoking rubble and say "Oooops!

Kingsley Amis

If you can't annoy somebody, there's little point in writing.

Cleveland Amory

I can't take a well tanned person seriously.

There are three terrible ages of childhood   1 to 10, 10 to 20, and 20 to 30.

Hans Christian Anderson

Every man's life is a fairy tale written by God's fingers.

Harry Anderson (Night Court as Judge Harold T. Stone)

Even a fool knows you can't touch the stars, but it doesn't stop a wise man from trying.

Jeremy S. Anderson

There are two major products that come out of Berkeley: LSD and UNIX. We don't believe this to be a coincidence.

Poul Anderson

I have yet to see any problem, however complicated, which, when you looked at it in the right way, did not become still more complicated.

Sparky Anderson

A great leader doesn't humiliate any single individual.

It's a leader's responsibility to earn respect.

Nothing is free, except for one thing   that's to be nice. It doesn't cost you anything to be nice.

AngelClare

It's kinda fun to squick the vanillas, and a vanilla who publically [sic] notifies us that he is squicked can be said to be making a contribution to the overall festivities.

Piers Anthony (www.HiPiers.com)

It was easier to do nothing, in a democracy, than to agree on any positive course of action.
-- Anthonology, "Beak by Beak"

Dr. **Robert Anthony** (http://www.drrobertanthony.com)

If you let other people do it for you, they will do it to you.

Once a person believes that something is true, whether or not it is, he then acts as if it were. He will instinctively seek to collect facts to support the belief no matter how false it may be.

Some people drink from the fountain of knowledge, others just gargle.

When you blame others, you give up your power to change.

Susan B. Anthony

[Bicycling] has done more to emancipate women than any one thing in the world. It gives her a feeling of self-reliance and independence the moment she takes her seat; and away she goes, the picture of untrammelled womanhood.

Cautious, careful people, always casting about to preserve their reputations...can never effect a reform.

I distrust those people who know so well what God wants them to do, because I notice it always coincides with their own desires.

If all the rich and all of the church people should send their children to the public schools they would feel bound to concentrate their money on improving these schools until they met the highest ideals.

The older I get, the greater power I seem to have to help the world; I am like a snowball -- the further I am rolled the more I gain.

Why should we not accept all in favor of woman suffrage to our platform and association even though they be rabid pro-slavery Democrats.

Laura M Antoniou (www.lantoniou.com)

And thank you *very* much for buying my books. Every sale goes toward making sure I don't have to cook my cat for Thanksgiving. (Although I'm gettin' pretty tired of Ramen noodles. . .)

The difference is not what you name things; it's how you live and what you value.

When someone calls me a sinner, or says that I make them "uncomfortable", or that they "feel sorry for me", I have the right to pinpoint exactly what they're really saying - that I'm less human than they, that I have less of a right to live my life than a life that they would choose for me.

Thomas Aquinas (From Summa Theologica)

Further, the existence of truth is self-evident. For whoever denies the existence of truth grants that truth does not exist: and, if truth does not exist, then the proposition "Truth does not exist" is true: and if there is anything true, there must be truth.

Now, in things, neither truth nor falsity exists, except in relation to the intellect.

Our natural knowledge begins from sense. Hence our natural knowledge can go as far as it can be led by sensible things.

The existence of truth in general is self-evident but the existence of a Primal Truth is not self-evident to us.

This is part of the infinite goodness of God, that He should allow evil to exist, and out of it produce good.

Arab proverb

Thank Allah, for in his wisdom he put death at the end of life, and not at the beginning.

The whisper of a pretty girl can be heard further than the roar of a lion.

Trust in Allah, but tie your camel.

Gaius Petronius Arbiter (Actually from a unknown British Army NCO)

We trained hard but it seemed that every time we were beginning to form into teams, we would be reorganized. I was to learn later in life that we tend to meet any new situation by reorganizing. And what a wonderful method it can be for creating the illusion of progress while producing confusion, inefficiency, and demoralization.

John Arbuthnot

All political parties die at last of swallowing their own lies.

Archimedes

Give me a lever and place to stand, and I will move the world.

Robert Ardrey

Human war has been the most successful of our cultural traditions.

But we were born of risen apes, not fallen angels, and the apes were armed killers besides. And so what shall we wonder at? Our murders and massacres and missiles, and our irreconcilable regiments? Or our treaties whatever they may be worth; our sympathies however seldom they may be played; our peaceful acres, however frequently they may be converted to battlefields; our dreams however rarely they may be accomplished. The miracle of man is not how far he has sunk but how magnificently he has risen. We are known among the stars by our poems, not our corpses.

Aristophanes

You have all the characteristics of a popular politician: a horrible voice, bad breeding, and a vulgar manner.

Aristotle

A democracy is a government in the hands of men of low birth, no property, and vulgar employments.

A proper wife should be as obedient as a slave...The female is a female by virtue of a certain lack of qualities - a natural defectiveness.

Anyone can become angry. That is easy. But to be angry with the right person, to the right degree, at the right time, for the right purpose and in the right way - that is not easy.

Dignity consists not in possessing honors, but in the consciousness that we deserve them.

Excellence is an art won by training and habituation. We do not act rightly because we have virtue or excellence, but rather we have those because we have acted rightly. We are what we repeatedly do. Excellence, then, is not an act but a habit.

How many a dispute could have been deflated into a single paragraph if the disputants had dared to define their terms?

It is the mark of an educated mind to be able to entertain a thought without accepting it.

It is not always the same thing to be a good man and a good citizen.

It is unbecoming for young men to utter maxims.

Man is by nature a political animal.

The gods too are fond of a joke.

There is a foolish corner in the brain of the wisest man.

There was never a genius without a tincture of madness.

We are what we repeatedly do. Excellence then, is not an act but a Habit.

We give up leisure in order that we may have leisure, just as we go to war in order that we may have peace.

What lies in our power to do, it lies in our power not to do.
- Nicomachean Ethics

Richard Armour

Beauty is only skin deep, and the world is full of thin-skinned people.

Neil Armstrong

I believe every human has a finite number of heartbeats. I don't intend to waste any of mine running around doing exercises.

Rebekka Armstrong (www.rebekkaarmstrong.com/)

Something hit me when I was 15, and I decided to become more feminine. So I wore a dress over the combat boots.

Tom Armstrong

Let me see if I've got this Santa business straight. You say he wears a beard, has no discernible source of income and flies to cities all over the world under cover of darkness? You sure this guy isn't laundering illegal drug money?
- "Marvin"

Ramona E. F. Arnett

The perception of a problem is always relative. Your headache feels terrific to the druggist.

Poncianá Arriaga

How can we have popular government when the people are naked, miserable, and starving?

Mike Ash

I think it would be more pleasant for everybody involved if you just stopped reading whatever it is that you don't like instead of erupting in a tirade every time somebody agrees with you.

Clifford W. Ashley, The Ashley Book of Knots

Without doubt my critics would have been entirely satisfied if I had announced that I proposed to write a book on the subject, for the urge to write a book is nowadays accepted as ample excuse for almost any delinquency.

Elizabeth Ashley

In a great romance, each person plays a part the other really likes.

Carole Ashmore

Hang in there. Don't let the overbearing cowhide fetishists get you down. Your decidedly perverse attraction to suits and ties (you **are** a masochist, right?) is no less a legitimate kink than their's [sic].

Robert Asprin

When things are blackest, I just tell myself 'cheer up, things could be worse!' And sure enough, they get worse.

John Astin

The world is, for the most part, a collective madhouse, and practically everyone, however "normal" his facade, is faking sanity.

Nancy Astor

I married beneath me-- all women do.

Chester G. Atkins

In presidential elections and in second marriages, people look for the exact qualities missing in their previous choices.

Brooks Atkinson

After each war there is a little less democracy to save.

When a pious visitor inquired sweetly, "Henry, have you made your peace with God?" he [Thoreau] replied, "We have never quarreled."

Mark Atwood

In my defense, I was posting fast from an unfamiliar computer while playing with a new cat.

St. Augustine

A thing is not necessarily true because badly uttered, nor false because spoken magnificently.

If the true is that which is, it will be concluded that the false exists nowhere; whatever reason may appear to the contrary.
-- Soliloq. ii, 8

Judge nothing before the end.

Out of all things is built up the admirable beauty of the universe, wherein even that which is called evil, properly ordered and disposed, commends the good more evidently in that good is more pleasing and praiseworthy when contrasted with evil.
-- Enchiridion 10, 11

Since God is the highest good, He would not allow any evil to exist in His works, unless His omnipotence and goodness were such as to bring good even out of evil.
-- Enchiridion xi

The good Christian should beware of mathematicians and all those who make empty prophecies. The danger already exists that mathematicians have made a covenant with the devil to darken the spirit and confine man in the bonds of Hell.

To many, total abstinence is easier than perfect moderation.

Truth is that whereby is made manifest that which is.
-- De Vera Relig. xxxvi

St. Augustus

A nation is an association of reasonable beings, peacefully sharing the things that they cherish. To determine the quality of the nation, these things have to be examined.

Marcus Aurelius

Adapt yourself to the environment in which your lot has been cast, and show true love to the fellow-mortals with whom destiny has surrounded you.

Jane Austen

One half of the world cannot understand the pleasures of the other.

I do not want people to be agreeable, as it saves me the trouble of liking them.

Run mad as often as you choose, but do not faint.

Amy Austin (http://prettybabies.blogspot.com)

I mean, you'd be irritable, too, if someone were trying to cut open your skull with a dull axe.

See, it's easier to just let everyone make their own choices. Then you have so much time free with which to run your own life...

The sum of your experience does not equal the sum of the diversity in the world.

Bernard Avishai

The danger from computers is not that they will eventually get as smart as men, but that we will meanwhile agree to meet them halfway.

The Avocado Avenger

My favorite thing about onion rings was taking the first bite and pulling out the sweet onion, then having breaded grease left to nibble on.

Lee Ayrton

I prefer my crap to be well written, peer-reviewed, footnoted crap.

Hint for homeowners buying their very own sawzall/tigersaw/&c: Hot blades look exactly the same as cold blades. Be careful when changing or tightening a recently used blade.

It isn't that we're going to Hell in a hand basket but that we arrived there long ago.

What happens if I stop believing in gravity?

~B~

Babylonian Proverb

The Gods do not deduct from a man's allotted span the hours spent in fishing.

Johan Sebastian Bach

There's nothing remarkable about it. All one has to do is hit the right keys at the right time and the instrument plays itself.

Richard Bach

Live never to be ashamed if anything you do or say is published around the world... even if what is published is not true.

Your friends will know you better in the first minute you meet than your acquaintances will know you in a thousand years.

Daniel Bacon

Female influence when judiciously exerted gives character to any spot.

Francis Bacon

A wise man will make more opportunities than he finds.

Imagination was given to man to compensate him for what he is not; a sense of humor to console him for what he is.

Knowledge itself is power.

Walter Bagehot

The reason why so few good books are written is that so few people who can write know anything.

George Bailey, "It's a Wonderful Life"

I'm shaking the dust of this crummy little town off my feet and I'm going to see the world!

Pearl Bailey

What the world really needs is more love and less paper work.

Alan Baker

If you raise the ceiling 4 feet, move the fireplace from that wall to that wall, you'll still only get the full stereophonic effect if you sit in the bottom of that cupboard.

Keiko Baker

Children don't play in Japan, they study.

Russell Baker (GFDL)

In America, it is sport that's the opiate of the masses.
- "The Muscular Opiate"

New York is the only city in the world where you can get deliberately run down on the sidewalk by a pedestrian.

Usually, terrible things that are done with the excuse that progress requires them are not really progress at all, but just terrible things.
- "The Fact About Progress"

Mikhail A. Bakunin

In politics, as in high finance, duplicity is regarded as a virtue.

Bill Baldwin

A foolish topicality is the hobgoblin of little minds.

As long as those people know that this is the wrong way and cheerfully admit it and secretly plot against the cat or the baby, I can make an exception.

Embrace your fogeyness.

Human birth control pills work on gorillas. Of course, looking at a female gorilla is pretty much all the birth control you need.

I am so confident of this that I am prepared to run like a screaming weenie from anyone who wants to fight over it.

I guess I knew that you weren't trying to say what you said. But I really don't know what it is you didn't say that you may have thought you said instead of what you did say which is what you didn't mean.

I like symmetry. Sometimes I try to see it when it's not there.

If black cats are demonized then only demons will have black cats.

If you suggest my wife has a reason to like vibrating coasters, I may have to punch you.

When you're smart, it's hard to accept that other smart people disagree with you. It threatens the whole basis of your opinions.

Without the garlic and lime, your guacomole will never taste like what you get at the taco stand or El Torito. I am so confident of this that I am prepared to run like a screaming weenie from anyone who wants to fight over it.

Why do I associate with fornicators and idolaters and the godless? Because I love you guys.

You've got to get up pretty early in the morning to make a lame joke before I do.

James Baldwin

Children have never been very good at listening to their elders, but they have never failed to imitate them.

The price one pays for pursuing any profession or calling is an intimate knowledge of its ugly side.

Stanley Baldwin

War would end if the dead could return.

Arthur Balfour

History does not repeat itself. Historians repeat each other.

David Ball

You know, it takes forever to get out of Texas. And then when you do, you're in Oklahoma.

Ivern Ball

A politician is a person who can make waves and then make you think he's the only one who can save the ship.

Ever notice that people never say "It's only a game when they're winning?"

These days, the wages of sin depend on what kind of deal you make with the publisher

Jerry Ball

If you're shooting a six shooter and it's got five bullets, is it a six shooter or a five shooter?

Sal Bando

[Baseball players chew tobacco because] You're outdoors where you can spit.

Tallulah Bankhead

Critics are like legless men who teach running.

If I had to live my life again, I'd make the same mistakes, only sooner.

It's the good girls who keep the diaries; the bad girls never have the time.

Henri Barbusse

Dampness rusts men like rifles, more slowly but more deeply.

Clive Barker

Be regular and orderly in your life, that you may be violent and original in your work.
- Jihad

Charles Barkley

Somebody hits me, I'm going to hit him back. Even if it does look like he hasn't eaten in a while.
(after blatantly elbowing an Angolan basketball player in the Olympics)

The Alamo I know rents cars.

Donald L. Barlett & James B. Steele
[Both of these gentlemen have said they did not utter the following quotation – which has been repeatedly attributed to them and no one else on the web.]

Worried that the people who represent you in Congress are taking care of themselves and their friends at your expense?

You're right.

Clive Barnes

Television is the first truly democratic culture; the first culture available to everybody and entirely governed by what the people want. The most terrifying thing is what people do want.

Scott Barnes

Sometimes misinformation can be hard to unlearn.

Joe Barr

Please remember to use complete sentences when flaming others for their grammar.

Jonetta Rose Barras

I came to know that we are all more alike than different

John Barrymore

The good die young because they see it's no use living if you've got to be good.

Randall Bart

I'm new around here, so I can't tell if you're joking or ignorant.

Mildred Barthel

Happiness is a conscious choice, not an automatic response.

R. S. Barton

Maybe Computer Science should be in the College of Theology.

Systems programmers are the high priests of a low cult.

Bernard Baruch

To me, old age is always 15 years older than I am.

Basque proverb

Beware of women with beards and men without them.

Charles Baudelaire

Life is a hospital in which every patient is possessed by the desire of changing his bed. One would prefer to suffer near the fire, and another is certain he would get well if he were by the window.

What is irritating about love is that it is a crime that requires an accomplice.

Jerry Bauer

Apparently, he was one hound-dog shy of a full porch.

Isn't Pearl Harbor where Hearst paid the Spanish to sink the Alamo and start the Civil War, so TDR could lead the Minute Men up Pork Chop Hill?

Bruce Baum

I don't know what's wrong with my television set. Last night I was getting C-Span and the Home Shopping Network on the same channel, and I actually bought a congressman.

L. Frank Baum

But Destiny had singled me out, humble though I was, for a grander fate!
- H.M. Wogglebug, T.E., The Marvelous Land of Oz

Dangers, when they cannot be avoided, are often quite interesting and I am willing to go wherever you two venture to go.
- Woot the Wanderer, The Tin Woodman of Oz

Everything in life is unusual until you get accustomed to it.
- The Scarecrow, The Marvelous Land of Oz

I am glad you find me conceited, for that proves I know my good qualities.
- Quox, Tik-Tok of Oz

I'm only a little girl from Kansas, and we've got more dignity at home than we know what to do with.
- Dorothy Gale, Ozma of Oz

If you love us, do not inflict your burdens on us; be unhappy all by yourself.
- Cowardly Lion, The Lost Princess of Oz

"It must be dreadful to be stuffed full of wisdom," remarked Wiljon reflectively, and eyeing the Frogman with a doubtful look. "It is my good fortune to know very little."
- The Lost Princess of Oz

Laws were never meant to be understood, and it is foolish to make the attempt.
- Nick Chopper (The Tin Woodman), The Marvelous Land of Oz

"Thoughtless people are not unusual," observed the Scarecrow, "but I consider them more fortunate than those who have useless or wicked thoughts and do not try to curb them."
- The Tin Woodman of Oz

To be individual, my friends, to be different from others, is the only way to become distinguished from the common herd. Let us be glad, therefore, that we differ from one another in form and disposition.
- Cowardly Lion, The Lost Princess of Oz

Well, I was born on a farm in Kansas, and I guess that's being just as 'spectable and haughty as living in a cave with your tail tied to a rock. If it isn't I'll have to stand it, that's all.
- Dorothy Gale, Dorothy and the Wizard In Oz

Pierre Bayle

No nations are more warlike than those professing Christianity.

Brett Bayne

I've gotta stop getting all of my botanical data from cartoons.

Dover Beach

22-year-olds have always been naive and self-centered, and getting their little snowflake asses kicked a few times on the job will wake them up.

As my mother has always said, blood is thicker than water, and lots nastier.

Do you think that all opinions are equally correct? I don't. Most people here don't. That's why we argue.

Have some gin and chocolate and simmer down, Ms Size Six.

I foresee parents getting pushed to quit telling the kids that they're special and instead tell them to suck it up and do some work even if they don't like it.

I know this is true because I have thought about it very hard.

I only watch bad movies that have giant ants.

Mostly I just eat Doritos and curse the darkness.

My outfits are cute and complicated.

Of all the things that I could do to drive men away, I think karaoke might work the fastest. It might work faster than bitching about how fat my thighs are, which is definitely in the top five men-repelling activities.

Peter S. Beagle

It is a great mistake to try to cure a man of paranoia, for it gives him just as clear an understanding of the innards of the universe as Psychology or religion.
- I See by My Outfit, copyright (c) 1965 Avicenna Development Corporation
(www.peterbeagle.com)

Louise Beal

Love thy neighbor as thyself, but choose your neighborhood.

Richard Beal and Robert Sward
[*Although both of these selections have been attributed to these two authors, both deny having written them. They were too good to leave out, so just remember that Richard Bean and Robert Sward did not write them*]

So you're cruising down the highway and you glance up in the rearview mirror. Uh oh, you're hair is a complete mess! It's not like you're some vain, conceited marketing dweeb, but really, it's a knotty, tangled mess! Do you wait until you get to the office and brush it out in the parking lot? Hell no, someone could see you and think to themselves, "Look at that slob, did squirrels nest in that hair?". The smart (and fashionable) thing to do is root around and find your brush, adjust your mirror so you can get a real good look at your head and start working on making you beautiful again.

Don't worry about the cars around you, they'll get out of your way while you deal with your hair. Your looks are much more important then their safety, obviously.

Why is it wrong to hate someone you don't know and wish that their head would pop like a raw egg in a microwave? Is it wrong? I don't think so. At least not when they drive like total boobs in front of you.

Charles Austin Beard

You need only reflect that one of the best ways to get yourself a reputation as a dangerous citizen these days is to go about repeating the very phrases which our founding fathers used in their struggle for independence.

General d'Armee **Andre Beaufre**

A gigantic technological race is in progress...a new form of strategy is developing in peacetime...There are no battles in this strategy...Its tactics are industrial, technical, and financial...A silent and apparently peaceful war is in progress.

Pierre-Augustin Caron De Beaumarchais

Drinking when we are not thirsty and making love all year round, madam; that is all there is to distinguish us from other animals.
- The Marriage of Figaro

Ralph Beaumont

Raise less corn and more hell.

Carl Becker

Idealism must always prevail on the frontier, because the frontier, whether geographical or intellectual, offers little hope to those who see things as they are. To venture into the wilderness, one must see it, not as it is, but as it will be.

Pete Becker

[B]usiness decisions based on opinions garnered from newsgroups are inherently more risky than business decisions based on sound legal advice. I don't understand why this is so controversial.

Most risky of all are the things you think you understand and don't.

Stephen Becker

If judges were required to sit stark naked we would have more justice.
- A Covenant With Death

Samuel Beckett

Human existence is a logical impossibility.

Sir Thomas Beecham

There are two golden rules for an orchestra: start together and finish together. The public doesn't give a damn what goes in between.

Henry Ward Beecher

Books are not made for furniture, but there is nothing else that so beautifully furnishes a house.

Hold yourself responsible for a higher standard than anybody else expects of you. Never excuse yourself. Never pity yourself. Be a hard master to yourself - and be lenient to everybody else.

In the ordinary business of life, industry can do anything which genius can do, and very many things which it cannot.

It is not merely cruelty that leads men to love war, it is excitement.

Many men are stored full of unused knowledge. Like loaded guns that are never fired off, or military magazines in times of peace, they are stuffed with useless ammunition.

Never forget what a man says to you when he is angry.

Where is human nature so weak as in a bookstore?

Brendan Behan

Critics are like eunuchs in a harem; they know how it's done, they've seen it done every day, but they're unable to do it themselves.

I have never seen a situation so dismal that a policeman couldn't make it worse.

I value kindness to humans first of all, and kindness to animals. I don't respect the law; I have total irreverence for anything connected with society except that which makes the roads safer, the beer stronger, the food cheaper, and old men and women warmer in the winter, and happier in the summer.

It's not that the Irish are cynical. It's rather that they have a wonderful lack of respect for everything and everybody.

Arnold Beichmen

The myth of socialism is far stronger than the reality of capitalism. That is because capitalism is not really an ism at all. It is what people do if you leave them alone.

Harry Belafonte

A group without a leader is but a mob. A mob with a leader is a country.

Alexander Graham Bell

When one door closes another door opens; but we so often look so long and so regretfully upon the closed door, that we do not see the ones which open for us.

James Warner Bellah

A dead soldier who has given his life because of the failure of his leader is a dreadful sight before God. Like all dead soldiers, he was tired, possibly frightened to his soul, and there he is on top of all that never again to see his homeland. Don't be the one who failed to instruct him properly, who failed to lead him well. Burn the midnight oil, so that you may not in later years look upon your hands and find his blood still red upon them.

Never apologize son, it's a sign of weakness.
- Nathan Brittles, "She Wore a Yellow Ribbon"

Hillaire Belloc

The standard of intellect in politics is so low, men of moderate mental capacity have to stoop to reach it.

Robert Benchley

A dog teaches a boy fidelity, perseverance, and to turn around three times before lying down.

It took me fifteen years to discover that I had no talent for writing, but I couldn't give it up because by then I was too famous.

The surest way to make a monkey of a man is to quote him.

There are several ways to apportion the family income, all of them unsatisfactory.

Benedict XVI

Christianity is not an intellectual system, a collection of dogmas, or a moral system. Christianity is an encounter, a love story, an event.

In a society which values personal freedom and autonomy, it is easy to lose sight of our dependence on others as well as the responsibilities that we bear towards them. . . . We were created as social beings who find fulfillment only in love -- for God and for our neighbor.

Only when their faith permeates every aspect of their lives do Christians become truly open to the transforming power of the Gospel.

Ruth Benedict

If we justify war it is because all peoples always justify the traits of which they find themselves possessed.

Stephen Vincent Benet

Make war on the men--the ladies have too-long memories.

There comes a point when driven men and women revolt against blood and horror.
- "We Aren't Superstitious"

Thomas Bennett

You Europeans are so smug, I mean smart.

William J. Bennett

Happiness is like a cat. If you try to coax it or call it, it will avoid you. It will never come. But if you pay no attention to it and go about your business, you'll find it rubbing up against your legs and jumping into your lap.

Honor never grows old, and honor rejoices the heart of age. It does so because honor is, finally, about defending those noble and worthy things that deserve defending, even if it comes at a high cost. In our time, that may mean social disapproval, public scorn, hardship, persecution, or as always, even death itself. The question remains: What is worth defending? What is worth dying for? What is worth living for?
- in a lecture to the United States Naval Academy November 24, 1997

Jack Benny

I really don't deserve this, but I have arthritis and I don't deserve that either.

Annie Benson-Lennaman

Anything can be wonderful in the short term. I mean, even a visit to the dentist can be relaxing in the short term, since you get to sit in a big old over-sized, mechanical chair and experience interesting levels of anesthesia legally. But then the dark side shows up, known as the drill. Or strings. Whatever. One minute you're just having fun, letting your body take you on a ride, then the next, blammo! You're in way over your head.

This is how people end up with root canals. Or married. And it happens to women too, as I'll gladly attest to when I'm drunk.

Jeremy Bentham

Every law is an infraction of liberty.

Lawyers are the only persons in whom ignorance of the law is not punished.

Ingrid Bergman

Happiness is good health and a bad memory.

David Berlind, Information Week and Tech Web & four-time father

Compared with sitting in front of a computer; I'd like to think there's something therapeutic about walking the aisles of Toys R Us.
- From an article in PC Week

You can't change the truth; just the list of people who know it.

Hector-Louis Berlioz

Time is the best teacher. Unfortunately, it kills all its pupils.

Daniel Bernstein <cs962091@ariel.cs>

Having worked for my university's helpdesk... I have to say that having an IQ as high as some adults doesn't mean very much...

Judge **Mark Bernstein**

The law in its majesty applies equally to highly paid executives and minimum wage clerks

Bert Beros

He'd heard us talk democracy - They preach it to his face -
Yet knows that in our Federal House there's no one of his race.
- "The Colored Digger"

May the mothers of Australia
when they offer up a prayer
Mention those impromptu angels
with their fuzzy wuzzy hair.
- "Fuzzy Wuzzy Angels"

Yogi Berra

Baseball is ninety percent mental. The other half is physical.

I didn't say everything I said.

If you don't know where you're going, you'll end up somewhere else.

It was impossible to get a conversation going, everybody was talking too much.

Nobody goes there anymore; it's too crowded.

You can observe a lot just by watching.

You got to be very careful if you don't know where you're going, because you might not get there.

Corlin O. Beum

A job not worth doing is not worth doing well.

Bhagavad-Gita

I have become Death, the Destroyer of Worlds.

Elizabeth Bibesco

Blessed are those who can give without remembering and take without forgetting.

Ambrose Bierce

Ah, that we could fall into women's arms without falling into their hands.

Education is that which discloses to the wise and disguises from the foolish their lack of understanding.

Slang is the speech of him who robs the literary garbage cans on their way to the dump.

Somebody has attempted to rob the safe in the office of the City and County Treasurer. This is rushing matters; the impatient scoundrel ought to try his hand at being a Supervisor first. From Supervisor to Thief the transition is natural and easy.

We give the same name to a woman's lack of temptation and man's lack of opportunity.

Josh Billings

The best way to convince a fool he is wrong is to let him have his way.

Love looks through a telescope; envy, through a microscope.

When I see a man of shallow understanding extravagantly clothed, I feel sorry - for the clothes.

Augustine Birrell

An ordinary man can...surround himself with two thousand books...and thenceforward have at least one place in the world in which it is possible to be happy.

Charles Bishop

I dunno, maybe I'll remember and be coherent, later.

When I'm on my deathbed, I'm going to regret the time I spent on this [Usenet] thread.

Bishop187 <bishop187@aol.com>

Racism is being blind and thinking you can see...

Otto von Bismarck

A little caution outflanks a large cavalry.

Bits & Pieces

One of the quickest ways to meet new people is to pick up the wrong ball on a golf course.

Shirley Temple Black

I stopped believing in Santa Claus at age six when my mother took me to see him in a store and he asked for my autograph.

Black Hawk, Oglala chief

These lands once belonged to the Kiowas and Crows, but we whipped these nations out of them, and in this we did what the white men do when they want the lands of the Indians.

Red Blaik

In its steep physical, mental and moral challenges, in its sacrifices, selflessness and courage, football, beyond any game invented by man, is closest to war.

William Blake

And we are put on earth a little space

That we may learn to bear the beams of love

How do you know but ev'ry bird that cuts the airy way

Is an immense world of delight, only clos'd by your senses five?

It is easier to forgive an Enemy than to forgive a Friend.

Man's perceptions are not bounded by organs of perception

He perceives more than sense (though ever so acute) can discover

Prisons are built with stones of Law, Brothels with bricks of Religion.
-"Proverbs of Hell"

Marc Bloch

Peasants and workers, whom one expects to be uncouth, are often remarkably sensitive.

Robert Bloch

I like to tell people I have the heart of a small boy...And then I tell them that I keep it in a jar on my desk.

William J. H. Boetcker

You cannot further the brotherhood of man by inciting class hatred.

Bruce Bogaert

Your own happiness increases the more you give your happiness away.

Humphrey Bogart

A hot dog at the ballpark is better than steak at the Ritz.

The difference between life and a movie script is that the script has to make sense.

Niels Bohr

Never express yourself more clearly than you think.

The opposite of a correct statement is a false statement. But the opposite of a profound truth may well be another profound truth.

You are not thinking. You are merely being logical.

Derek Bok, Harvard President Emeritus

If you think education is expensive, try ignorance.

[He writes that Ann Landers attributed this to him, but he doesn't remember saying this.]

Tommy Bolt

I never threw a golf club that didn't deserve it.

If you are going to throw a club, it is important to throw it ahead of you, down the fairway, so you don't have to waste energy going back to pick it up.

Erma Bombeck

I do not participate in any sport with ambulances at the bottom of a hill.

Dieuwke Wendelaar Bonga, Eight Prison Camps: A Dutch Family in Japanese Java

I sincerely hope that whoever reads my story may learn that hate destroys, that wars should not be fought, they should be prevented.

Wherever we live on this planet, we will observe cruelty, envy, hunger, thirst, humiliation, fear, and darkness. I experienced it all and the memory will always stay with me. And even if God did not always seem to be there with us in the camps when were so forlorn, we kept our faith. We hope, we loved and, through prayer, we became survivors in our weakest hours.

Buckaroo Bonzai

No matter where you go, there you are.

Book of Leviathan

Short is the pain, long is the ornament

Daniel J. Boorstin

A wonderful thing about a book, in contrast to a computer screen, is that you can take it to bed with you.

I write to discover what I think. After all, the bars aren't open that early.

Reading is like the sex act - done privately, and often in bed.

We easily forget that smog is the price of freedom of our streets from manure, and from the flies and diseases it brought.

Elayne Boosler

I have six locks on my door all in a row. When I go out, I lock every other one. I figure no matter how long somebody stands there picking the locks, they are always locking three.

When women are depressed they either eat or go shopping. Men invade another country.

Maj. **Stephen Booth**, USAF Chaplain

When I say "the body of Christ," the proper response is "amen" not "hoo ah."

William H. Borah

The marvel of all history is the patience with which men and women submit to burdens unnecessarily laid upon them by their governments.

James H. Boren

Guidelines for bureaucrats:
1) When in charge ponder
2) When in trouble delegate
3) When in doubt mumble.

Nathaniel Borenstein

The most likely way for the world to be destroyed, most experts agree, is by accident. That's where we come in; we're computer professionals. We cause accidents.

Victor Borge

Santa Claus has the right idea. Visit people once a year.

Alan Bostick

It is very difficult to do good science involving human sexual behavior. Unfortunately, this doesn't seem to stop a lot of researchers in the field.

Alec Bourne

It is possible to store the mind with a million facts and still be entirely uneducated.

Randolph Bourne

If you are not an idealist by the time you are twenty you have no heart, but if you are still an idealist by the time you are thirty, you don't have a head.

Jim Bouton

Life is a big s*** sandwich, the more bread you got, the less s*** you eat.

You see, you spend a good piece of your life gripping a baseball, and in the end it turns out that it was the other way around all the time.

Francis Bowen

To become a thoroughly good man is the best prescription for keeping a sound mind and a sound body.

Paul Bowers

When the law supports idiots, idiotic things happen

S. Clint Bradford

A fool and his money are soon partying.

Bo Bradham

Does the idea of a financial adviser named Skip make anyone else nervous?

You know, I started this thread and I don't even remember what it is about.

F.H. Bradley

The secret of happiness is to admire without desiring.

Omar Bradley

The way to win an atomic war is to make certain it never starts.

Bobby Bragan

The biggest ovation I ever got came in Milwaukee when I told them I was leaving, but it got real quiet when I said I was taking the team with me to Atlanta.

Gloria Brame

Aha, so you're sucking up? A very attractive quality in a man, I must say.

As anyone who's ever had sex knows, sex is fundamentally mysterious. We don't know just how and why it all works, all we know is that it seems to work differently for different people.

I've often wondered whether those people who compulsively collect thimbles are really so very different from foot fetishists who compulsively collect shoes.

If you ask me, EVERYTHING from our spirituality to our eating habits is connected to our sexuality.

There are different types of consent and different levels of consent...

Yes, I always wonder about those people who spent hours and hours poring through messages and then condemn them as being sick.

Justice **Louis D. Brandeis**

Our government...teaches the whole people by its example. If the government becomes the lawbreaker, it breeds contempt for law; it invites every man to become a law unto himself; it invites anarchy.

The greatest dangers to liberty lurk in insidious encroachment by men of zeal, well meaning but without understanding.

The most important political office is that of private citizen.

The right most valued by civilized men is the right to be let alone.

Aaron Brandon

I will gladly start a flame war over brussels sprouts. Those little balls of bitter hell deserve the Agent Orange treatment...In fact, I propose that we wage war on Belgium (the Phlegms) for lending their name to what is clearly Satan's vegetative manifestation on earth

Dick Brandon

Documentation is like sex: when it is good, it is very, very good; and when it is bad, it is better than nothing.

Mike Brandt

The Lawrence Welk Show is Barney for adults.

W. C. Brann

Baylor University stands four square against heresy, the Papacy and lunacy, but up to its neck in hypocrisy.

Werner von Braun

Crash programs fail because they are based on the theory that, with nine women pregnant, you can get a baby a month.

The best computer is a man, and it's the only one that can be mass-produced by unskilled labor.

Bertholt Brecht

He who laughs has not yet heard the bad news.

If there are obstacles, the shortest line between two points may be a crooked line.

It isn't important to come out on top. What matters is to be the one who comes out alive.

The finest plans have always been spoiled by the littleness of those that should carry them out. Even emperors can't do it all by themselves.

There are times when you have to choose between being human and having good taste.

War is like love, it always finds a way.

Justice **William Brennan**

We do not consecrate the flag by punishing its desecration, for in doing so, we dilute the freedom this cherished emblem represents.

Richard Brenner

Canada is a country so square that even the female impersonators are women.

brerbear@netcom.com

I tried to tell them that having a funeral on Sunday was a bad idea. Least during football season.

Still remember the day my nephew got it. We all sat around crying and watching CSU whup them Arizona boys to win themselves a WAC title.

Cryin' an' cheerin'. What a night.

Joe Bob Briggs

Satire is the moral equivalent of a stink bomb in a crowded theater.

Peter Brimelow, Editor, VDARE.COM

The modern definition of 'racist' is someone who is winning an argument with a liberal.

David Brin

We have to go forth and crush every world view that doesn't believe in tolerance and free speech.
[David Brin was reluctant to give permission to use this quotation since, "it is absolutely dependent upon a sense of whimsey, either in the tone of voice or in the paragraphs that surround it.
Taken by itself, only half the readers will "get it" or see that it is both true and toweringly ironic.
The rest will see only a hypocritical and self-contradictory raving, alas."]

Dave Bristol

Boys, baseball is a game where you gotta have fun. You do that by winning.

Michael Britton

Mom knows twice as much as you think she does, and half as much as she thinks she does.

Dave Broadfoot

If you don't like the way you are -- you're probably not alone.

Tom Brokaw

It is not enough to wire the world if you short-circuit your souls.

Rosa Brooks

How does a democracy come to adopt a policy of torturing detainees? To paraphrase Hillary Clinton, it takes a village.

Brigid Brophy

I refuse to consign the whole male sex to the nursery. I insist on believing that some men are my equals.

Whenever people say we mustn't be sentimental, you can take it they are about to do something cruel. And, if they add, we must be realistic, they mean they are going to make money out of it.

Dr. Joyce Brothers (GFDL)

Trust your hunches. They're usually based on facts filed away just below the conscious level.

A.L. Brown

If you can't return a favour, pass it on.

Fredric Brown, "Knock"

The last man on Earth sat alone in his room. There was a knock at the door...

H. Rap Brown

Violence is as American as cherry pie.

Jerry Brown

Prisons don't rehabilitate, they don't punish, they don't protect, so what the hell do they do?

Jim Brown

I learned a long time ago that acting like a victim gets you nowhere. I pay my taxes, so I want my damn rights. Success is a journey, not a destination.

You can be dumb, or you can be smart.

Mike Brown

I just think that most older folks don't go to raves for the same reason that they stop listening to punk rock: they've been there, done that, and it scares the hell out of them to think of what *this* generation is doing.

Pat Brown

I am invariably misquoted on something I never should have said in the first place.

1969 Brown and Williamson document

Doubt is our product since it is the best means of competing with the "body of fact" that exists in the mind of the general public
-- http://tobaccodocuments.org/bw/332506.html, Page 4

Truth is our message because of its power to withstand a conflict and sustain a controversy.
-- page 5

Christopher Browning

The scholar's quest is not a multiple-choice exam.
- Ordinary Men

Robert Browning

Ah, but a man's reach should exceed his grasp, Or what's a heaven for?

Lenny Bruce

Communism is like one big phone company.

The liberals can understand everything but people who don't understand them.

Giordano Bruno

It is proof of a base and low mind for one to wish to think with the masses or majority, merely because the majority is the majority. Truth does not change because it is, or is not, believed by a majority of the people.

Jan Harold Brunvand

The truth never stands in the way of a good story.

William Jennings Bryan

I do not think about things I don't think about.
- during the Scopes Trial

No one can earn a million dollars honestly.

Science is a magnificent force, but it is not a teacher of morals. It can perfect machinery, but it adds no moral restraints to protect society from the misuse of the machine. It can also build gigantic intellectual ships, but it constructs no moral rudders for the control of storm tossed human vessel.

William F. Buckley, Jr.

I am obliged to confess I should sooner live in a society governed by the first two thousand names in the Boston telephone directory than in a society governed by the two thousand faculty members of Harvard University.

It had all the earmarks of a CIA operation; the bomb killed everybody in the room except the intended target.

Life can't be all bad when for ten dollars you can buy all the Beethoven sonatas and listen to them for ten years.

The temptation is to think the worst of someone one loves to hate.

When Abraham Lincoln died...the nation was for a period buoyed by the sentiments he expressed in his second inaugural address, but it was not long before Reconstruction became the ugly thing it was.

Buddha

Believe nothing merely because you have been told it... Do not believe what your teacher tells you merely out of respect for the teacher. But whatsoever, after due examination and analysis, you find to be kind, conducive to the good, the benefit, the welfare of all beings -- that doctrine believe and cling to, and take it as your guide.

If a viper lives in your room and you wish to have a peaceful sleep, you must first chase it out.

Let yourself be open and life will be easier. A spoon of salt in a glass of water makes the water undrinkable. A spoon of salt in a lake is almost unnoticed.

The secret of health for both mind and body is not to mourn for the past, not to worry about the future, or not to anticipate troubles, but to live the present moment wisely and earnestly.

There is nothing more dreadful than the habit of doubt. Doubt separates people. It is a poison that disintegrates friendships and breaks up pleasant relations. It is a thorn that irritates and hurts; it is a sword that kills.

Thousands of candles can be lighted from a single candle, and the life of the candle will not be shortened. Happiness never decreases by being shared.

You cannot travel the path until you have become the path itself.

Ferris Bueller

Understanding is what makes it possible for people like us to tolerate a person like yourself.

Alan Bullock

Men are perfectly capable in public life of holding two incompatible beliefs. And most of the day, I do.

Edward Bulwer-Lytton

The man who seeks one, and but one, thing in life may hope to achieve it; but he who seeks all things, wherever he goes, only reaps, from the hopes which he sows, a harvest of barren regrets.

The true spirit of conversation consists in building on another man's observation, not overturning it

J. Buffet

I like to be in touch with what makes me scream.

John R. Bumgarner

I protested that rank among lieutenants was like virtue among courtesans.
- Parade of the Dead

John Bunyan

If we have not quiet in our minds, outward comfort will do no more for us than a golden slipper on a gouty foot.

Michael Burger

Freedom of speach [sic] is carefully worded to give the appearance of a guaranteed right to verbally challenge injustice without actually granting that right.

Life is a learning experience, And it seems I'm still in school.

Edmund Burke

Nobody makes a greater mistake than he who does nothing because he could only do a little.

The only thing necessary for the triumph of evil is for good men to do nothing.

The true danger is when liberty is nibbled away, for expedients, and by parts.

They defend their errors as if they were defending their inheritance.

To read without reflecting is like eating without digesting.

Your representative owes you, not his industry only, but his judgment; and he betrays, instead of serving you, if he sacrifices it to your opinion.
- to the voters of Bristol, 1774

Frances H. Burnett

At first people refuse to believe that a strange new thing can be done, then they begin to hope it can be done, then they see it can be done-----then it is done and all the world wonders why it was not done centuries ago.

E. Burns

There has been a great proliferation of lawyers in the past 20 years, just as there has been a proliferation of computers. But unlike computers, lawyers do not get twice as intelligent and half as expensive every two years.

George Burns

I'd go out with women my age, but there are no women my age.

Pat Burns

[Winnipeg is] the only town where you can watch your dog run away for three days.

Robert Burns

There is no such uncertainty as a sure thing.

The best-laid schemes o' mice an' men gang aft a-gley.

William S. Burroughs

And beware of the middle roads, the roads of moderation, common sense and careful planning.

A paranoid is a man who knows a little of what's going on.

Robert Burton

A blow with a word strikes deeper than a blow with a sword.

Barbara Bush

I married the first man I ever kissed. When I tell my children that, they just about throw up.

George W.H. Bush

People must be free to work, to save, to own their own home, to take risks, to invest in each other and, in essence, to control their own lives.

When I need a little free advice about Saddam Hussein, I turn to country music.

George W. Bush

A world where some live in comfort and plenty, while half of the human race lives on less than two dollars a day, is neither just, nor stable.

Comte de Bussy-Rabutin

Absence is to love what wind is to fire; it extinguishes the small, it enkindles the great.

Bustan of Sadi

Beware of the fool whose volume of words is as that of ten men, a hundred arrows shot and each one wide of the target. If thou art wise, shoot one and that one straight.

Dick Butkus

I wouldn't ever set out to hurt anybody deliberately unless it was, you know, important - like a league game or something.

Ellis Parker Butler

You could have hit him over the head with it and he wouldn't have minded. He never did mind being hit with small things like guns and axe handles.
-- "That Pup of Murchison's"

Geoff Butler

Forgive me if I misunderstood myself, but I don't think I was arguing in favour of that.

Nicholas Murray Butler

Brigands demand your money or your life; women require both.

Samuel Butler (1612-1680)

He that complies against his will

Is of his own opinion still.

Samuel Butler

The next best thing to knowing something is knowing where to find it.

Smedley Butler, War is a Racket

War is a racket. ...It is the only one in which the profits are reckoned in dollars and the losses in lives.

War, like any other racket, pays high dividends to the very few ... The cost of operations is always transferred to the people who do not profit.

Richard Lee Byers, Foragers

I wished that she and all the other stay at homes could experience the war as it truly was. After they'd marched in the rain and slept in the mud, caught a case of lice or the itch, taken a wound and grown a crop of maggots inside it, then we could all have a nice long talk about how important it was to subdue the Rebels...

Lord Byron

I've seen your stormy seas and stormy women

And pity lovers rather more than seamen.

If I am fool, it is, at least, a doubting one; and I envy no one the certainty of his self approved wisdom.

~C~

James Branch Cabell

Patriotism is the religion of Hell.
- Jurgen: a comedy of justice

The optimist proclaims that we live in the best of all possible worlds; and the pessimist fears this is true.
- The Silver Stallion

Nicolas Cage

We've become so glorified in the movie-star system that it's become this artificial royalty. The truth is that we're circus clowns.

John Cairns, British biochemist

[Cities are the] graveyards of mankind.

California Department of Consumer Affairs

In this chapter, the present tense includes the past and future tenses, and the future, the present; the masculine gender includes the feminine, and the feminine, the masculine, and the singular includes the plural, and the plural the singular.

Huey Callison

Explain things in plain English, and where you need a diagram, keep that simple too.

Facts are for wimps. Real usenet posters just say stuff that sounds right.

For every thing, there is a URL, and a time for every purpose under heaven.

Geeks no longer work at Radio Shaft. That whole company fell out of geek-chic somewhere between ten and fifteen years ago, when all the geeks got into computers and Radio Shack got out of them...

Hey, this is USENET, remember? The less he knows, the better qualified he is to give advice!

I, on the other hand, am still a man, even while wearing pants.

I'm a 3rd-shift computer network admin, and in reality I could probably wear a bathrobe and slippers to work and get away with it. I don't do this, but I do wear what pleases me, and if it makes me look like an out-of-work truck driver, _so_?

I have very little desire to eat my fellow airline passengers, so I make it a point to never fly over the Andes.

Just once, when a sports reporter asks a coach some inane question about tonight's game, I wanna hear the coach say "I think the key here is that we need to score more points than the other team, and we need to keep them from scoring more points than us. I think if we can do those two things, we'll have a pretty good chance of being able to win."

Lucky I had that doghouse to shingle to get all of that "holy crap this is cool. Let's put a bunch of nails in things!" out of my system.

People are stupid. It's one of the fundamental facts of life. No matter where you go, no matter what you do, you're going to encounter stupid people.

People who intend to commit crimes should be allowed to kill themselves without our intervention, so long as they don't hurt anybody else.

Purely in the interests of science, I'm going to blow up a shop-vac.

Somebody guessed my password, so I had to rename my dog.

The real lesson is "Don't be a lazy idiot, because that doesn't pay very well". Being an economics major don't enter into it.

That we're in a war doesn't mean that we should encourage hell.

[T]here will always be idiots in your life, and some of them will be your teachers and your bosses. And you need to learn to deal with them.

Wisconsin is an Indian word meaning "Land of Many Bars."

Robert Calmes

God may have created man, but Samuel Colt made 'em equal.

Dom Heider Camara

If I feed the hungry, people call me a saint. If I ask why they have no food, people call me a Communist.

Joseph Maxwell Cameron

Energetic stupidity, once invested with authority and allowed to accumulate experience, can do a convincing imitation of a hard driving professional soldier...
- The Anatomy of Military Merit

Simon Cameron

An honest politician is one who, when he is bought, will stay bought.

Chris Campbell

Soap operas are proof that the world we live in is just your typical primate troop with concrete trees.

Joseph Campbell

Computers are like Old Testament gods; lots of rules and no mercy.

Pat Campbell (associate counsel of the Major League Umpires Association)

I mean, if an umpire shot a player on the field, could he be terminated? I guess under those circumstances I would have a tough time saying he couldn't.

Mrs. Patrick Campbell

Marriage is the deep, deep peace of the double bed after the hurly-burly of the chaise lounge.

Albert Camus

Do not wait for the last judgment, it takes place every day.

Don't walk in front of me, I may not follow. Don't walk behind me, I may not lead. Walk beside me, and just be my friend.

It is a kind of spiritual snobbery that makes people think they can be happy without money.

It is not man who must be protected, but the possibilities within him.

It is the job of thinking people, not to be on the side of the executioners.

Nobody realizes that some people expend tremendous energy merely to be normal.

To be happy, we must not be too concerned with others

We used to wonder where war lived, what it was that made it so vile. And now we realize that we know where it lives, that it is inside ourselves.

Candido Cannavo, "La Gazzetta dello Sport"

Italy's elimination [from the European Soccer Championship] bears the stamp of the enormous sin of pride felt by the coach and transmitted to the squad with devastating psychological consequences.

Truman Capote

It's a scientific fact that if you stay in California you lose one point of your IQ every year.

Al Capp

Abstract art? A product of the untalented, sold by the unprincipled to the utterly bewildered.

Cardinal **Carlo Caraffa** (16th Century), Nephew of Pope Paul IV

Populus vult decipi, decipiatur. [The people want to be deceived, let them be deceived.]

Costas Caramanlis (Greek Prime Minister)

The movie's lesson is: Fight for your country, even if it's a losing battle, and have enough swords and hotel rooms on hand for tourists...
[Commenting on "The 300"]

BrigadierGeneral **J. Ronald Carey**

The Army has more fat than there is at a Jenny Craig convention.

[Referring to the Army's RCAS and SBIS systems]

Thomas Carlisle

Make yourself an honest man, and then you may be sure that there is one less scoundrel in the world.

Dana W. Carpender

Anyway, anyone who says, "I should be allowed to dress any way I want to, because it's an expression of who I am" has just lost all right to not be judged by t he way they look. If it's an expression of who you are, I have the right to draw opinions about you from it, just as I would from your writings.

Indeed, if we really want to find out how ever-horny American men are, all we have to do is have all the women in American make a pass at their man when he's settled in his leather recliner, with a beer, waiting for the kickoff of the superbowl.

One of the major jobs of childhood is differentiating one's self from one's sibs. Therefore, if #1 is, as first children tend to be, responsible and productive, one only has irresponsible slackerdom left.

This makes us sound like a society of hard-working slackers, which is pretty odd when you think about it.

You'll make more money with a college degree -- almost any college degree -- than without one, largely because it's a strong signal to Corporate America and its overseas relatives that you're the sort of person who can deal with almost unlimited bureaucratic bullshit.

Carr

There exists a curious lot of witless or perhaps psychopathic characters who love to run over box turtles on the roads to hear them pop, and there is probably nothing more that can be done about these people except to hope they skid.

Jonathan Carroll

You have to walk carefully in the beginning of love; the running across fields into your lover's arms can only come later when you're sure they won't laugh if you trip.

Lewis Carroll

Consider anything, only don't cry.

Here you need all the running you can to stay in the same place.

C. Carsrud

It's Saturday night and we're at the K-Mart cafeteria.

James Earl "Jimmy" Carter, Jr

Penalties against possession of a drug should not be more damaging to an individual than the use of the drug itself.

We hope someday, having solved the problems we face, to join a community of galactic civilizations.
- 1977

George Washington Carver

Ninety-nine percent of failures come from people who have the habit of making excuses.

Richard Casady

My grandmother taught me if all I want out of life is just three meals a day and a roof, just shoot a policeman.

You have the basic food groups, consisting of sugar, salt, grease, alcohol, nicotine, marijuana, coffee, and of course, starch.

Willa Cather

The are only two or three human stories, and they go on repeating themselves as fiercely as if they had never happened before.

Catherine the Great

I praise loudly, I blame softly

Marcus Porcius Cato

To say that private men have nothing to do with government is to say that private men have nothing to do with their own happiness or misery; the people ought not to concern themselves whether they be naked or clothed, fed or starved, deceived or instructed, protected or destroyed.

Mike Causey

And, if the only job I could get was flipping burgers, and somebody has to do it, hearing some guy making more in six weeks than I do in a year complain about being inconvenienced wouldn't sit well with me. In fact, if he ever came to my burger-flipping window, he might get some extra condiments he didn't ask for.

Dick Cavett

There's so much comedy on television. Does that cause comedy in the streets?

Conte **Camillo Benso di Cavour**

I have discovered the art of deceiving diplomats. I speak the truth, and they never believe me.

Bennett Cerf

Coleridge was a drug addict. Poe was an alcoholic. Marlowe was killed by a man whom he was treacherously trying to stab. Pope took money to keep a woman's name out of a satire then wrote a piece so that she still could be recognised anyhow. Chatterton killed himself. Byron was accused of incest. Do you still want to be a writer-----if so, why?"

Miguel de Cervantes

Drink moderately, for drunkenness neither keeps a secret, nor observes a promise.

Many go out for wool, and come home shorn themselves.
- Don Quixote

Jackie Chan

American stuntmen are smart -- they think about safety. When they do a jump in a car, they calculate everything: the speed, the distance...But in Hong Kong, we don't know how to count. Everything we do is a guess. If you've got the guts, you do it. All of my stuntmen have gotten hurt. I say, "Do it! Camera, action, jump!" Boom! Ambulance! Hospital! Next stuntman!

Raymond Chandler

Alcohol is like love: the first kiss is magic, the second is intimate, the third is routine. After that you just take the girl's clothes off.
- The Long Goodbye

Chess is as elaborate a waste of human intelligence as you can find outside an advertising agency.

Tun Channareth

We appeal to all of you who really love Cambodia to stop producing mines and planting them in our land.

Rev. John Chaplin

You know that...thing about propriety that you penalize people for speaking out and never penalize them for keeping quiet?

Ian Chappel

If you're fit, three or four beers don't hurt anyone. You'd be better off having three or four beers than three or four Cokes.

Pierre Teilhard de Chardin

Love is the most universal, the most tremendous and the most mysterious of the cosmic forces

Charles V (Holy Roman Emperor)

I speak Spanish to God, Italian to women, French to men and German to my horse.

Mary Chase

In my life I have found two methods--being oh, so smart or oh, so pleasant. For years I tried smart. I recommend pleasant. And you may quote me
-- Elwood P. Dowd, "Harvey"

Paddy Chayefsky

Television is democracy at its ugliest.

Samuel Checker

Different people have different recipes for guacamole. Yours, of course, is wrong. My second will contact your second.

You know, this is how the sum total of human knowledge is increased. Not with idle speculation and meaningless chatter, but with a medium-sized hammer and some free time.

You were a psych major too? I should show you my senior thesis: Convincing Attractive Young Women That They Are Research Assistants. Got me an A and three restraining orders.

Without politics work would be a pleasant experience and we'd all have a lot more money. This is why there will always be politics.

Anton Chekhov

Doctors are just the same as lawyers; the only difference is that lawyers merely rob you, whereas doctors rob you and kill you too.

Philip Dormer Stanhope, 4th Earl of Chesterfield

As to running after women, the consequences of that vice are only the loss of one's nose, the total destruction of health, and, not unfrequently, the being run through the body.
- February 24, 1747

But remember, at the same time, that errors and mistakes, however gross, in matters of opinion, if they are sincere, are to be pitied, but not punished nor laughed at. The blindness of the understanding is as much to be pitied as the blindness of the eye; and there is neither jest nor guilt in a man's losing his way in either case.
- September 21, 1747

I hope you employ your whole time, which few people do; and that you put every moment to, profit of some kind or other. I call company, walking, riding, etc., employing one's time, and, upon proper occasions, very usefully; but what I cannot forgive in anybody is sauntering, and doing nothing at all, with a thing so precious as time, and so irrecoverable when lost.
- December 9, 1746

Learning is acquired by reading books; but the much more necessary learning, the knowledge of the world, is only to be acquired by reading man, and studying all the various editions of them.

The character which most young men first aim at, is that of a man of pleasure; but they generally take it upon trust; and instead of consulting their own taste and inclinations, they blindly adopt whatever those with whom they chiefly converse, are pleased to call by the name of pleasure; and a man of pleasure in the vulgar acceptation of that phrase, means only, a beastly drunkard, an abandoned whoremaster, and a profligate swearer and curser.
- March 27, 1747

G.K. Chesterton

I regard golf as an expensive way of playing marbles.

If a thing is worth doing, it is worth doing badly.

Journalism largely consists in saying 'Lord Jones Dead' to people who never knew that Lord Jones was alive.

Poets have been mysteriously silent on the subject of cheese.

The Bible tells us to love our neighbors, and also to love our enemies; probably because they are generally the same people.

The only people who seem to have nothing to do with the education of the children are the parents.

The word good has many meanings. For example, if a man were to shoot his grandmother at a range of five hundred yards, I should call him a good shot, but not necessarily a good man.

Without education, we are in the horrible and deadly danger of taking educated people seriously.

Chinese proverb

Do not employ handsome servants.

Do not use a hatchet to remove a fly from your friend's forehead.

If you suspect a man, don't employ him, and if you employ him, don't suspect him.

If you wish to succeed, consult three old people.

Nakedness is seldom seen but often noticed.

Never be boastful; someone may come along who knew you as a child.

Never write a letter while you are angry.

Teachers open the door, but you must enter by yourself.

There is no economy in going to bed early to save candles if the result is twins.

When you want to test the depths of a stream, don't use both feet.

Avram Noam Chomsky

Propaganda is to a democracy what the bludgeon is to a totalitarian state.

Stanley Chow

Even excellent documentation is useless, unless you can find it again.

Agatha Christie

Every murderer is probably somebody's old friend.

chk@xs4all.nl (Christine)

I wonder if there's somebody here who still knows what's going on.

It's very useful to have bruises and marks to remind you of the good time you had.

People who live in glass houses, should draw the curtains before they undress, lest they frighten the horses.

Bob Church

We either learn from history or, uh, well, something bad will happen.

Winston Churchill

Don't talk to me about Naval Tradition, it's nothing but rum, sodomy, and the lash.
[Even though this is often attributed to Churchill, he didn't actually say it – although, according to his assistant Anthony Montague-Browne, he wished he had.]

Everyone has his day and some days last longer than others.

Give me the facts, Ashley, and I will twist them the way I want to suit my argument.

History will be kind to me for I intend to write it.

I like pigs. Dogs look up to you. Cats look down at you. Pigs look at you as an equal.

It is a good thing for an uneducated man to read books of quotations.
- "My Early Life"

It is a mistake to look too far ahead. Only one link in the chain of destiny can be handled at a time.

Let us therefore brace ourselves to our duty, and so bear ourselves that if the British Commonwealth and its Empire lasts for a thousand years, men will still say, "This was their finest hour."
- House of Commons, 18 June 1940

Men occasionally stumble over the truth, but most of them pick themselves up and hurry off as if nothing happened.

No one can guarantee success in war, but only deserve it.

The Almighty in His infinite wisdom did not see fit to create Frenchmen in the image of Englishmen.

The Americans will always do the right thing...after they've exhausted all the alternatives.

The greatest lesson in life is to know that even fools are right sometimes.

The truth is incontrovertible. Malice may attack it. Ignorance may deride it. But in the end, there it is.

There may well be a landslide and they have a perfect right to kick us out. That is democracy. That is what we have been fighting for. Hand me my towel.

When a nation has allowed itself to fall under a tyrannical regime, it cannot be absolved from the faults due to the guilt of the regime.
- speech, July 28, 1944

Writing a book is an adventure. To begin with, it is a toy and an amusement. Then it becomes a mistress, then it becomes a master, then it becomes a tyrant. The last phase is that just as you are about to be reconciled to your servitude, you kill the monster, and fling him to the public.

Marcus Tullius Cicero

A room without books is like a body without a soul.

I prefer the most unfair peace to the most righteous war.

Laws are silent in time of war.

No one is so old that he does not think he could live another year.

No sane man will dance.

To know nothing of what happened before you were born is to remain ever a child.

The national budget must be balanced. The public debt must be reduced; the arrogance of the authorities must be moderated and controlled. Payments to foreign governments must be reduced, if the nation doesn't want to go bankrupt. People must again learn to work, instead of living on public assistance.

Paul Ciszek

If a bank refuses a deposit, made in valid US currency, it really is time to find a different bank.

Rich Clancey

Cats will hunt, and once they get a taste of it, you may have trouble keeping them indoors. But the real problems arise when you come home and find them watching baseball and drinking beer.

Arthur C. Clarke

A faith that cannot survive collision with the truth is not worth many regrets.

Any sufficiently advanced technology looks like magic.

Politicians should read science fiction, not westerns and detective stories.

Reading computer manuals without the hardware is as frustrating as reading sex manuals without the software.

The earth is simply too small and fragile a basket for the human race to keep all its eggs in.

When a distinguished but elderly scientist states that something is possible, he is almost certainly right. When he states that something is impossible, he is very probably wrong.
- 'Profiles of the Future' (Clarke's First Law)

Appius Claudius

If you would have peace, be thou then prepared for war.

Karl von Clausewitz, On Strategy

Everything in war is very simple, but the simplest thing is difficult.

The fact that slaughter is a horrifying spectacle must make us take war more seriously, but not provide an excuse for gradually blunting our swords in the name of humanity. Sooner or later someone will come along with a sharp sword and hack off our arms.

The subordination of the political point of view to the military would be contrary to common sense.

War is a continuation of policy by other means. It is not merely a political act but a real political instrument.

War is nothing but a duel on a larger scale.

War is the realm of chance. No other human activity gives it greater scope; no other has such incessant and varied dealings with this intruder. Chance makes everything more uncertain and interferes with the whole course of events.

Eldridge Cleaver

If you're not part of the solution, you're part of the problem.

Georges Clemenceau

I don't know whether war is an interlude during peace, or peace is an interlude during war.

La guerre est finie, la guerre continue.

War is too important to be left to the generals.

Samuel Clemens - See **Mark Twain**

Grover Cleveland

He mocks the people who proposes that the Government shall protect the rich and that they in turn shall care for the laboring poor.

It is better to be defeated standing for a high principle than to run by committing subterfuge.

William Jefferson Clinton

It is clear that we cannot police the world.
- 1994

No government really rooted in limited, parliamentary democracy should have the power to make its citizens fight and kill and die in a war they may oppose, a war which even possibly may be wrong, a war which, in any case, does not involve immediately the peace and freedom of the nation.
- Dec 3, 1969

We can't be so fixated on our desire to preserve the rights of ordinary Americans...

Howell Cobb, Major General, CSA

[West Pointers] are very sociable fellows...but never have I seen men who had so little appreciation of merit in others. Self sufficiency and self aggrandizement are their...controlling characteristics.

Peter Coffee, Technology Editor, "eWEEK"

Controlling my children's access to online information is my job, not the government's. The government won't be able to do it well, and I wish it wouldn't try.

It's cheaper to avoid making enemies of your workers than to prosecute them once the damage has been done.

Software's speed is sometimes better measured with a calendar than a stopwatch.

Word Processors like DeScribe or Microsoft Word. . .make it easy to do the irrelevant...

Rep. **William Cohen**

When the chief executive of the country starts to investigate private citizens who criticize his policies or authorizes his subordinates to do such things, then I think the rattle of the chains that would bind up our constitutional freedoms can be heard. . .

Rocky Colavito

Swing and a miss. . . called strike three.

There's a two hopper to [Duane] Kuiper, who fields it on the first bounce.

Colette

Time spent with cats is never wasted.

G. Norman Collie

Every man has one thing he can do better than anyone else - and usually it's reading his own handwriting.

Colonial American proverb

You will always be lucky if you know how to make friends with strange cats.

Charles Caleb Colton

For what are the triumphs of war, planned by ambition, executed by violence, and consummated by devastation? The means are the sacrifice of many, the end, the bloated aggrandizement of the few.

The Commune of Marseilles

We propose to burn the academic libraries, because Theology is only fanaticism, History is lies, Philosophy is dreams, and Science is unnecessary.

Communication Briefings

The mind is like a TV set when it goes blank, it's a good idea to turn off the sound.

Confucius

In a country well governed, poverty is something to be ashamed of. In a country badly governed, wealth is something to be ashamed of.

Learning without thought is labor lost; thought without learning is perilous.

No one ever really minds seeing a friend fall off a roof.

Real knowledge is to know the extent of one's ignorance.

The superior man is distressed by the limitation of his ability; he is not distressed by the fact that men do not recognize the ability he has.

To know what is right and not to do it is the worst cowardice.

To see what is right and not to do it is want of courage.
- Analects

Bill Conlin, Philadelphia Daily News

[during Mickey Mantle's prime playing years] The food tasted better. The beer was colder. The girls were prettier. And a dollar went much farther. There was nothing you couldn't get rid of with a penicillin shot. There were no skyjackings, carjackings or drive by massacres performed by junior high school kids.

Sean Connery

Love may not make the world go round, but I must admit that it makes the ride worthwhile.

Cyril Connolly

All charming people have something to conceal, usually their total dependence on the appreciation of others.

The reward of art is not fame or success but intoxication
-- "The Unquiet Grave"

We are all serving a life sentence in the dungeon of life.

Joseph Conrad

The belief in a supernatural source of evil is not necessary; men alone are quite capable f every wickedness.

Cynthia Conyers

Sylvia's skin was exquisite, soft and pretty. Leonard loved the way it looked tacked up on his wall.

Rich Cook

Programming today is a race between software engineers striving to build bigger and better idiot-proof programs, and the Universe trying to produce bigger and better idiots. So far, the Universe is winning.

Alistair Cooke

A professional is someone who can do his best work when he doesn't feel like it.

Calvin Coolidge

I have never been hurt by anything I didn't say.

Stephen Coonts

An American's enthusiasm for law and order is directly proportional to the degree to which he believes his personal safety or his livelihood is threatened.
- Under Siege

Marie Corelli

I never married because there was no need. I have three pets at home which answer the same purpose as a husband. I have a dog which growls every morning, a parrot which swears all afternoon and a cat that comes home late at night.

What a fool cannot learn he laughs at, thinking that by his laughter he shows superiority instead of latent idiocy.

Pierre Corneille

To win without risk is to triumph without glory.

Cornish Prayer

From ghoulies and ghosties and long-leggety beasties

And things that go bump in the night,

Good lord deliver us!"

Bernard Cornwell and Susannah Kells

The English have a sneaking suspicion that we know something about life and elegance and beauty that they do not know, and it is every Frenchman's duty to continue the illusion.
- Campion, The Fallen Angels

There were few things in life more dangerous than the idle, bored young men of London society.
- The Fallen Angels

Pat Corrales

Talent always beats experience. Because by the time you get experience, the talent's gone.

James Cort

Like most computer techie people, I'll happily spend 6 hours trying figure out how to do a 3 hour job in 10 minutes.

Geoffrey Cottrell

In America, only the successful writer is important, in France all writers are important, in England no writer is important, and in Australia you have to explain what a writer is.

Ann Coulter

They're not Americans. They're liberals!

Jacques Cousteau

Man, of all the animals, is probably the only one to regard himself as a great delicacy.

Harold Covington, National Socialist White Peoples Party

The real purpose of Holocaust revisionism is to make National Socialism an acceptable political alternative again.

Noel Coward

People are wrong when they say that the opera isn't what it used to be. It is what it used to be. That's what's wrong with it.

Tommy Craggs

Cheering for the [American University] Eagles now is like cheering for Brussels sprouts and condoms.

Monta Crane

There are three ways to get something done: do it yourself, employ someone to do it, or forbid your children from doing it.

Stephen Crane

A man said to the universe "Sir, I exist."

"However," the universe replied, "the fact has not created in me a sense of obligation"

Karen J. Cravens

And at least when they do move in football, they pretty much all do. Baseball? You got one, maybe two guys going anywhere most of the time. Now, if the whole other team could tackle the runner, that would make it more interesting. Of course, he'd have had to have been allowed to keep the bat with him, to make it fair.

A bus with carousel animals for seats would be *way* cooler than the trolley buses.

Joan Crawford

Love is a fire. But whether it is going to warm your hearth or burn down your house, you can never tell.

Crazy Horse

One does not sell the land people walk on.

Mandell Creighton

No people do so much harm as those who go about doing good.

Robert X. Cringely

All women eventually meld into variations of June Cleaver.

Not that America has any particular dibs on the birth of Christ, who as I last recall, was neither a Methodist nor a member of the National Rifle Association.

If the automobile had followed the same development cycle as the computer, a Rolls-Royce would today cost $100, get a million miles per gallon, and explode once a year, killing everyone inside.

I've noticed that most people, including me, are a little bit stupider in the summer months. More gullible, too.

Quentin Crisp

Never keep up with the Jones. Drag them down to your level.

When I told the people of Northern Ireland that I was an atheist, a woman in the audience stood up and said, "Yes, but is it the God of the Catholics or the God of the Protestants in whom you don't believe?"

David Crockett

We have rights, as individuals, to give as much of our own money as we please to charity; but as members of Congress we have no right so to appropriate a dollar of public money.

Oliver Cromwell

None climbs so high as he who knows not wither he is going.

Though peace be made, yet it is interest that keeps peace.

You have been here too long for any good you have been doing. Depart, I say and let us have done with you! In the name of God, go!
- to the Long Parliament

Your pretended fear lest error might step in is like the man who would keep all wine out of the country lest men should be drunk.

Zuseke Crone, quoted in The Way of A Boy by Ernest Hillen

All things are possible except biting off your own nose.

In the concert of life no one gets a program.

Whores and crooks are always talking about honor.

Robert Crowe

Cats and 'acts normally' are a nearly tangential intersection on a VERY enlarged Venn diagram.

Crowfoot, Blackfoot orator

What is life? It is the flash of a firefly in the night. It is the breath of a buffalo in the wintertime. It is the little shadow which runs across the grass and loses itself in the sunset.

Liz Crown

My kid's room looks like something put up a major death struggle there following a protracted food fight.

e e cummings

to be nobody but myself in a world which is doing its best, night and day to make you everybody else means to fight the hardest battle which any human being can fight, and never stop fighting.

Father **Jerome Cummings**

A friend is one who knows us, but loves us anyway.

Keith Cummings

Don't forget the most important rule to live by. . .never believe anything you read on the Internet.

Ed Cunningham

Friends are those rare people who ask how we are and then wait to hear the answer.

Michael Cunningham

I told the teacher that my son wasn't very smart, and she said something about the acorn not falling far from the tree. Since I never studied treeology, I don't have a clue what that means.

Randall Cunningham

I'm thinking of changing my middle name to "Boo" so when I play in Philly, it'll sound like they're cheering me.

Will Cuppy

Aristotle. . .taught that the brain exists merely to cool the blood and is not involved in the process of thinking. This is true only of certain persons.

J.W. Curran

There are, of course, several things in Ontario that are more dangerous than wolves. For instance, the stepladder.

Emmanuel Custer

I have every confidence in my dear son Autie, surrounded as he is by temptations . . . but, Libbie, I want you to counsel Thomas. I want my boys to be, foremost, soldiers of the Lord.
["Autie" was George A. Custer]

George A. Custer

"I suppose you think I am of a very forgiving disposition. Well, perhaps I am. I often think of the beautiful expression uttered by President Lincoln--"With malice toward none; with charity toward all. . ." and I hope this may ever be mine to say."
- in a letter to Elizabeth Custer, September 28, 1873, Ft Abraham Lincoln

I would rather have a good education and no money than a fortune and be ignorant.

I wrote a very strong letter recently against an Indian War, depicting as strongly as I could the serious results that would follow . . ."
- Letter to Elizabeth, May 1, 1867, Fort Hays, KS

If I were an Indian I often think I would greatly prefer to cast my lot among those of my people adhered to the free open plains rather than submit to the confined limits of a reservation, there to be the recipient of the blessed benefits of civilization, with its vices thrown in without stint or measure.

The Methodists are holding a revival. Capts. Moylan and Smith and Lt. Varnum attended last night, and will go again, from the same motives as if attending a circus.
- Letter to Elizabeth, Feb 9, 1873, Elizabethtown, KY

Mary Custer

It is sweet to toil for those we love.

A. Cygni

Resting on one's laurels makes for an uncomfortable bed, and only crushes the laurels.

(Back To Table of Contents)

~D~

Daniel D'Errico

Power corrupts, but we need electricity.

[Probably not original to him, but he is the source for this quotation]

Leonardo da Vinci

Just as courage imperils life, fear protects it."

Jeffery Dahmer

I feel it's wrong for people who commit crimes to try to shift the blame to someone else, onto their parents, or onto their upbringing or living circumstances. I think that's just a cop out. I take full responsibility.
-- in an interview with Stone Phillips on Dateline

Dalai Lama

Ignorance...can't be dispelled through simple prayer.

Salvador Dali

The only difference between me and a madman is that I am not mad.

Danish Proverb

Advice after injury is like medicine after death.

If you put ten Norwegians together, eleven would call themselves kings and lead fifteen armies to war against each other.

Georges Jacques Danton

Show my head to the people, it is worth seeing.
- at his beheading

We must dare, dare again, and always go on daring.

Tony Danza

I'm a washed up boxer who hasn't fought for 15 years. Do you know what that makes me today? It makes me a contender.

darmsted@shadow.net

Why spank a child, they don't appreciate it. I know lots of adults who would gladly stand in.

Clarence Darrow

Do you think about things you do think about?
- to William Jennings Bryan during the Scopes Trial

Even if you do learn to speak correct English, whom are you going to speak it to?

He was eminently qualified; he had never read a line on the subject, and very little on any other
- The Story of My Life

He who raises his voice against what he believes to be the injustice of the present and the wrongs of the past is the one who hunches the world along.

History repeats itself; that's one of the things that's wrong with history.

I don't like spinach, and I'm glad I don't, because if I liked it I'd eat it, and I just hate it.

I have never killed a man, but I have read many obituaries with great pleasure.

I have suffered from being misunderstood, but I would have suffered a hell of a lot more if I had been understood.

The first half of our life is ruined by our parents and the second half by our children.

There is no such thing as justice in or out of court.

To think is to differ.

When I was a boy I was told that anybody could become President; I'm beginning to believe it.

Charles Darwin

A mathematician is a blind man in a dark room looking for a black cat which isn't there.

From the war of nature, from famine and death, the most exalted object which we are capable of conceiving, namely, the production of the higher animals, directly follows.

Dale Dauten

Criticizing lawyers for lawsuits is like criticizing linebackers for knocking people down.

Different isn't always better, but better is always different.

Just as certainly as spiders are born to weave webs, so we are genetically predisposed to create environments of which we want no part. In other words, it is natural that organizations tend to suck.

There's nothing less impressive than trying to be impressive.

The job market is the used car lot of employment.

Robertson Davies

If you attack Stupidity you attack an entrenched interest with friends in government and every walk of public life.
- The Diary of Samuel Marchbanks

The dog is a yes-animal. Very popular with people who can't afford a yes man.

Adelle Davis

Thousands upon thousands of persons have studied disease. Almost no one has studied health.

We are indeed much more than what we eat, but what we eat can nevertheless help us to be much more than what we are.

To say that obesity is caused by merely consuming too many calories is like saying that the only cause of the American Revolution was the Boston Tea Party.

Nutrition. . .has been kicked around like a puppy that cannot take care of itself. Food faddists and crackpots have kicked it pretty cruelly...

If this country [America] is to survive, the best-fed-nation myth had better be recognized for what it is: propaganda designed to produce wealth not health.

Angela Davis

What this country needs is more unemployed politicians.

Jefferson Davis

We must prepare to meet the emergency and maintain, by the final arbitratement of the sword, the position which we have assumed among the nations of the earth.
- Provisional Inaugural

Miles Davis

Sometimes you have to play a long time to be able to play like yourself.

Stephen S. Davis

People's choices should be respected, and the default assumption should be that each person has a better knowledge of what they need than do others (especially those others who don't know the person intimately), and relationships should not be interfered with save in some cases where there is compelling evidence that destructive choices have been made.

Clarence Day

If your parents didn't have any children, there's a good chance that you won't have any.

Honoré de Balzac

Behind every great fortune there is a crime.

Bureaucracy is a giant mechanism operated by pygmies.

Equality may perhaps be a right, but no power on earth can ever turn it into a fact.

It is easier to be a lover than a husband for the simple reason that it is more difficult to be witty every day than to say pretty things from time to time.

No man should marry until he has studied anatomy and dissected at least one woman.

Woman must be a genius to create a good husband.

L. Sprague de Camp

Laws are passed and constitutions adopted to enlarge the power of the ruled majority over their own destinies; but the ruling minority somehow keeps a grip on power, whether they pass under the name of counts, colonels, capitalists, or commissars.
- Ras Thavas in "Sir Harold of Zodanga,"

Charles De Gaulle

How can you govern a country which has 246 varieties of cheese?

In order to become the master, the politician poses as the servant.

Since a politician never believes what he says, he is surprised when others believe him.

Jules De Gaultier

Imagination is the one weapon in the war against reality.

Thomas De Quincey

In this state of imbecility, I had, for amusement, turned my attention to political economy.
- "Confessions of an English Opium Eater"

Marquis de Sade

It seemed that everything must give in to me, that the whole world must flatter my whims, and that it was up to me alone to conceive and satisfy them.

There is no more lively sensation than that of pain. Its impressions are certain and dependable.

Peter de Vries

There are times when parenthood seems nothing but feeding the mouth that bites you.

Eugene V. Debs

The rights of one are as sacred as the rights of a million.

Wars throughout history have been waged for conquest and plunder...the master class has always declared the wars; the subject class has always fought the battles.

Stephen Dedman

You're a lawyer, I'm a vampire. There is such a thing as professional courtesy.
- "Never Seen by Waking Eyes"

David Denslow

Most felons are not Republicans. If they are, they've retired to Bermuda.

Attributed to **Erik Dern** (Who probably doesn't exist)

I had never really thought about it before, but obviously, giving an elephant an enema can be a very dangerous activity -- and not something that should be attempted alone.

Michael Dertouzos

Email is an open duct into your central nervous system. It occupies the brain & reduces productivity.

Rene Descartes

A state is better governed which has few laws, and those laws strictly observed.

It is not enough to have a good mind; the main thing is to use it well.

Stephen A. Devaux

War, famine, disease and death are but toothaches when compared with emoticons.
- in rec.sport.cricket

Sir James Dewar

Minds are like parachutes. They only function when they are open.

Bill Diamond

I'm disinclined to live anywhere where people can ice skate to work.

It's a good place to go, once. Preferably with people who you don't want to frequently visit or who have a refined sense of bad taste.

Some things just shouldn't be faced medicated.

The Republicans are completely turning me off sex altogether.

Jared Diamond, The Third Chimpanzee

Along with drinking a strychnine cocktail, poking an adult rhino or Cape buffalo with a spear ranks as one of the most effective means of suicide that I know.

Any social system with rules of conduct is open to the risk of individual's cheating when they find the advantages of cheating to outweigh the burden of sanctions.

Mass extinctions have coincided with each major extension of human lebensraum during the last ten thousand years and possibly much longer.

Our desire to read about sex is surpassed only by our desire to practice it.

The difference between a kleptocrat and a wise statesman, between a robber baron and a public benefactor, is merely one of degree; a matter of just how large a percentage of the tribute extracted from producers is retained by the elite and how much the commoners like the public uses to which the redistributed tribute is put.
- Guns, Germs, and Steel

Phillip K. Dick

Reality is that which refuses to go away when I stop believing in it.

Charles Dickens

Minds, like bodies, will often fall into a pimpled, ill-conditioned state from mere excess of comfort.

R.J. Dickens

Never believe in anything you can't eat.

Rob Dickerson

By the time you get an application up on a mainframe, it's going to take nuclear weapons to dislodge that thing.

Jeff Dickerson, Team Spotter and Agent for Kyle Busch

It doesn't matter if it's Friday, Saturday or Sunday – we want to get a trophy, and we want a picture taken with a pretty girl.

Paul C. Dickie

[Germans] don't have stupid laws. They might have stupid lawyers, but that's an affliction that affects nearly every country!

You've generally made yourself about as welcome as a flea would be in a space suit and then you're amazed when you get the sort of treatment that one would mete out to any other parasite.

Emily Dickinson

Dying is a wild night and a new road.

Gordon R. Dickson

Some people like my advice so much that they frame it upon the wall instead of using it.

Denis Diderot

Gold is everything; without gold there's nothing.

Marlene Dietrich

In America sex is an obsession, in other parts of the world it is a fact.

Howard Dietz

Composers shouldn't think too much -- it interferes with their plagiarism.

Tom Digby

Consider, for example, the semi literate mechanic who can figure out almost any mechanical device by taking it apart and seeing how the pieces fit together. Is such a person less intelligent than someone else who can quote the classics all day long but has no idea which end of a screwdriver is which?

Phyllis Diller

Never go to bed mad. Stay up and fight.

Charles Wm. Dimmick

A cat's brain is much smaller than that of a sheep, but you will never find a cat trying to graze in the middle of a paved road.

Don't EVER invite someone to play the bagpipes indoors.

It is part of the job description of sitting on a council, board, or commission that you have to sit and listen to a great deal of nonsense and not interrupt.

There is absolutely nothing wrong with being a cynical old fart.

Edward A. Dimmick

Recall that a majority often simply means that all the fools are thinking alike.

David Dinkins

I haven't committed a crime. What I did was fail to comply with the law.

Benjamin Disraeli

I will not go down to posterity talking bad grammar.

If every man were straightforward in his opinions, there would be no conversation.

It is much easier to be critical than to be correct.

Little things affect little minds.

Never apologize for showing feeling. When you do so you apologize for truth.

Never complain and never explain.

Nobody has money who ought to have it.

The wisdom of the wise and the experience of the ages are perpetuated by quotations.

There are three kinds of lies: lies, damned lies and statistics.

What we anticipate seldom occurs; what we least expected generally happens.

Dorothy Dix

The reason husbands and wives do not understand each other is because they belong to different sexes.

Missy Camp Dizick

Dogs come when they are called; cats take a message and get back to you.

Some people say that cats are sneaky, evil, and cruel. True, and they have many other fine qualities as well.

John Dodge

[Office97 is] the poster child for computing's overindulgence...The overriding emphasis on power and features should not sacrifice reliability and leanness.
- "PC Week," 1/27/97

Victimization via downsizing is as random as getting mugged.

Danilo Dolci

Children will not accept a broken reality.

Knowing with the head is not enough. One must know some things with the bones.

Bob Dole

Irreverence is in my blood.

Aelius Donatus

Confound those who have said our remarks before us.

John Donne

As peace is of all goodness, so war is an emblem, a hieroglyphic, of all misery.

Vince Dooley

To err is human, to forgive is divine. But to forgive a football coach is unheard of.

Feodor Dostoyevsky

The main thing is the play itself. I swear that greed for money has nothing to do with it, although heaven knows I am sorely in need of money.

Pat Dougherty

I'd like to see one of those PETA folks walk into a biker bar with their spray cans. If they are as fanatic as they claim [it] should be a natural logical step. After all bikers wear quite a lot of leather clothing. Then again little blue haired old ladies won't wrap a chain around you and drag you behind their Harley.

Frederick Douglass

Those who profess to favor freedom, and yet depreciate agitation, are men who want rain without thunder and lightning. They want the roar of the ocean without the roar of its many waters.

Glenn Dowdy

I also see Government as a whole bunch of federal employees whose job doesn't change much after elections, some of whom are mindless drones, some of whom take pride in their work for good or ill, some of whom really want to help people. A lot of these folks do jobs others wouldn't do for love or money, jobs essential to the somewhat successful running of the government.

I'll be 73 when my youngest hits 30. I might not be around for grandkids, so I've got to irritate them now. And embarrass them in junior high and high school. I'm going to buy gangsta chic when it goes out of style and save it for parent-teacher conferences.

I'm not claiming you're crazy. I'm letting you make that decision.

Shooting at warplanes flying over your own country strikes me as somehow different than unrestricted submarine warfare. But I'm crazy like that.

These are the times that put schadenfreude in men's souls

You know what I hate? When I click on the drop down menu for year of birth and I have to scroll down to get to mine.

Arthur Conan Doyle

It is a capital mistake to theorize before one has data.

Take away what is impossible, and whatever remains, however improbable, is the truth.

David Drake

In the field, the only purpose of a salute was to target a hated officer for an enemy sniper...

Politics were a part of human life. People who thought they didn't play politics, simply played politics badly.

Sometimes you have to charge straight uphill into a gun position. Then it's nice if you've got people along who think that's a good idea.

The use of force is always an answer to problems. Whether or not it's a satisfactory answer depends on a number of things, not least the personality of the person making the determination.

Wars result when one side either misjudges the chances or wishes to commit suicide; and not even Masada began as a suicide attempt. In general, both warring parties expect to win. In the event, they are wrong more than half the time.

R.H. Draney

As long as you can remember a few esoteric terms, it matters not a whit if you know what they mean. . .I find "eigenvalue" and "Dirichlet condition" very effective when someone needs a blast of warm BS. . .

I defer to your plainly more vivid memories of topless women with whips...

Daniel M Drucker

Tell the users you love them. Say it with flowers. Send them a Triffid**

Peter Drucker

Most of what we call management consists of making it difficult for people to get their work done.

Rank does not confer privilege or give power. It imposes responsibility.

The most important thing in communication is hearing what isn't said.

There is nothing so useless as doing efficiently that which should not be done at all.

When a subject becomes totally obsolete we make it a required course.

John Dryden

Beware the fury of a patient man.

There is a pleasure in being mad that only madmen know.

Ardant Du Picq

Four brave men who do not know each other will not dare to attack a lion. Four less brave, but knowing each other well, sure of their reliability and consequently of mutual aid, will attack resolutely. There is the science of the organization of armies in a nutshell.

Man taxes his ingenuity to be able to kill without running the risk of being killed.

The man is the first weapon of battle. Let us study the soldier, for it is he who brings reality to it.

Cheng Duanli

Gambling and chess games are lowly pastimes and should be avoided by our students.

Marc Dufour

I prefer to give a bit of my liberty to an elected government rather than to unaccountable corporations.

John Foster Dulles

The world will never have lasting peace so long as men reserve for war the finest human qualities.

Alexandre Dumas

I prefer the wicked rather than the foolish. The wicked sometimes rest.

Men's minds are raised to the level of the women with whom they associate.

Will Durant

One of the lessons of history is that nothing is often a good thing to do and always a clever thing to say.

Leo Durocher

Baseball is like church. Many attend. Few understand.

Buy a steak for a player on another club after the game, but don't even speak to him on the field. Get out there and beat them to death.

I believe in rules. Sure I do. If there weren't any rules, how could you break them?

Dutch proverb

Don't do to others that which you don't want done to yourself.

No one can have peace longer than his neighbor pleases.

Bob Dylan (GFDL)

Ah, but I was so much older then, I'm younger than that now.

All I can do is be me, whoever that is.

But even the President of the United States sometimes must have to stand naked.

I think of a hero as someone who understands the degree of responsibility that comes with his freedom.

Just because you like my stuff doesn't mean I owe you anything.

You don't count the dead When God's on your side.

Freeman Dyson

In the long run, life depends less on an abundant supply of energy than on a good signal to noise ratio.

Feliz Dzerzhanova

We also believe 'so called criminals' are just troubled, misunderstood people searching for peace, happiness and a work free lifestyle, which might involve beating, robbing and killing you. Don't make it hard for them by owning and using the destructive semi automatic weapons of violence called guns.

~E~

Rachel E.

The rain falls alike upon the Just and Unjust, but mostly upon the Just because the Unjust steals the Just's umbrella.

Amelia Earhart

Courage is the price that life exacts for granting peace.

You do not have to live a small life.

Clint Eastwood (GFDL)

There's only one way to have a happy marriage and as soon as I learn what it is I'll get married again.

Abba Eban

A consensus means that everyone agrees to say collectively what no one believes individually.

His ignorance is encyclopedic.

Dick Ebersol, NBC Sports

They have good music in Nashville, but I don't think Loretta Lynn will be returning kickoffs.

Nicholas Eberstadt.

The world population explosion did not take place because people suddenly started breeding like rabbits--it happened because they finally stopped dying like flies.

Roger Ebert

Show me a man who is not afraid of being eaten by an alligator in a sewer, and I'll show you a fool.

Umberto Eco

I don't even have an e-mail address. I have reached an age where my main purpose is not to receive messages.

In the past men were handsome and great (now they are children and dwarfs)...
- Adso in The Name of the Rose

The real hero is always a hero by mistake; he dreams of being an honest coward like everybody else.
- "Travels in Hyper Reality"

Neal Eckhardt

Another fine Sony feature. Rootkits that can't be deleted and exploding batteries that can't be extinguished. Not real good business models.
[Neal says this isn't original with him. Since I can't find the original of this, I left it under his name.]

Isn't having a smoking section in a restaurant like having a peeing section in a swimming pool?

The only thing pennies are good for is to stop people from giving you more of them.

Tammy Jo Eckhart

Love, Peace, Hugs, Kisses, Whips, and Chains,

Charles Edison

People will inevitably associate me with my father [Thomas A. Edison], but I would not have anyone believe that I am trading on the name Edison. I would rather have you know me merely as the result of one of my father's earlier experiments.

Thomas Edison

I haven't failed. I've found 10,000 ways that don't work.

Just because something doesn't do what you planned it to do doesn't mean it's useless.

Results! Why man, I have gotten a lot of results. I know several thousand things that won't work

Opportunity is missed by most people because it is dressed in overalls and looks like work.

Winners form the habit of concentrating on what they want to happen; losers concentrate on what they don't want to happen. In a pressure situation, winners call up past wins; losers recall past losses. Both are self-fulfilling.

Robert C. "Bob" Edwards
(Not to be confused with Robert A. "Bob" Edwards of radio fame.)

A little learning is a dangerous thing, but a lot of ignorance is just as bad.

If you want anything done well, do it yourself. This is why most people laugh at their own jokes.

Chester G. Edwards

Let's face the obvious. Yesterday we were nerds. Today we're the cognitive elite. Let's conquer.

John Edwards

Those who believe that real change starts with Washington politicians have been in Washington too long and are living a fairy tale

Egyptian Proverb

Friendship doubles joy and halves grief.

Adolf Eichmann

I must state that I consider this murder, this extermination of the Jews, to be one of the most heinous crimes in the history of mankind.
- July 13, 1961

Albert Einstein (GFDL)

Any man who reads too much and uses his own brain too little falls into lazy habits of thinking.

Common sense is the collection of prejudices acquired by age 18.

Education is what remains after one has forgotten everything one learned in school.

God is subtle but He is not malicious

God punished me for my contempt for authority by making me an authority.

I am enough of an artist to draw freely upon my imagination. Imagination is more important than knowledge. Knowledge is limited. Imagination encircles the world.

If A equals success, then the formula is: A=X+Y+Z. X is work. Y is play. Z is keep your mouth shut.

If only I had known, I should have become a watchmaker

If my theory of relativity is proven successful, Germany will claim me as a German and France will declare that I am a citizen of the world.

If we knew what it was we were doing, it would not be called research, would it?

Insofar as the laws of mathematics are certain, they do not refer to reality; and insofar as they refer to reality, they are not certain.

It is my conviction that killing under the cloak of war is nothing but an act of murder.

It should be possible to explain the laws of physics to a barmaid.

Nationalism is an infantile sickness. It is the measles of the human race.

Nothing is more destructive of respect for the government and the law of the land than passing laws which cannot be enforced.

Peace cannot be kept by force. It can only be achieved by understanding.

Put your hand on a hot stove for a minute, and it seems like an hour. Sit with a pretty girl for an hour, and it seems like a minute. THAT'S relativity.

Sometimes one pays most for the things one gets for nothing.

The answer is 'yes' or 'no', depending on the interpretation.

The only reason for time is so that everything doesn't happen at once.

The secret to creativity is knowing how to hide your sources.

Too many of us look upon Americans as dollar chasers. This is a cruel libel, even if it is reiterated thoughtlessly by the Americans themselves.

Two things are infinite: the universe and human stupidity; and I'm not sure about the universe.

Where am I? Oh, here I am.

Whoever is careless with the truth in small matters cannot be trusted with important matters.

Whoever undertakes to set himself up as a judge of Truth and Knowledge is shipwrecked by the laughter of the gods.

Wire telegraph is a kind of a very, very long cat. You pull his tail in New York and his head is meowing in Los Angeles. Do you understand this? And radio operates exactly the same way: you send signals here, they receive them there. The only difference is that there is no cat.

John Eisenberg, Baltimore Sun

Whiners, beware! You're entering a no excuse zone.

Why should a player feel any loyalty to his team when a shoe company is making him rich and famous.

Dwight D. Eisenhower

An intellectual is a man who takes more words than necessary to tell more than he knows

I think that people want peace so much that one of these days government had better get out of their way and let them have it.

Though force can protect in emergency, only justice, fairness, consideration and cooperation can finally lead men to the drawn of eternal peace.

We develop weapons, not to wage war, but to prevent war. Only in the clear light of this greater truth can we properly examine the lesser matter of the testing of our nuclear weapons.

We seek peace, knowing that peace is the climate of freedom.

When people speak to you about a preventive war, you tell them to go and fight it. After my experience, I have come to hate war. War settles nothing.

George Eliot (Marian Evans)

Every man who is not a monster, a mathematician, or a mad philosopher, is the slave of some woman or other.
- Scenes of Clerical Life

Prophesy is the most gratuitous of errors.
- Middlemarch

Hassan El-Ashmawi

Individual freedom must assert itself before the challenges of both the metaphysical and tangible worlds.

[Theologians and jurists] speak of bringing about God's dominion on earth, but have they explained what this means? Does God want to rule the earth in a specific way? Did He draw up a plan for government? With total confidence, I say no, and I challenge anyone to furnish me with proof of the contrary.

T.S. Eliot

College football is becoming so complicated, players will find it a recreation to go to class.

Half the harm that is done in this world is due to people who want to feel important. They don't mean to do harm -- but the harm does not interest them. Or they do not see it, or they justify it because they are absorbed in the endless struggle to think well of themselves.

Immature poets imitate; mature poets steal.

Some editors are failed writers, but so are most writers.

Linda Ellerbee

If men can run the world, why can't they stop wearing neckties? How intelligent is it to start the day by tying a little noose around your neck?

Duke Ellington

If it sounds good, it is good.

So naturally, I don't have to tell you that one never snaps one's fingers on the beat... it's considered aggressive. Never push it, just let it fall on the afterbeat, thus.

Elynne

An animal who grooms rather than responding to a "come here" command, or who climbs onto your newspaper and grooms, is training you to be a good human pet.

Ralph Waldo Emerson

A child is a curly, dimpled lunatic.

A foolish consistency is the hobgoblin of little minds, adored by little statesmen and philosophers and divines.
- Self-Reliance

By necessity, by proclivity, and by delight, we all quote. In fact, it is as difficult to appropriate the thoughts of others as it is to invent.

I hate quotations. Tell me what you know.

Make the most of yourself, for that is all there is of you.

Money often costs too much.

Nothing can bring you peace but yourself.

People do not deserve to have good writing, they are so pleased with bad.

Society everywhere is in conspiracy against the manhood of everyone of its members.

The louder he talked of his honor, the faster we counted our spoons.

The tragedy of war is that it uses man's best to do man's worst.

This time, like all other times, is a very good time, if we but know what to do with it.

The torments of martyrdom are probably most keenly felt by the bystanders.

The true test of civilization is the kind of man the country turns out.

War educates the senses, calls into action the will, perfects the physical constitution, brings men into such swift and close collision in critical moments that man measures man.

We are shut up in schools and college recitation rooms for ten or fifteen years, and come out at last with a bellyful of words and do not know a thing.

Peter Eng

Does a pebble know what its ripples do?

English proverb

In a cat's eye, all things belong to cats.

Money is the sinew of love as well as of war.

Epictetus

He is a man of sense who does not grieve for what he has not, but rejoices in what he has.

Epicurus

Most men are in a coma when they are at rest and mad when they act.

Erasmus

Scitum est inter caecos luscum regnare posse. (It is well known, that among the blind the one-eyed man is king.)

When I get a little money, I buy books. If I have any left over, I buy food and pay the rent.

Susan Ertz

Millions long for immortality who do not know what to do with themselves on a rainy Sunday afternoon.

M.C. Escher

I don't use drugs; my dreams are frightening enough.

Chuck Estrada, Texas Rangers pitching coach

We had a very scientific system for bringing in relief pitchers. We used the first one who answered the phone.

Estron

Sometimes, "you will learn stuff here" that you didn't want to know.

Melissa Etheridge

I guess I'm just addicted to the pain of delight

Edith Evans

When a woman behaves like a man, why doesn't she behave like a nice man?

Richard Ewell, Lieutenant General, CSA

Women--I tell you, sir, women would make a grand brigade--if it was not for snakes and spiders. They don't mind bullets--women are not afraid of bullets; but one big black-snake would put a whole army to flight.

~F~

Clifton Fadiman

The German mind has a talent for making no mistakes but the very greatest.

Tom Fagan

In pre-war days, or more particularly before becoming a POW of the Japanese, no-one could ever have convinced me I would see grown, supposedly educated men, go to such lengths to cause hardship and horror, or to perpetrate, deliberately, demoniacal acts of unbelievable violence toward men, women, children or animal life.
-- Tom Fagan's POW diary, unpublished

Charles Fair

Conversely, the man who is by temperament and physique close to the going tribal norms tends to rise no matter how stupid he is, it being only in the eleventh hour that his unfitness comes to be seen, to the consternation and loss of all concerned.

It is perhaps asking too much of a naturally stupid man to expect him to make proper allowance for his own stupidity.

One of the chief differences between ourselves and the ancients lies not (unfortunately) in human nature, but rather in the proliferation of our skills, and our institutions, and therefore in the number of niches in which the incompetent can now install themselves as persons of consequence.

Barry Farber

In a Russian tragedy, everybody dies. In a Russian comedy, everybody dies too. But they die happy.

The Farmer's Almanac

Don't worry about avoiding temptation. As you grow older, it starts avoiding you.

David Fasold

Intellectual brilliance is no guarantee against being dead wrong .

Guy Fawkes

A desperate disease requires a dangerous remedy.

Mary Featherston

When you're proven to be wrong, just change the definitions of what you're arguing about.

James K. Feibleman

A myth is a religion in which no one any longer believes.

Jules Feiffer

Christ died for our sins. Dare we make his martyrdom meaningless by not committing them?

Federico Fellini

Only when man understands that he is free can he know where he stands and then make a free choice. Only at this point can he jump into faith. This faith can be religious, political, or whatever. That choice exists is the point.

Anne E. Ferguson

I've always assumed (despite the pretty paintings) that angels must look scarey as hell, since the first words out of their mouths are invariably "Be not afraid"

Miriam A. "Ma" Ferguson

If the King's English was good enough for Jesus, it's good enough for me!

Al Ferrara

I wanted to be a big league ball player so I could see my picture on a bubble gum card.

Mike Fester

Sometimes life doesn't give a choice between good and bad; it's between bad and "you gotta be kidding me".

Uncle Fester

Someday, I hope you'll know the indescribable joy of having children and paying somebody else to raise them.

Jim Fiebig

It takes a big man to admit when he's wrong, and an even bigger one to keep his mouth shut when he's right.

You own a dog; you feed a cat.

W.C. Fields

A woman drove me to drink and I didn't even have the decency to thank her.

I never vote *for* anybody, I always vote against.

If you're a real good kid, I'll give you a piggy-back ride on a buzz-saw.

Madam, there's no such thing as a tough child -- if you parboil them first for seven hours, they always come out tender.

The cost of living has gone up another dollar a quart.

Women are like elephants to me   I like to look at 'em, but I wouldn't want to own one.

Bill Finnegan

We're New Yorkers...A little poison in water won't kill us.

Martin H. Fischer

A conclusion is the place where you got tired of thinking.

John Arbuthnot Fisher

Naval supremacy is the best security for the peace of the world...If...you are ready for instant war, with every unit of your strength in the first line and waiting to be first in, and hit your enemy in the belly and kick him when he is down, and boil your prisoners in oil (if you take any) and torture his women and children, then people will keep clear of you.

The essence of war is violence. Moderation in war is imbecility.

Joshua Fishman

A language is a dialect with an army and a navy

[Maybe from Joshua Fishman, maybe not. The saying was first publicized by Max Weinreich in 1945 and he says it was from one of his students. Joshua Fishman said he was the student. Scholars differ on the issue.]

Nick FitzGerald
[a former editor of Virus Bulletin]

Put very simply, I think a lot of the "problems" I hear described, along with the attendant expectation that any computer user should be able to fix them, are akin to expecting any car owner to be able to fix anything that may go wrong with their car (and only using a screwdriver at that!).

Gustave Flaubert

The whole dream of democracy is to raise the proletarian to the level of stupidity attained by the bourgeois.

Peter Fleming

It is impossible, or at any rate highly dangerous, to tell a lie until you know what the truth is going to be.

Marshal **Ferdinand Foch**, Professor of Strategy, *Ecole Superieure de Guerre*, Supreme Commander of Allied Forces in France, 1918

Airplanes are interesting toys but of no military value.

My centre is giving way, my right is in retreat; situation excellent. I shall attack.

Alan Follett

You are speaking lightly, madam, of the beer which I most revere as an ice cream float ingredient!

Carla Fong

God has angels to help with her work, the devil has politicians

Bernard le Bovier de Fontenelle

Exactness is the sublimity of fools.

Henry Ford

Exercise is bunk. If you're sick you shouldn't take it and if you're healthy you don't need it.

It is not the employer who pays the wages. Employers only handle the money. It is the customer who pays the wages.

Whether you think that you can, or that you can't, you are usually right.

George Foreman

I want to keep fighting because it is the only thing that keeps me out of the hamburger joints. If I don't fight, I'll eat this planet.

C. S. Forester

I now pronounce you man and wife. Proceed with the execution.
-- the German captain, The African Queen

Fortran manual for Xerox Computers

The primary purpose of the Data statement is to give names to constants; instead of referring to pi as 3.141592653589793 at every appearance, the variable Pi can be given that value with a Data statement and used instead of the longer form of the constant. This also simplifies modifying the program, should the value of pi change.

Harry Emerson Fosdick

Hating people is like burning down your own house to get rid of a rat.

Michel Foucault

No power is exercised without the extraction, appropriation, distribution or retention of knowledge.

Gene Fowler

An editor should have a pimp for a brother, so he'd have someone to look up to.

Writing is easy. All you do is stare at a blank sheet of paper until drops of blood form on your forehead.

Michael J. Fox

I wish I had a dime for every time I've been called 'diminutive.' I'm not - I'm just damn short.

Michael W. Fox

The life of an ant and that of my child should be granted equal consideration

Anatole France

All writers of confessions, from Augustine on down, have always remained a little in love with their sins.

An education isn't how much you have committed to memory, or even how much you know. It's being able to differentiate between what you know and what you don't.

If fifty million people say a stupid thing, it is still a stupid thing.

It is his reasonable conversation which mostly frightens us in a madman.

Shallow men believe in luck, believe in circumstances -- it was somebody's name, or he happened to be there at the time, or it was so then, and another day would have been otherwise. Strong men believe in cause and effect.

The law in its majestic equality, forbids the rich as well as the poor to sleep under bridges, to beg in the streets, and to steal bread.

When a thing has been said and said well, have no scruple. Take it and copy it.

St. Francis of Assisi

Lord, grant me the serenity to accept the things I cannot change, the courage to change the things I can, and the wisdom to know the difference.

Ed Frank

We're lucky, in the long run, that the Bomb got used at the end of a war rather than the beginning of one...
[a librarian and historian in Memphis, Tennessee, and a lifelong student of WWII writing about the USA's first use of nuclear bombs]

Victor Frankl

An abnormal reaction to an abnormal situation is normal behavior.

Aretha Franklin

I've always felt rock and roll was very, very wholesome music.

Benjamin Franklin

A countryman between two lawyers, is like a fish between two cats.

Beer is proof that God loves us and wants us to be happy.

Dost thou love life? Then do not squander time, for that's the stuff life is made of.

Guests, like fish, begin to stink on the third day.

If Jack's in love, he's no judge of Jill's beauty.

In this world nothing is certain but death and taxes.

Remember, that time is money. He that can earn ten shillings a day by his labor, and goes abroad, or sits idle, one half of that day, though he spends but six pence during his diversion or idleness, ought not to reckon that the only expense; he has really spent, or rather thrown away, five shillings besides.

We must, indeed, all hang together, or most assuredly we shall hang separately.

Whoever would overthrow the liberty of a nation must begin by subduing the freeness of speech.

Frederick the Great

It is disgusting to note the increase in the quantity of coffee used by my subjects and the amount of money that goes out of the country in consequence. Everybody is using coffee. If possible, this must be prevented. My people must drink beer.

John L. Freiler

Peeps just get crabby from time to time. Sadly, the government frowns on the obvious corrective action of dumping them in boiling water and devouring them with loads of melted butter.

Public school doesn't teach history. They feed a smidge of pablum along with a host of urban legends and generally they strive to avoid *any* issue where the kids parents may have been direct participants.

There are sore losers everywhere.

You're entitled to your incredibly wrong opinon.[sic]

Sigmund Freud

Never underestimate the power of the need to obey.

The great question...which I have not been able to answer...is, "What does a woman want?"

The liberty of the individual is no gift of civilization. It was greater before there was any civilization.

What a distressing contrast there is between the radiant intelligence of the child and the feeble mentality of the average adult.

Betty Friedan

When she stopped conforming to the conventional picture of femininity, she finally began to enjoy being a woman.

Dr **David D. Friedman**, Economist (www.daviddfriedman.com)

it is rational to be ignorant when the information costs more than it is worth.
[explaining why voters are rationally ignorant]

Kinky Friedman

There is no shame in being from Texas, only in going back.

Milton Friedman

Nothing is so permanent as a temporary government program.

There is nothing that does so much harm as good intentions.

Erich Fromm

The deepest need of man is the need to overcome his separateness, to leave the prison of his aloneness.
- "The Art of Loving"

David Frost

There have been many definitions of hell, but for the English the best definition is that it is the place here the Germans are the police, the Swedish are the comedians, the Italians are the defense force, Frenchmen dig the roads, the Belgians are the pop singers, the Spanish run the railways, the Turks cook the food, the Irish are the waiters, the Greeks run the government, and the common language is Dutch.

Robert Frost

By working faithfully eight hours a day, you may eventually get to be a boss and work twelve hours a day.

I hold it to be the inalienable right of anybody to go to hell in his own way.

Christopher Fry

You mustn't let it make you conceited. Pride is one of the deadly sins. And it's better to go for the lively ones.

Northrop Frye

Men will die loyally for a wicked or cruel man, but not for an amiable backslapper. Those who are able to attract most devotion from others are those who are able to suggest in their manner that they have no need of it.

J.F.C. Fuller

Nelson did not fight in order to carry out a plan, instead he planned in order to carry out a fight...
- The Decisive Battles of the Western World and Their Influence Upon History, Vol 2, 1792-1944

Paul Fussell

Chess is seldom found above the upper middle class: it's too hard.

~G~

Zsa Zsa Gabor (GFDL)

Husbands are like fires. They go out if unattended.

I am a marvelous housekeeper. Every time I leave a man I keep his house.

I never hated a man enough to give him diamonds back.

Macho does not prove mucho.

To a smart girl men are no problem -- they're the answer.

John Lewis Gaddis

In the Soviet System...incompetence can be institutionalized for years without anyone being able to do anything about it.

William Gaddis

Justice? You get justice in the next world, in this world you have the law.

John Kenneth Galbraith (GFDL)

If all else fails, immortality can always be assured by spectacular error.

The salary of the chief executive of a large corporation is not a market award for achievement. It is frequently in the nature of a warm personal gesture by the individual to himself.

The modern conservative is engaged in one of man[1]s oldest exercises in moral philosophy; that is, the search for a superior moral justification for selfishness.

Wealth is not without its advantages, and the case to the contrary, although it has often been made, has never proved widely persuasive.

Dorothy Gale

What would you do with a brain if you had one?
- "The Wizard of Oz"

Galileo Galilei

I do not feel obliged to believe that the same God who has endowed us with sense, reason, and intellect has intended us to forgo their use.

The Sun, with all the planets revolving around it, and depending on it, can still ripen a bunch of grapes as though it had nothing else in the Universe to do.

Pierre Gallois (GFDL)

If you put tomfoolery into a computer, nothing comes out but tomfoolery. But this tomfoolery, having passed through a very expensive machine, is somehow ennobled and no one dares criticize it.

Indira Gandhi

There are two kinds of people, those who do the work and those who take the credit. Try to be in the first group: there is less competition there.

Mohandas K. Gandhi

Anger and intolerance are the enemies of correct understanding.

For me the different religions are beautiful flowers from the same garden. Therefore they are equally true, and yet being received and interpreted through human instruments, equally imperfect.

Freedom is not worth having if it does not include the freedom to make mistakes.

I believe in equality for everyone, except reporters and photographers.

I object to violence because when it appears to do good, the good is only temporary; the evil it does is permanent.

If you don't find God in the next person you meet, it is a waste of time looking for him further.

In matters of conscience, the law of majority has no place.

It is easy enough to be friendly to one's friends. But to befriend the one who regards himself as your enemy is the quintessence of true religion. The other is mere business.

Morality is contraband in war.

No doubt religion has to answer for some of the most terrible crimes in history. But that is the fault not of religion but of the ungovernable brute in man.

The good man is the friend of all living things.

War is an unmitigated evil. But it certainly does one good thing. It drives away fear and brings bravery to the surface.

What difference does it make to the dead, the orphans and the homeless, whether the mad destruction is wrought under the name of totalitarianism or the holy name of liberty or democracy?

When I despair, I remember that all through history, the way of truth and love has always won. There have been murderers and tyrants, and for a time they can seem invincible. But in the end they always fall. Think of it, always.

Shanta Gandhi

I'm afraid that art is very, very pale compared to real life sometimes. Very pale indeed.

Jerry Garcia

Somebody has to do something, and it's just incredibly pathetic that it has to be us.

Ed Gardner

Opera is when a guy gets stabbed and instead of bleeding, he sings.

James Alan Gardner

Given time, a ship's crew will attach sexual innuendo to anything. It makes their jobs more exciting.
-- Expendable

Stanley Marion Garn

If the aborigine drafted an IQ test, all of Western civilization would presumably flunk it.

Lieutenant. Colonel **Joe C. Garrett**, staff Veterinarian for AAFES Europe

Moldy juice is more of an aesthetic problem, unless somebody's superallergic to the mold. It's good penicillin. It'll kill whatever's in you.

Roger Gary

Any dog that won't eat ice cream or chips is up to something.

Bill Gates

The software is where the magic is.

General **James Gavin**

When we jumped into Sicily, the units became separated, and I couldn't find anyone. Eventually I stumbled across two colonels, a major, three captains, two lieutenants, and one rifleman, and we secured the bridge. Never in the history of war have so few been led by so many.

Bill Gawne

The amount of ignorance masquerading as knowledge in this discussion is just amazing.

Bob Geary

Someone told me that the headaches were my body telling me I should quit drinking coffee, which was clearly wrong - my body was saying explicitly, "Get some coffee, dumbass!

Sam "Sully" Gehring

Women are just like cats. To win them, you must first make them purr.

R. Geis

Death is life's way of telling you you've been fired.

Gensha

If you understand, things are as they are. If you do not understand, things are as they are.

Mary Gentle

Prejudice is stronger than guns.
- Grunts

Dr. **Darren S. A. George**

Of course, since Death Stars don't really exist, and I've never been in space, I'm quitting this thread and getting a life.

James George

There's nothing bad that happens that isn't somehow good for lawyers.

German Proverb

Old wine and young women are the best ways to pass time.

David Gerrold

Being crazy is a great way to get attention without having to be responsible.

The constitution guarantees every citizen the right to make a damn fool of himself, in public or in private, however he or she chooses.

Fairness is a concept invented by human beings. Nature doesn't believe in it.

If God is really watching us, the least we can do is be entertaining.

Life is hard. Then you die. Then they throw dirt in your face. Then the worms eat you. Be grateful it happens in that order.

No matter how hard we try, the government cannot be fair to everybody. Cannot. The very best we can do is treat everybody equally unfairly.

There isn't any such thing as sanity. What there is, is the ability to be appropriate to the situation.

There's one thing to be said for ignorance. It starts a lot of interesting arguments.

J. Paul Getty

If you can count your money, you don't have a billion dollars.

Bob Getz

About wearing a cap indoors, ma'am, some rooms can be awfully sunny, and you have to admit caps are sure cheaper than curtains.

For those few who might not recognize the name Ernest Hemingway, he was a hunter and a fisherman who also did some writing...

Rap is to music what demolition derbies are to transportation.

To the victor belongs the rubble.

Kathryn Ghent

A scrubbing brush and elbow grease is the only way to get our floors clean. Which is why thy're [sic] not.

Every now and again I want to continue an xpost and drag us kicking and screaming into a huge flame war.

Edward Gibbon

The wind and the waves are always on the side of the ablest navigators.

John Gibbons, Toronto Blue Jays Manager

The thing about the Yankees, one of the reasons they're so respected, is they do things right. Always have. They've got a lot of pride and a lot of class. They play the game hard.

Kahlil Gibran

Keep me away from the wisdom which does not cry, the philosophy which does not laugh and the greatness which does not bow before children.

You give but little when you give of your possessions. It is when you give of yourself that you truly give.

James G. Gilbert

The "Defense of Marriage Act" before Congress was co-sponsored by the divorced Bob Dole and the divorced House Speaker Newt Gingrich. The bill, if it passes, has been promised to be signed by the renowned skirt-chaser President Bill Clinton. These men tell us that they support the bill because committed, monogamous same-sex unions are an affront to the sacred institution of heterosexual marriage. Am I the only one a bit confused here?

W. S. Gilbert

I always voted at my party's call,

And I never thought of thinking for myself at all.
-- HMS Pinafore

Hank Gillette

The government says you can do it. You trust your government, don't you?

You've seen nothing until you've seen volleyball played at a nude beach.

Richard Gilliam

Pet names for children are part of the risk of growing up Southern.

Alexis A. Gilliland

The trouble with hell is that the ambient temperature is above the flash point of alcohol. Which means you can't linger over your drink.

Jean Giraudoux

Only the mediocre are always at their best.

Washington Gladden

It is better to say, "This one thing I do" than to say, "These forty things I dabble in."

Michael Glaser

Though SUV's offer marginally greater utility, I think they are bought because husbands found a way to get a truck in the family.

Jackie Gleason

I have a 'Play the melody' philosophy. It means don't over-arrange, don't make life difficult. Just play the melody -- and do it the simplest way possible.

If you have it, and you know you have it, you have it. If you don't have it and think you have it, you have it. But if you have it and don't know you have it, you don't have it.

The second day of a diet is always easier than the first. By the second day you're off it.

Thin people are beautiful, but fat people are adorable.

Mike Godwin

The First Amendment was designed to protect offensive speech, because nobody ever tries to ban the other kind.

Josef Goebbels

The lie can be maintained only for such time as the State can shield the people from the political, economic and/or military consequences of the lie. It thus becomes vitally important for the State to use all of its powers to repress dissent, for the truth is the mortal enemy of the lie, and thus by extension, the truth becomes the greatest enemy of the State.

We can do without butter, but despite all our love of peace, not without arms. One cannot shoot with butter but with guns.

Hermann Göring

Naturally the common people don't want war...but after all it is the leaders of a country who determine policy, and it is always a simple matter to drag the people along...All you have to do is tell them they are being attacked, and denounce the pacifists for lack of patriotism and exposing the country to danger.

Johann Wolfgang von Goethe

A person can stand almost anything except a succession of ordinary days.

He is the happiest, be he king or peasant, who finds peace in his home.

If you start to think about your physical or moral condition, you usually find that you are sick.

In politics as on the sickbed people toss from one side to the other, thinking that they will be more comfortable.

"Know thyself?" If I knew myself, I'd run away.

Let everyone sweep in front of his own door, and the whole world will be clean.

Nature goes her own way and all that to us seems an exception is really according to order.

Nothing is more revolting than the majority; for it consists of few vigorous predecessors, of knaves who accommodate themselves, of weak people who assimilate themselves, and the mass that toddles after them without knowing in the least what it wants.

One ought, every day at least, to hear a little song, read a good poem, see a fine picture, and, if it were possible, to speak a few reasonable words.

The intelligent man finds almost everything ridiculous, the sensible man hardly anything.

The sagacious reader who is capable of reading between these lines what does not stand written in them, but is nevertheless implied, will be able to form some conception.
-- Truth and Beauty

We do not have to visit a madhouse to find disordered minds; our planet is the mental institution of the universe.

When an idea is wanting, a word can always be found to take its place.

When ideas fail, words come in very handy.

Isaac Goldberg

Diplomacy is to do and say the nastiest thing in the nicest way.

Emma Goldman

If voting changed anything, they'd make it illegal.

William Goldman

Life is pain, highness. Anyone who says differently is selling something.
-- Westley, The Princess Bride

Oliver Goldsmith

Honor sinks where commerce long prevails.

There is nothing so absurd or ridiculous that has not at some time been said by some philosopher.

Bobcat Goldthwait

The only reason clowns perform in hospitals is that's the only place kids can't get up and run away from them.

Barry Goldwater

America is a country where anyone can become president - except me.

Anyone who tries to make politics out of God ought to go to hell.

I don't care if a soldier is straight, as long as he can shoot straight.

If you don't mind smelling like a peanut for a few days, peanut butter makes a darn fine shaving cream.

Samuel Goldwyn

A bachelor's life is no life for a single man.

I can give you a definite maybe.

Baron **Kolmar von der Goltz**

Modern wars have become the nations' way of doing business.

Lee Gomes

While modern technology has given people powerful new communication tools, it apparently can do nothing to alter the fact that many people have nothing useful to say.

Alberto Gonzalez, US Attorney General

President Washington, President Lincoln, President Wilson, President Roosevelt have all authorized electronic surveillance on a far broader scale.

Jane Goodall

We are the only species able to change the natural world and able to understand what we've done, so we must be the stewards of the world.

Ellen Goodman

Sports is the male icebreaker and leveler of class, race and age...It's what many men who have little in common have in common.

Robert Goodman

And of course people who don't know what they're talking about might complain about anything.

It bugs me that BAD term papers are now offered for cheating.

James "Heavy" Goodwin

One benefit of being with the Marines is that I get a two hour lunch break. The Marines have to do an hour of PT at lunch. I just do lunch twice.

Laura Goodwin (http://lauragoodwin.org)

Forget diamonds: whips and rope are a girl's best friend!

I have learned that the majority of people DON'T CARE about your sex life, or if they do care, it's because they are fascinated. It's a tiny, nasty, mean-spirited, and incredibly ignoble little bunch of skunks who are actively out to get [you].

If our right to go to hell in our own way is attacked, so is our right to go to heaven in our own way.

Mikhail Gorbachev

The market is not an invention of capitalism. It has existed for centuries. It is an invention of civilization.

Rick Gordon

Crossposting isn't inherently evil, in the same sense that necrophilia doesn't really hurt anybody. One wonders only whether it's appropriate to the occasion.

David Ormsby Gore, 5th Baron Harlech

It would indeed be a tragedy if the history of the human race proved to be nothing more than the story of an ape playing with a box of matches on a petrol dump.

Maxim Gorky

When a woman gets married it is like jumping into a hole in the ice in the middle of winter; you do it once and you remember it the rest of your days.
- " The Lower Depth"

Greg Goss

Dogs have owners. Cats have staff.

Geek status comes from digesting massive quantities of widely varying information and throwing it out at random to see if it would be recognized

So how can a guy get concussed by a hamburger but survive a roof collapse?

Some of us don't see the big deal about big tits. Are they perky?

Stephen Jay Gould

I'm not inclined to write pompous books about unanswerable questions. That strikes me as a tremendous waste of time.

John D. Goulden

Microsoft is going to write the software that spies on me? I feel better already.

Graey (slayer@luvewe.eglobe.com)

The moment you deign to voice your opinions, you are giving everyone who hears (or in this case reads) them the right to bash you for them. If you don't want ridicule and criticism, lurk. With the freedom of speach [sic] comes the freedom to flame the [expletive deleted] out of someone for speaking.

Douglas Graham

One of the things that amazed me is how many bullets can be fired during a firefight without anyone getting hurt.

Ulysses S. Grant

I have never advocated war except as a means of peace.

I know only two tunes: One is Yankee Doodle, and the other isn't.

There was never a time, in my opinion, some way could not be found to prevent the drawing of the sword.

GrapeApe@AOL.com

If you are going to pretend to be southern, you have to use those well worn Southern seasoning agents, salt and pepper and fat.

There is something about a baseball cap that automatically lowers the apparent IQ of the wearer at least 20 points, even if there is a practical need for it.

Bill Graves

This is a terrible, tragic, embarrassing solution to a problem that did not exist.
- On the Kansas BOE decision to drop evolution from the state assessment criteria.

John S. Gray

Restitution and compensation can work wonders for a wronged person. But common sense, the rights of the innocent, and the compelling necessity of breaking the vendetta chain dictate that the eligibility for compensation expire with the life of the wronged person. If my ancestor stole your ancestor's cow, I am not the thief and you are not the victim of thievery...Only the redress of present wrongs can do anything for the living and unborn. But even this taxes all the insight, understanding, and patience that both sides can muster...

Greek Proverb

Ignorance of one's misfortunes is clear gain.

Steven J. Green

If at first you don't succeed, try again. Then delegate. No sense making a fool out of yourself.

Graham Greene

In Italy for thirty years under the Borgias they had warfare, terror, murder and bloodshed, but they produced Michelangelo, Leonardo da Vinci and the Renaissance. In Switzerland they had brotherly love, they had five hundred years of democracy and peace, and what did they produce? The cuckoo clock.
- Harry Lime to Holly Martins, The Third Man

Greenville County, SC, Department of Social Services

Your food stamps will be stopped effective March, 1992, because we received notice that you passed away. May God bless you. You may reapply if there is a change in your circumstances.

Germaine Greer

Man made one grave mistake: in answer to vaguely reformist and humanitarian agitation he admitted women to politics and the professions. The conservatives who saw this as the undermining of our civilization and the end of the state and marriage were right after all; it is time for the demolition to begin.

One may not reach the dawn save by the path of the night.

Dick Gregory

I never believed in Santa Claus because I knew no white man would be coming into my neighborhood after dark.

Wayne Gretzky

You miss 100 percent of the shots you never take.

Corporal **Daniel Grimes**

I'd rather be sleeping on rocks without air conditioning than not being able to have Internet.

Lewis Grizzard

I don't think I'll get married again. I'll just find a woman I don't like and give her a house.

Matt Groening

Love is a perky elf dancing a merry little jig and then suddenly he turns on you with a miniature machine gun.

When authorities warn you of the sinfulness of sex, there is an important lesson to be learned. Do not have sex with the authorities.

groo

I am not a kook, but I play one on usenet.

I have come to the inescapable conclusion that a significant fraction of the population consists of self-absorbed idiots.

I heard part of a segment on NPR yesterday about some substance that scientists have found that when applied topically induced mouse skin cells to produce melanin. I kept imagining little tanned mice wearing sunglasses.

I will sometimes switch ears, but the left dominates.

I try to not get too involved in the details of doll/dinosaur sex.

Jell-O also makes me giggle, but only if applied properly.

The distinction between a bar and most frat houses is vanishingly small.

The innocent suffer for the evils of the wicked. No longer will you be able to count on receiving an answer to the burning question "But what does groo think?" when faced with a thorny conundrum, a moral dilemma, or a question about nonexistent sheep.

Who ya gonna trust, me or some big old book with teeny print?

Lieutenant Colonel **Dave Grossman**, On Killing

But we must also remember that death has its place in the natural order of life.

To sponsors, media executives claim that just a few well-placed seconds can control how American will spend its hard-earned money. But to Congress and other watchdog agencies they argue that they are not responsible for causing viewers to change the way they will respond to any emotionally charged, potentially violent circumstance that they may subsequently find themselves in.

War has often been a sexist environment, but death is an equal opportunity employer.

War is an environment that will psychologically debilitate 98 percent of all who participate in it for any length of time. And the 2 percent who are not driven insane by war appear to have already been insane...before coming to the battlefield.

Lieutenant Colonel **Dave Grossman and Gloria DeGaetano**, Stop Teaching Our Children to Kill

How can there even be any more argument when everyone in the industry agrees that thirty-second television commercials change adult behavior. If rapidly moving images and inane jingles slashed on a small two-dimensional screen can get adults to do things, why would violent images watched for hours on screens large and small have no impact on the behaviors of children and teens.

Hustler is another manufacturer that does not claim any "right" to sell their product to your kids; they accept restraints on their industry, but the TV, movie, and video game industries fall short of even the moral standard set by Hustler.

Let's face it, we live in a violent world. We can see it in many aspects of our surroundings, and if we miss it we have a chance to see it played out again and again in the media.

Some blame [intensified violence] on increased access to guns. Such access is never a good thing, but we're missing the point if we blame guns; the availability of guns has been a constant factor in the violence equation in the United States. The question we should be asking is why kids want to pick up weapons in the first place.

Leslie Richard Groves

People who talk of outlawing the atomic bomb are mistaken--what needs to be outlawed is war.

David Guaspari

Comparing information to knowledge is like asking whether the fatness of a pig is more or less green than the designated hitter rule.
- Risks digest 8.55

Ernesto "Che" Guevara

Go on, shoot coward. You're only killing a man!
- reported last words

Silence is argument carried out by other means.

Francesco Guicciadini

We are at a great disadvantage when we make war on people who have nothing to lose.

Ronald F. Guilmette

That is an entirely sensible idea, and that in turn undoubtedly explains why it hasn't been done.

Guindon

The good Lord never gives you more than you can handle. Unless you die of something.

Sacha Guitry

When a man steals your wife, there is no better revenge than to let him keep her.

You can pretend to be serious; you can't pretend to be witty.

Doug Gwyn

Truth is not determined by majority vote.

~H~

C. Hacking

While preceding your entrance with a grenade is a good tactic in Quake, it can lead to problems if attempted at work.

Major **D. Lee Hackle**

Unlike mainstream America, the military is not about individual and personal rights, it is about accomplishing the mission.

Uta Hagen

We must overcome the notion that we must be regular. It robs you of the chance to be extraordinary and leads you to the mediocre.

Ernie Hai

[Singapore's official lack of Internet access is] not to control, but to protect the citizens of Singapore. In our society, you can state your views, but they have to be correct.

Haida Indian saying

We do not inherit this land from our ancestors; we borrow it from our children.

H.R. Haldeman

We are getting into semantics again. If we use words, there is a very grave danger they will be misinterpreted.

Matt Hall

I love the Internet. Useless info at the speed of light.

Rich Hall, from Self Help for the Bleak

Get up every morning with a purpose, not a reason. If you don't know the difference, picture a robbery taking place in an alley. The guy holding the gun is being "purposeful." The guy forking over his wallet is being "reasonable."

Robert W. Hall

I don't have my doctorate yet, but as far as I can tell, you sound pretty sick. You probably should watch 'Barney and Friends' daily, check yourself into a hospital, join the Hari Krishnas/Jehovahs Witlesses, or commit suicide.

Mike Hallman, (President, Microsoft)

Users of information are probably not, nor do they want to be computer scientists.

William F. "Bull"Halsey

All problems, personal, national, or combat, become smaller if you don't dodge them, but confront them. Touch a thistle timidly, and it pricks you; grasp it boldly, and its spines crumble. Carry the battle to the enemy! Lay your ship alongside his!

Alexander Hamilton ("The Federalist No. 84")

To bereave a man of life . . . or by violence to confiscate his estate, without accusation or trial, would be so gross and notorious an act of despotism as must at once convey the alarm of tyranny throughout the whole nation; but confinement of the person, by secretly hurrying him to jail, where his sufferings are unknown or forgotten, is a less public, a less striking, and therefore a more dangerous engine of arbitrary government.

Robert M. Hamilton

A book of quotations . . . can never be complete.

Jon Hammond

The early bird gets the worm, but the second mouse gets the cheese

Christopher Hampton

Asking a working writer what he thinks about critics is like asking a lamp post how it feels about dogs.

M C Hamster

But still, I was right, even if I was wrong.

I feel nothing but dread about almost everything. But understand I'm a Cubs fan *and* a Democrat.

Charles J. Hanley

Terrorists, too, can boost productivity through technology.

Barry Hansen (Dr. Demento)

And let's face it a song like 'Poisoning Pigeons in the Park' never really goes out of style.
[Mr. Hanson was not advocating cruelty to animals and was concerned that people not think so. Rather, he was commenting on people's taste in music.]

Captain Tameichi Hara

The beatings will continue until the morale improves.

Donna Haraway

We unmasked the doctrines of objectivity because they threatened our budding sense of collective historical subjectivity and agency, and we ended up with one more excuse for not learning any post Newtonian physics.
- "Situated Knowledges: The Science Question in Feminism as a Site of Discourse on the Privilege of Partial Perspective," *Feminist Studies* 14, no.3 (1988): 575-99.

Larry Hardiman

The word 'politics' is derived from the word 'poly' meaning 'many', and the word 'ticks' meaning 'blood sucking parasites'.

Tonya Harding

God just told me I had to go into that bar.

Augustus Hare

Half the failures of this world arise from pulling in one's horse as he is leaping.

Michael Harrington

Clothes make the poor invisible...America has the best-dressed poverty the world has ever known.

If there is a technological advance without a social advance, there is, almost automatically, an increase in human misery.

One cannot raise the bottom of society without benefiting everyone above.

Our affluent society contains those of talent and insight who are driven to prefer poverty, to choose it, rather than to submit to the desolation of an empty abundance. It is a strange part of the other America that one finds in the intellectual slums.

Sydney Harris

A person who is going to commit an inhuman act invariably excuses himself by saying, "I'm only human, after all."

Richard Harrison

Maybe my greatest contribution to cinema was not doing "Fistful of Dollars", and recommending Clint [Eastwood] for the part

William Henry Harrison

I believe and I say it is true Democratic feeling, that all the measures of the Government are directed to the purpose of making the rich richer and the poor poorer.

Max Hastings (Bomber Command)

Most civilised men would agree that there is a significant moral distinction between the incidental and deliberate destruction of civilian life in war, and it is hard to look back across a generation on such a night's work as the destruction of Darmstadt with any pride.

Hatori Miho

You can go for a week without love - you will die without food.

Dave Hatunen

In the land of the blind, the one eyed man is king... Until they find out he can see, then they kill him.

It must be nice to be young, ignorant, and believe the world began in 1980.

One can only find so many ways to hide one's crotch without looking obvious.

Stanley Hauerwas

Consider the problem of taking showers with [Christians]. They are, after all, constantly going on about the business of witnessing in the hopes of making converts to their God and church. Would you want to shower with such people? You never know when they might try to baptize you.
- The Hauerwas Reader

I'm a pacifist because I'm a violent son of a bitch.

One reason why we Christians argue so much about which hymn to sing, which liturgy to follow, which way to worship is that the commandments teach us to believe that bad liturgy eventually leads to bad ethics. You begin by singing some sappy, sentimental hymn, then you pray some pointless prayer, and the next thing you know you have murdered your best friend.

Stephen Hawking

God still has a few tricks up his sleeve.

I think computer viruses should count as life. I think it says something about human nature that the only form of life we have created so far is purely destructive. We've created life in our own image.

Jane E. Hawkins

You can't always get what you want, but, if you try, sometimes you can want what you get.

S.I. Hayakawa

Inaccuracy in communication is not merely a mistake. It is a crime, because when we do not understand another person's reality, we can easily run it over with our own.

Woody Hayes

Statistics always reminds me of the fellow who drowned in a river whose average depth was only three feet.

Admiral **Thomas Hayward**, Chief of Naval Operations

I am tired of talking about what the threat is. Let us be the threat. I want to read about how Admiral Gorshkov stays awake nights worrying about our threat to his Navy.

Michael J. Haze, Chief of Fort Carson Housing Office

In reality, we're the biggest slumlords in the country.

SarahAnn Hazelwood

The Grimace. Barney. Jonestown Kool-Aid. I fear purple.

Vicki Hearne and Elizabeth Marshall Thomas

The difference between difficult dogs and vicious human beings is that difficult dogs do not rise to positions of prominence in the community.
- Bandit

Friedrich Hebbel

It's incredible how much intelligence is used in this world to prove nonsense.

Georg Wilhelm Friedrich Hegel

We learn from history that we do not learn from history.

What experience and history teach is this - that nations and governments have never learned anything from history, or acted upon any lessons they might have drawn from it.

Heinrich Heine

One should forgive one's enemies, but not before they are hanged.

Wherever they burn books, they will also, in the end, burn people.

Robert A. Heinlein (GFDL)

A desire not to butt into other people's business is at least eighty percent of all human wisdom...and the other twenty percent isn't very important.

A true confession story should never be tarnished by any taint of truth.

All females are anarchists in their hearts, with no innate respect for law and order...

Never try to outstubborn a cat.

Never try to teach a pig to sing. It wastes your time and annoys the pig.
- Time Enough for Love

We all know that there isn't any great difference between one female and another save possibly in their cooking.

When in danger or in doubt, run in circles, scream and shout.
- The Number of the Beast

You can't ever pay anything Back...therefore, you pay it Forward.

Joseph Heller

Some men are born mediocre, some men achieve mediocrity, and some men have mediocrity thrust upon them.
– Catch 22

They told me it would disrupt my life less if I got killed sooner.

Lillian Hellman

Writers are interesting people, but often mean and petty.

Leona Helmsley

We don't pay taxes. Only the little people pay taxes.

Ernest Hemingway

Always do sober what you said you'd do drunk. That will teach you to keep your mouth shut.

I would like to take the great DiMaggio fishing.
-- Santiago, The Old Man and the Sea

One cat just leads to another.

Don Henley

A man with a briefcase can steal millions more than any man with a gun.

Lawsuits should not be used to destroy a viable and independent distribution system. The solution lies in the marketplace and not the courtroom.

There are no facts. There is no truth. Just data to be manipulated.

Manfred Hennecke

Do insects experience romantic love? It is commonly assumed that some European, especially Mediterranean, insects really do. American, British, Japanese, Russian, or German insects probably not.

Henri IV of France

It is my wish that in my kingdom there should be no peasant so poor that he cannot have a chicken in his pot every Sunday.

Patrick Henry

Is life so dear, or peace so sweet, as to be purchased at the price of chains and slavery? Forbid it, Almighty God! I know not what course others may take; but as for me, give me liberty or give me death!

Katharine Hepburn

If you follow all the rules of life, you miss all the fun.

Sometimes I wonder if men and women really suit each other. Perhaps they should live next door and just visit now and then.

Heraclitus

No man ever steps in the same river twice, for it's not the same river and he's not the same man.

The road uphill and the road downhill are one and the same.

There is nothing permanent, except change.

Winfried Herget, Mainz University professor

The Americans brought strange habits [after World War II]. For example, men took out the garbage and 'the women could cook and talk on the phone at the same time.'

Michael Herr

The Marine Corps is the finest instrument ever devised for killing young Americans.
-- Dispatches

A.R. Herring

At the moment I kind of feel like Wile E. Coyote holding up that little umbrella.

Richard Hershberger

I have to say, the combination of firearms, homemade booze, and Billy Ray playing the bagpipes spells 'fun' to me.

I too generally dislike inspirational or religious or irreligious messages accompanying my purchase of fungible consumer products.

Part of being an adult is realizing that you don't have to watch a show simply because other people are.

Play the ad hominem card or don't. But play it while complaining about it will only make people point at you and laugh.

When your whole argument is that the sky is falling, you have a problem when it stubbornly refuses to fall: a lot of people are eventually going to notice.

Orel Hershiser

Hello, my name is Orel Hershiser, and I'm a reformed Dodger. I spent three years in Cleveland in detox, and I'm much better now.

Reverend **Theodore Hesburgh**

The most important thing a father can do for his children is to love their mother.

Hermann Hesse

Eternity is a mere moment, just long enough for a joke.
- Steppenwolf

If you hate a person, you hate something in him that is a part of yourself. What isn't part of ourselves doesn't disturb us.
- Demian

The deity is within you, not in ideas and books. Truth is lived, not taught.
- Magister Ludi (The Glass Bead Game)

They knew a tremendous number of things — But was it worthwhile knowing all these things if they did not know the one important thing, the only important thing?
- Siddhartha

Wisdom is not communicable. The wisdom which a wise man tries to communicate always sounds foolish... Knowledge can be communicated, but not wisdom.
- Siddhartha

Charlton Heston

A war put off is not a war avoided.

History shows that one out of three Hollywood conservatives become President.

Hiawatha aka Dr H

Just because something has always been done one way before, does that mean it always has to be done that way forever? Is there no way of growing, evolving, improving things? Are we incapable of learning and change? Do we really believe that things are as good as they can possibly be right now, and there is no hope of ever making them better?

"suit" is as much an attitude as a style of dress. Every industry has it's [sic] share of suits; some of them wear jeans and Birkenstocks.

Bob Hiebert, Jr.

I absolutely hate it when I go to a football game and a baseball game breaks out.

Cullen Hightower

We may not imagine how our lives could be more frustrating and complex- but Congress can.

Hans Hildebrandt

If you want a German to tell you what he thinks is wrong with Germany, say something positive about Germany. Works every time and with every nation.

Benny Hill

Do unto others, then run.

The odds against there being a bomb on a plane are a million to one, and against two bombs a million times a million to one. Next time you fly, cut the odds and take a bomb.

John N. Hill, Jr.

If you confront evil you can stop it. If you don't confront it, it grows like weeds.

Sir Edmund Hillary

It is not the mountain we conquer but ourselves.

Hillel (gazit@cs.duke.edu)

In every revolution those who are very committed tend to keep the guillotine working extra hours.

Heinrich Himmler

The best political weapon is the weapon of terror. Cruelty commands respect. Men may hate us. But, we don't ask for their love; only for their fear.

Emperor **Hirohito**

The war situation has developed not necessarily to Japan's advantage.
- August 14, 1945

Steve Hiser, Wichita PD

It's not illegal to accidentally shoot yourself in the leg.

Alfred Hitchcock

I have a perfect cure for a sore throat; cut it.

I must apologize for the lack of bloodshed in tonight's program. We shall try to do better next time.

The paperback is very interesting, but I find it will never replace the hardcover book; it makes a very poor doorstop.

There are several differences between a football game and a revolution. For one thing, a football game usually lasts longer and the participants wear uniforms. Also there are more injuries at a football game.

Adolf Hitler

I regard Henry Ford as my inspiration.

Mankind has grown strong in eternal struggles and it will only perish through eternal peace.

Nature is cruel; therefore we are also entitled to be cruel. When I send the flower of German youth into the steel hail of the next war without feeling the slightest regret over the precious German blood that is being spilled, should I not also have the right to eliminate millions of an inferior race that multiplies like vermin?

The size of the lie is a definite factor in causing it to be believed, for the vast masses of a nation are in the depths of their hearts more easily deceived than they are consciously and intentionally bad. The primitive simplicity of their minds renders them more easily prey to a big lie than a small one, for they themselves often tell little lies but would be ashamed to tell a big one.
- Mein Kampf

We shall not capitulate - no, never, we may be destroyed, but if we are, we shall drag a world with us - a world in flames. (1932)

What luck for rulers that men do not think.

Who remembers the Armenians? The world did nothing then. It will do nothing now.

Paula Hitler

The autobahn and the VW are probably the best things my brother left behind.

Arthur D. Hlavaty

Sometimes it's a good idea to revere the sacred crazy from a safe distance.
- 1980 Turing Award lecture

C.A.R. Hoare

Premature optimization is the root of all evil.

There are two ways of constructing a software design: One way is to make it so simple that there are obviously no deficiencies, and the other way is to make it so complicated that there are no obvious deficiencies.

Jeannie Hobbs

I have been known to run over my own feet with my office chair.

Interesting things happen when you eat a quantity of bright blue food coloring.

John Oliver Hobbes (pen name for **Pearl Mary Teresa Craigie**)

A man with a career can have no time to waste upon his wife and friends; he has to devote it wholly to his enemies.

Thomas Hobbes

Force and fraud are in war the two cardinal virtues.

Prof. **Jack Hodges**, San Francisco State University

The vast majority of users are Internet illiterate or inarticulate.

Eric Hoffer

A low capacity for getting along with those near us often goes hand in hand with a high receptivity to the idea of the brotherhood of men.

An empty head is not really empty; it is stuffed with rubbish. Hence the difficulty of forcing anything into an empty head.

It is easier to love humanity as a whole than to love one's neighbor.

Passionate hatred can give meaning and purpose to an empty life.

Talk shows don't exist to present guests, or convey information, or for any other reason usually presented. Talks shows exist to make the host look good.

When people are free to do as they please, they usually imitate each other.

Abbie Hoffman

I believe in compulsory cannibalism. If people were forced to eat what they killed, there would be no more wars.

Random action produces random political results...Why waste even a rock?
-- Steal This Book

Sacred cows make the best hamburger.

The first duty of a revolutionary is to get away with it.

Frank J Hollis

These opinions have not been passed by 3 committees, 7 subcommittees and 5 continuous improvement teams. So they can't be the opinions of my employer.

Lizz Holmans

I can 'splain it to you, but I can't understand it for you.

You are forgiven. Go out and sin some more--just check your crossposting afore you do it.

John Andrew Holmes

It is well to remember that the entire universe, with one trifling exception, is composed of others.

Oliver Wendell Holmes

Men do not quit playing because they grow old; they grow old because they quit playing.

Public policy sacrifices the individual to the general good.
- The Common Law

The mind of the bigot is like the pupil of the eye; the more light you pour upon it, the more it will contract.

The most stringent protection of free speech would not protect a man in falsely shouting fire in a theater and causing a panic...The question in every case is whether the words used are used in such circumstances and are of such a nature as to create a clear and present danger that they will bring about the substantive evils that Congress has a right to prevent.
- Schenck v. United States, 1919.

To obtain a man's opinion of you, make him mad.

Lou Holtz

Ability is what you're capable of doing. Motivation determines what you do. Attitude determines how well you do it.

You'll never get ahead of anyone as long as you're trying to get even.

Jenny Holzer

Some days you wake and immediately start to worry. Nothing in particular is wrong. It's just the suspicion that forces are aligning quietly and there will be trouble.
- "The Living Series"

Daniel B. Holzman

Love does not subtract, it multiplies.

Herbert Hoover

Blessed are the young, for they shall inherit the national debt.

Older men declare war. But it is the youth that must fight and die.

J. Edgar Hoover

Justice is incidental to law and order.

Bob Hope

If you watch a game it's fun. If you play it, it's recreation. If you work at it, it's golf.

John Hopkin

As for romantic sub-plots, they're usually completely silly. It sometimes looks as if you can't go to the local shop for a newspaper and a carton of milk without some kind of sexual tension and will-she-won't-she or some crap like that.

Cats are perfectly happy living indoors 24 hours a day. When they meow at the door, they're not asking to be let out - they're just thanking you for confining them so effectively. And when you open the door and they rush out, they just want to check that the outside of the door is in the same excellent condition as the inside.

Decent doner kebabs are just too good to give up when modern antibiotics are readily available and toilet paper is so cheap.

Film critics are rarely noted for their intellectual powers. Most think "irony" describes the taste of broccoli.

Fisher's reputation for high-quality audio gear took a nosedive when they merged with Price.

Hang on, I'll just threaten a weasel and see what happens.

If Bush told you that sticking carrots in your nostrils would defeat terrorism, you'd be first in line at the vegetable patch, wouldn't you?

I'm not happy with testing 240V with the meter. I'd need someone to stand here and show me what to do, because I don't trust myself not to get something wrong and suddenly end up at the other end of the room with a new hairdo.

I bought one of those "add water and stir" beer kits a few years ago. Amazing things. You get a plastic polypin with some powder in it, and you add water, leave it to ferment for ten days, and then you try a sip and pour the whole lot down the toilet. It was bloody awful.

That's not jazz, it's plain wanking.

There are plenty of stupid people in the world, and many of them have internet connections

Admiral **Grace Hopper**

It is easier to get forgiveness than permission.

Horace

Carpe diem, quam minimum credula postero! (Seize the day, put no trust in the morrow!)

Harlan Howard

Country music is three chords and the truth.

Edgar Watson Howe

There is always a type of man who says he loves his fellow men, and expects to make a living at it.

Fred Hoyle

There is a coherent plan in the universe, though I don't know what it is a plan for.

Elbert Hubbard

A pessimist is one who has been intimately acquainted with an optimist.

Every man is a damned fool for at least five minutes every day. Wisdom consists in not exceeding the limit.

Genius may have its limitations, but stupidity is not thus handicapped.

God will not look you over for medals, degrees or diplomas but for scars.

If you cannot answer your opponent's argument with reason, all is not lost; you can still call him vile names.

Never explain, your friends do not need it, and your enemies will not believe you anyway.

The idea that is not dangerous is not worthy of being called an idea at all.

Kin Hubbard

A grouch escapes so many little annoyances that it almost pays to be one.

Next to a circus there ain't nothing that packs up and tears out any quicker than the Christmas spirit.

Some folks seem to have descended from the chimpanzee later than others.

Juergen Hubert

[P]laying bagpipes in closed rooms should count as aggravated assault

Look, if there is one thing I have learned on Usenet, then it is that people who start cross-posting threads en masse by merely quoting what someone else has said are _never_ worth the effort. In most cases, they are only pathetically desperate for attention, and the only thing they deserve is to be mocked.

Oh, and I would keep away from microwave ovens, aluminium foil, flourides, salicylates, Beta-type videotapes, windmills, the number 23, sharp objects, and people named Bob if I were you. It will be healthier for you in the long run...

Today I woke up at 6.30 am to the lovely sound of a chainsaw, wielded by a man who cut some bushes near the town hall (which is opposite to my house).

I would have killed him, but he was better armed.

Mike Huckabee

But there's no crying in baseball, and no politics in music.

It's not that we can't be Christians. The sad fact is most of us don't want to be enough to try our faith to the point of patience and perseverance.

Fred A. Hufnagel, Sr.

Be nice to everyone on your way to the top because you pass them all on the way down.

Charles Evans Hughes

When we lose the right to be different, we lose the privilege to be free.

Victor Hugo

One is not idle because one is absorbed. There is both visible and invisible labor. To contemplate is to toil. To think is to do.

The greatest happiness of life is the conviction that we are loved--loved for ourselves, or rather, loved in spite of ourselves.

To love another person is to see the face of God!
- Les Miserables

When dictatorship is a fact, revolution becomes a right.

Cordell Hull

Never insult an alligator until you've crossed the river.

Hubert Humphrey

The impersonal hand of government can never replace the helping hand of a neighbor.

The right to be heard does not include the right to be taken seriously.

Collis P. Huntington

Whatever is not nailed down is mine. Whatever I can pry loose is not nailed down.

Robert Maynard Hutchins

Whenever the urge to exercise comes upon me, I lie down for a while and it passes.

Aldous Huxley

Facts do not cease to exist because they are ignored.

Thought is barred in this city of Dreadful Joy [Los Angeles], and conversation is unknown.

HWM

Fortunately my idiocy is eternally recorded in several newsservers around the globe.

~I~

I Ching

Perseverance alone does not assure success. No amount of stalking will lead to game in a field that has none.

IBM maintenance manual

All parts should go together without forcing. You must remember that the parts you are reassembling were disassembled by you. Therefore, if you can't get them together again, there must be a reason. By all means, do not use a hammer.

<ibm@svpal.org>

In pre-1945 Berlin you had the jack-booted troops of a murderous totalitarian regime goose-stepping down the Unter der Linden in funny helmets whereas in post-1945 Germany you had ...

Oh....

Neeeever mind....

Vincent Icke

Physics is not difficult, it is just weird.
- "The force of symmetry"

imp@charm.net (the impudent guttersnipe)

One could just try to deal with people on the Net in the same manner as one does in person; i.e. don't be a complete and utter jerk. If we spoke to each other in person the way some of us do here in Cyberia, there'd be a lot of broken noses.

Indian proverb

Call on God, but row away from the rocks.

William Ralph Inge

It is useless for sheep to pass resolutions in favor of vegetarianism while wolves remain of a different opinion.

IRS training manual for tax auditors

You will find it a distinct help...if you know and look as if you know what you are doing.

John Irving

Imagining something is better than remembering something.
- The World According to Garp

Washington Irving

A kind heart is a fountain of gladness making everything in its vicinity freshen into smiles.

Issa

Yes: The young sparrows

If you treat them tenderly

Thank you with droppings.

Italian Proverb

If the hours are long enough and the pay is short enough, someone will say it's women's work.

Susan Ivanova ("Babylon 5")

I'm in the middle of fifteen things, all of them annoying.

Molly Ivins

I believe all Southern liberals come from the same starting point -- race. Once you figure out they are lying to you about race, you start to question everything.

~J~

Jon Jacobs

Consensual [non consent] is an oxymoron only to those who have not experienced it.

Those who can't deal with the substance must deal with irrelevancies around the edges.

Andrew Jackson

It is a damn poor mind indeed which can't think of at least two ways to spell any word.

Holbrook Jackson

Man is a dog's idea of what God should be.

Justice **Robert H. Jackson**

In our country are evangelists and zealots of many different political, economic, and religious persuasions whose fanatical conviction is that all thought is divinely classified into two kinds that which is their own and that which is false and dangerous.

Thomas J. Jackson

I am very ignorant, but I can make it up in study. I know I have the energy and I think I have the intellect.

Let us go over the river and rest in the shade of the trees.
- Last words

I have since my entry into this land seen sights that would melt the heart of the most inhuman of beings: my friends dying around me and my brave soldiers breathing their last on the bloody fields of battle, deprived of every human comfort, and even now I can hardly open my eyes after entering a hospital, the atmosphere of which is generally so vitiated as to make the healthy sick.

You may be whatever you resolve to be.

Reggie Jackson

Fans don't boo nobodies.

Susan Jacoby

Get thee behind me, Satan. And thou who put tuxedos on thy dogs.

Christopher Jahn

A little rudeness and disrespect can elevate a meaningless interaction to a battle of wills and add drama to an otherwise dull day

jak1616@aol.com (JAK1616)

Here's a novel concept: Instead of searching the Web for information, READ A BOOK!!

William James

A great many people think they are thinking when they are merely rearranging their prejudices.

The God whom science recognizes must be a God of universal laws exclusively, a God who does a wholesale, not a retail business. He cannot accommodate His processes to the convenience of individuals.
- The Varieties of Religious Experience, 1902

<james@msmags.demon.co.uk>

I'm not sure though, that the old and established American oligarchy ergo the richest and most powerful group on the planet are terribly phased by democracy. After all, the majority have always been for sale, and cheap.

The only thing legislators have ever legislated against are things they can get themselves regardless of legislation.

Jeff Janes

Prisons serve two useful functions. They keep prisoners away from society for 24 hours a day. They keep prison employees away from society for 8 hours a day.
- in alt.fan.cecil-adams, May 2, 2000

I. L. Janis

The military group provides powerful incentives for releasing forbidden impulses, inducing the soldier to try out formerly inhibited acts which he originally regarded as morally repugnant.
- "Group Identification under Conditions of External Danger," British Journal of Medical Psychology 36

Arthur Janov

Death is evidently not a real tragedy for those who do not feel life.

Japanese Proverb

Deceive the rich and powerful if you will, but don't insult them.

jbrush@aros.net

If I spelled a word wrong and you want to make a fuss about it, send all comments to genius@dropdead.com

Thomas Jefferson

A little revolution now and then is a healthy thing

Few politicians die, and none resign.

I have sworn before the altar of god, eternal hostility against every form of tyranny over the mind of man.

I tremble for my country when I reflect that God is just.

If we are to guard against ignorance and remain free, it is the responsibility of every American to be informed.

I'm a great believer in luck, and I find the harder I work, the more I have of it.

Information is the currency of democracy.

It does me no injury for my neighbor to say there are twenty gods, or no God. It neither picks my pocket nor breaks my leg.

Rebellion to tyrants is obedience to God.

The man who reads nothing at all is better educated than the man who reads nothing but newspapers

The natural progress of things is for liberty to yield and government to gain ground.

The spirit of resistance to government is so valuable on certain occasions, that I wish it to be always kept alive. It will often be exercised when wrong but better so than not be exercised at all.

The tree of liberty must be refreshed from time to time with the blood of patriots and tyrants. It is its natural manure.

Rich Jeni

The Web brings people together because no matter what kind of a twisted sexual mutant you happen to be, you've got millions of pals out there. Type in 'Find people that have sex with goats that are on fire' and the computer will say, "Specify type of goat."

Sir Patrick Alfred Jennings

The real reasons I never married are (a) I never met a woman I hated that much and (b) I'm just not that fond of celibacy.

Jerome K. Jerome

It is always the best policy to tell the truth, unless of course, you are an exceptionally good liar.

Tim Jerzyk

The E. coli strain appears to have passed through our system,

Larry W. Jewell

One planet couldn't hold all the nuts you see on Usenet.

Jewish proverb

If God lived on earth, people would break his windows.

If you are bitter at heart, sugar in the mouth will not help you.

jmalia@dimensional.com

There's no place, anything like this place, anywhere near this place, so this must be the place!

John XXIII

Distrustful souls see only darkness burdening the face of the earth.

John Paul II

People must not attempt to impose their own 'truth' on others. The right to profess the truth must always be upheld, but not in a way that involves contempt for those who may think differently. Truth imposes itself solely by the force of its own truth.

Karl Johnson

A virus can be useful to a species by thinning it out.

Lyndon B. Johnson

As man increases his knowledge of the heavens, why should he fear the unknown on earth? As man draws nearer to the stars, why should he not also draw nearer to his neighbor?

If one morning I walked on top of the water across the Potomac River, the headline that afternoon would read: "PRESIDENT CAN'T SWIM."

If we are to live together in peace, we must come to know each other better.

Organized crime constitutes nothing less than a guerilla war against society.

The guns and bombs, the rockets and the warships, all are symbols of human failure.

This Administration here and now declares unconditional war on poverty in America.

We live in a world that has narrowed into a neighborhood before it has broadened into a brotherhood.

Martin Johnson

One of the few joys of approaching the ripe age of 48 is that curmudgeonliness comes much more naturally than it used to and I get a good strong dose of it every time the NCAA basketball tournament nears.
- "The Root", "I Don't Do Brackets and Here's Why", March 14, 2008

Norm Johnson, Pittsburgh Steelers

I'm not one of those kickers who will tell you I want every game to come down to my kick at the end. Those guys aren't truthful. I don't want this in every game. I don't want to die early from stress or a heart attack.

Robert E. Johnson

Sure, I know all the answers. Why do you ask?

Samuel Johnson

A fishing rod is a stick with a hook at one end and a fool at the other.

Go into the street and give one man a lecture on morality and another a dollar, and see which will respect you most.

Hope is itself a species of happiness, and, perhaps, the chief happiness which this world affords: but, like all other pleasures immoderately enjoyed, the excesses of hope must be expiated by pain; and expectations improperly indulged must end in disappointment.

I am very fond of the company of ladies. I like their beauty, I like their delicacy, I like their vivacity, and I like their silence.

Marriage may have many pains, but celibacy has no pleasure.

Mutual cowardice keeps us in peace.

Nature has given women so much power that the law has very wisely given them little.

No man but a blockhead ever wrote except for money.

The Irish are a fair people they never speak well of one another.

What I gained by being in France was learning to be better satisfied with my own country.

When a man says he had pleasure with a woman he does not mean conversation.

Alison Jolly

Anyone who has lived through an English winter can see the point of building Stonehenge to make the Sun come back.

Al Jolson

Outside of my liking for wine, women, and racehorses, I'm a regular husband.

Bertil Jonell

It can be shown that for any nutty theory, beyond-the-fringe political view or strange religion there exists a proponent on the Net. The proof is left as an exercise for your kill-file.

Andrea Jones

I once attempted to pick up a guy just because he drove a Hummer. When it became apparent that there was no way I was going to get ahold of the vehicle keys, I moved on.

Veni, vidi, Tomahawk deduci.
(I came, I saw, I took it out with a Tomahawk.)

Beverly Jones

Romance, like the rabbit at the dog track, is the elusive fake, and never attained reward which, for the benefit and amusement of our masters, keeps us running and thinking in safe circles.

Canada Bill Jones

Tie? You want me to wear a TIE? Listen: there's only one time in a man's life when he should have a rope knotted around his neck, and that time ain't come for me.

Franklin P. Jones

Experience is that marvelous thing that enables you to recognize a mistake when you make it again.

The most efficient labor-saving device is still money.

James Earl Jones

Once you begin to explain or excuse all events on racial grounds, you begin to indulge in the perilous mythology of race.

When I read great literature, great drama, speeches, or sermons, I feel that the human mind has not achieved anything greater than the ability to share feelings and thoughts through language.

John Paul Jones

I wish to have no connection with any ship that does not sail fast; for I intend to go in harm's way.

Stef Jones

Considering another's needs equal to one's own does not mean putting another's needs before one's own.

The simple fact that someone has expectations does not obligate me to adhere to those expectations; especially if I'm unaware of them.

Chief Joseph

All men where made by the same Great Spirit Chief. We are all brothers. The earth is the mother of all peoples. All people should have equal rights upon it.

I hear my voice in the depths of the forest but no answering voice comes back to me; all is silent around me. My words therefore must be few; I can now say no more.

Our chiefs are killed...The little children are freezing to death. My people...have no blankets, no food...My heart is sick and sad...I will fight no more forever.

Understand me fully in my affection for the land. I never said the land was mine to do with it as I chose. The one who has the right to dispose of it is the one who has created it. I claim a right to live on my land, and accord you the privilege to live on yours.

Joseph Joubert

Children need models rather than critics.

Kindness is loving people more than they deserve.

The aim of an argument or discussion should not be victory, but progress.

Benjamin Jowett

One man is as good as another until he has written a book.

The way to get things done is not to mind who gets the credit for doing them.

Leona Joy

Cry 'bother', and loose the Poohs of heck.

I believe that Man's destiny is to _become_ better, not just _do_ better. We are here to learn and grow.

I like to play with sharp, dangerous toys.

If there is no censure for the behavior of rude people there is no incentive for positive change.

Jealousy Is *NOT* an expression of love. It's an expression of insecurity, of low self esteem (sometimes), of fear.

Just 'cuz it don't float your boat don't mean someone else ain't swept along happily in the tide.

Life does not always happen according to your comfort schedule.

A man worthy of respect can afford to be gracious.

[Massive cuteness] has occasionally been a problem for me in my work. You see, I do event planning part of the year ... and some of the events are weddings. When the bride wants a "Precious Moments" motif, I gag, retch, and try as delicately as I can to mitigate my reaction...

No matter _what_ a person looks like, it is what dwells in their souls, and how that manifests in this world, that make the telling difference.

Real life is where we get off, get hurt, get loved, get real, get abused, get to *live*.

Sometimes honorable people are compelled to strong action.

When someone has violated the social contract, they have abrogated their rights and expectations to courtesy in return. I am under no obligation to be kind to someone that is rude to me. Now, it may indeed serve me to be kind to a rude individual, but that's a case by case call, in my estimation.

James Joyce

Christopher Columbus, as everyone knows, is honoured by posterity because he was the last to discover America.

Ireland has the honor of being the only country which never persecuted the Jews   because we never let any in.

Mistakes are the portals of discovery.

No pen, no ink, no table, no room, no time, no quiet, no inclination.

A man of genius makes no mistakes. His errors are volitional and are the portals of discovery.

Benito Juárez

Among nations, as among individuals, respect for the rights of others is peace.

Walter H. Judd

People often say that, in a democracy, decisions are made by the majority of the people. Of course, that is not true. Decisions are made by a majority of those who make themselves heard and who vote--a very different thing.

Carl Jung

Religion is a defense against the experience of God.

Show me a sane man and I will cure him for you.

Junius

The integrity of men is to be measured by their conduct, not by their professions.

Norton Juster, The Phantom Tollbooth

As long as the answer is right, who cares if the question is wrong? If you want sense, you'll have to make it yourself.
- The Dodecahedron

If you only do the easy and useless jobs, you'll never have to worry about the important ones which are so difficult. You just won't have the time. For there's always something to do to keep you from what you really should be doing. . .
- Terrible Trivium

Just because you have a choice, it doesn't mean that any of them has to be right.
- The Dodecahedron

You'll find that the only thing you can do easily is be wrong, and that's hardly worth the effort.
- The Mathemagician

~K~

Vladimir Kabaidze, Director of the Ivanovo Machine Works

We cannot tolerate the proliferation of this paperwork any longer. It is useless to fight the forms. We must kill the people producing them.
- speech at the Communist Party Congress, 1936.

Franz Kafka

A book should serve as an axe to the ice inside us.

Every revolution evaporates and leaves behind only the slime of a new bureaucracy.

You are free and that is why you are lost.

Philippe Kahn

BASIC is to programming what crack is to your brain.

Katharine Kalweit

Many times, our [library's] sex ed. books have disappeared, occasionally after we have defended carrying them to an irate patron. The same people who are outraged by the "moral decline" evidenced by our having such "filth" on our shelves seem to have no problem at all stealing the books to "protect" the innocent.

Ezra Kanagy

We feel that anyone who is capable of making a decent living, helping his neighbors in need, raising a family that will be an asset to the community, and living at peace with God and his fellow men has attained about the most practical and best education there is to get.

Wassily Kandinsky

Nothing that is Human is Alien to me.

Cindy Kandolf

It didn't kill me. It didn't make me stronger, either. But it *did* get the boys out in the water, if for no other reason than to Shut. Mom. UP.

It's now official: I had a boring childhood.

karenw@ibm.net

A degree in political science or philosophy makes you qualified to write a paper, but it doesn't make you intelligent or educated in [other areas]

Napoleon Kaufman

People nowadays are too greedy. They are not happy with the opportunities they are getting.

Mickey Kaus

I am living in my own "psychic reality." Watch out for the snipers.

Alan Kay

A new point of view is worth 80 IQ points.

Don't worry about what anybody else is going to do... The best way to predict the future is to invent it. Really smart people with reasonable funding can do just about anything that doesn't violate too many of Newton's Laws!

I invented the term Object-Oriented and I can tell you I did not have C++ in mind.

The real question is whether [the computer interface] can be more useful than annoying.

You just can't get rid of anything that's once worked.

Mary Ellen Kelly

Natives who beat drums to drive off evil spirits are objects of scorn to smart Americans who blow horns to break up traffic jams.

Walt Kelly

There is no need to sally forth, for it remains true that those things which make us human are, curiously enough, always close at hand. Resolve then, that on this very ground, with small flags waving and tinny blasts on tiny trumpets, we shall meet the enemy, and not only may he be ours, he may be us.
- Pogo

Stan Kelly Bootle

We can still dream of the ideal tech support solution: an ever present Jeevesian type, with patience, sympathy, degrees from MIT in computer science and electronic engineering, OS/2 accredited, Novell certified, and always ready with the perfect cup of tea.

Lord William Thompson Kelvin, president, Royal Society, 1895

Heavier than air flying machines are impossible.

I often say that when you can measure what you are speaking about, and express it in numbers, you know something about it; but when you cannot express it in numbers, your knowledge is of a meagre and unsatisfactory kind ...

Murray Kempton

Every social war is a battle between the very few on both sides who care and who fire their shots across a crowd of spectators.

H. Kendall

People who take issue with control of population do not understand that if it is not done in a graceful way, nature will do it in a brutal fashion.

John F. Kennedy

Arms alone are not enough to keep the peace. It must be kept by men.

Dick Nixon is the victim of the worst press that ever hit a politician in this country.

Forgive your enemies, but remember their names.

It is an unfortunate fact that we can secure peace only by preparing for war.

Mankind must put an end to war or war will put an end to mankind.

Our most basic common link is that we all inhabit this planet. We all breathe the same air. We all cherish our children's future. And we are all mortal.

Peace does not rest in charters and covenants alone. It lies in the hearts and minds of the people.

Peace is a daily, a weekly, a monthly process, gradually changing opinions, slowly eroding old barriers, quietly building new structures.

The mere absence of war is not peace.

The supreme reality of our time is our indivisibility as children of God and the common vulnerability of this planet.

We choose to go to the moon in this decade, not because it is easy, but because it is hard.

We have the power to make this the best generation of mankind in the history of the world--or to make it the last.

We prefer world law in the age of self-determination--we reject world war in the age of mass extermination

We seek not the worldwide victory of one nation or system but a worldwide victory of men.

Joseph Kennedy

It's not what you are, it's what people think you are that counts.

Robert Kennedy

Few will have the greatness to bend history itself, but each one of us can work to change a small portion of events, and in the total of all those acts will be written the history of this generation.

What we need is not division. What we need is not hatred. What we need is not violence but love and wisdom and compassion toward one another and a feeling of justice toward those who still suffer within our country, whether they be black or they be white.

Rose Kennedy

Things don't happen; they are made to happen.

Sister **Elizabeth Kenny**

Some minds remain open long enough for the truth not only to enter but to pass on through by way of a ready exit without pausing anywhere along the route.

Johanne Kepler

Astronomy would not provide me with bread if men did not entertain hopes of reading the future in the heavens.

Kermit

Time's fun when you're having flies.

Jean Kerr

I'm tired of all this business about beauty being only skin deep. That's deep enough. What do you want--an adorable pancreas?

Marrying a man is like buying something you've been admiring for a long time in a shop window. You may love it when you get it home, but it doesn't always go with everything else in the house.

Merle Kessler

Football players, like prostitutes, are in the business of ruining their bodies for the pleasure of strangers.

Thomas Kettenring

Geologists are amazing. They know hundreds of words for different sorts of dirt and hundreds of words for things it does when left alone for a few million years.

Charles F. Kettering

I have never heard of anyone stumbling on something while sitting down.

The future can be anything we want it to be, providing we have the faith and that we realize that peace, no less than war, required "blood and sweat and tears."

kettir@geocities.com

Perhaps...just perhaps...they are going to start penalizing people for being stupid. Please, god

John Maynard Keynes

The avoidance of taxes is the only pursuit that still carries any reward.

The politics of power are inevitable, and there is nothing very new to learn about [World War I] or the end it was fought for; England had destroyed, as in each preceding century, a trade rival.

Genghis Khan

The greatest happiness is to scatter your enemy, to drive him before you, to see his cities reduced to ashes, to see those who love him shrouded in tears, and to gather into your bosom his wives and daughters.

Omar Khayyam

The Moving Finger writes; and, having writ,
Moves on: nor all thy Piety nor Wit
    Shall lure it back to cancel half a Line,
Nor all they Tears wash out a Word of it.
- The Rubaiyat of Omar Khayyam

Ayatollah **Ruhollah Khomeini**

If a fly gets into the throat of one who is fasting, it is not necessary to pull it out.

Nikita Khrushchev

If we believed in God, He would be on our side.

Politicians are the same all over. They promise to build bridges, even when there are no rivers.

Whether you like it or not, we will be present at your burial.
[Misreported as "We will bury you."]

Soren Kierkegaard

Life can only be understood backwards; but it must be lived forwards.

kilroy@ix.netcom.com

Just for the record, the greatest advances of science all through history were presented by singular men of exceptional vision and courage who were scoffed at by their shortsighted peers, purveyors of such axioms as "No, you will fall of the edge of the earth," "If man was meant to fly he would have wings," and "We're from the government and we're here to help you."

Kim

England is part of Europe, right?

I like the order rather than the chaos and unpredictability. Much more comfortable and familiar to me.

I'd love to be vice president. Mostly because you get to shoot people in the face.

It's one thing to observe crazy in the wild, it's quite another to have crazy googling on your computer.

So, when I was sick, I continued to make him dinner, and take the dogs out, and keep the woodstove running, but now *he's* sick and he's been on the couch all day wondering why ... we don't have a little bell he can ring when he needs something from me, because it's just so inconvenient for him to have to yell, what with his throat being scratchy. And I just smile and wonder what the learning curve is on a plasma cutter, because I could easily see myself sawing his ass up and putting him in the tub with a bunch of lye.

Trees, Canadians, what's the difference?

Well it's just that gorillas don't do well with cash.

While redecorating, I realized my husband and I have drastically different tastes in furniture. I wanted to keep only the pieces that reflected the French provincial theme I was creating. He wanted to keep all the stuff we'd had sex on.

Admiral **Husband E. Kimmel**

How could they possibly be Japanese planes?
-- December 7, 1941

Dave Kindrid, Sporting News

[Soccer] is not art, as its partisans insist. This game is not chess played by sprinters. It's a marathon in quicksand.

Charlie King

America is a melting pot, the people at the bottom get burned while all the scum floats to the top.

Eben King

I'm not a lurker, but if I were, I would support you in email.

If you want flexible kids, you have to warp them a bit from time to time.

Martin Luther King, Jr.

Almost always the creative, dedicated minority has made the world better.

Peace is not merely a distant goal that we seek, but a means by which we arrive at that goal.

Pity may represent no more than the impersonal concern which prompts the mailing of a cheque, but true sympathy is the personal concern which demands the giving of one's soul.

We must learn to live together as brothers or perish together as fools.

Stephen King

Only enemies speak the truth; friends and lovers lie endlessly, caught in the web of duty.

We're all going to die; I'm just trying to make it a little more interesting.

Alan Kingsley

The Alamo tragedy was the result of an error made by the government allowing too many aliens, legal and illegal, to come into Texas from across the border

Kingston Trio

Los Angeles really is quite an intellectual town, and we were lucky enough to run into him down there.

Dr. **Alfred Charles Kinsey**

The only unnatural sexual act is the one that which you cannot perform.

Rudyard Kipling

For it's Tommy this, an' Tommy that, an' 'Chuck him out, the brute!'

But it's "Savior of 'is country,' when the guns begin to shoot;
-- "Tommy"

The female of the species is more deadly than the male.
-- "The Female of the Species"

To take your chance in the thick of a rush, with firing all about,
Is nothing so bad when you've cover to 'and an' leave an' likin' to shout;
But to stand an' be still to the Birken'ead drill is a damn' tough bullet to chew,
An' they done it, the Jollies—'Er Majesty's Jollies—soldier and sailor too!
-- "Soldier and Sailor Too"

Words are, of course, the most powerful drug used by mankind.

Neil Kirby, Lucent Technologies

The difference between a printing press and a modern digital longdistance network is that the press produces money much more slowly.

Russel L. Kirlin

You can't have Wyoming be a pristine, untouched area and still be a major natural gas producer. You have to decide what you want.

Oleg Kiselev

How do you know what *I* find attractive? Where did you get the idea that I share the sick fixation on anorexic, skin cancer candidate built like Barbie doll that Big Media is pushing on weak minded men of this society?

Henry Kissinger

Henceforth the adequacy of any military establishment will be tested by its ability to preserve the peace.

Nobody will ever win the Battle of the Sexes. There's just too much fraternizing with the enemy.

Power is the ultimate aphrodisiac.

University politics are vicious precisely because the stakes are so small.

Howard Kleinberg

Traditionalists...want to keep soccer as the world's most popular boring sport.

Dr. **John Knowles**, President, Rockefeller Foundation

The cost of sloth, gluttony, alcoholic intemperance, reckless driving, sexual frenzy and smoking is now a national and not an individual responsibility. This is justified as individual freedom but one man's freedom in health is another man's shackle in taxes and insurance premiums.

Don Knuth

It seems to me that 15 years of email is plenty for one lifetime.
[explaining why he does not have an e-mail address]

The most important thing in the programming language is the name. A language will not succeed without a good name. I have recently invented a very good name and now I am looking for a suitable language.

You don't finish a program, you give up on it.

Anita Koddick

If you think you're too small to have an impact, try going to bed with a mosquito in the room.

Helmut Kohl

My weight is a state secret.

Ted Koppel

Our society finds truth too strong a medicine to digest undiluted. In its purest form, truth is not a polite tap on the shoulder. It is a howling reproach.

Kojima Takeo, Captain, Imperial Japanese Army

We were given training to get our courage up. We were ordered to watch beheadings...Then we had bayonet practice. Victims had their hands tied behind them around a tree, and were used as bayonet targets...This was normal training in the Japanese army.

Michael Korda

An ounce of hypocrisy is worth a pound of ambition.

One of the first rules of playing the power game is that all bad news must be accepted calmly, as if one already knew and didn't care.

Pete Kott, Speaker of the Alaska House of Representatives

I had to cheat, steal, beg, borrow and lie...Exxon's happy. BP's happy. I'll sell my soul to the devil.

Karl Kraus

Chastity always takes its toll. In some it produces pimples; in others, sex laws.

One of the most common of all diseases is diagnosis.

Since the law prohibits the keeping of wild animals and I get no enjoyment from pets, I prefer to remain unmarried.

Stupidity is an elemental force for which no earthquake is a match.

The secret of the demagogue is to make himself as stupid as his audience so that they believe they are as clever as he.

Krystal Ann Kraus

If you want a high performance woman, I can go from zero to bitch in less than 2.1 seconds.

Bob Kravitz

Chess would be a whole lot more exciting if they allowed trash talking.

Christmas Gifts You Really Didn't Want: Dominatrix Barbie (leather not included).

I'm reading about this dead dog rule in the Iditarod and I'm wondering if we can't apply it to the Denver Nuggets.

If you feel the need to rip your teammates, do it on a cable-access show. In Kuala Lumpur. Speaking an obscure dialect.

It's safe to assume the folks at Auburn handled news of Alabama's probation with great grace, style and equanimity. Right after the week long block party ended.

When life is ugly, the news is ugly.

When snowboarding becomes an Olympic sport in 1998, will cutting into a lift line be one of the competitions?

You know you've been watching too much football when your dreams begin involving Brent Musburger.

Kris Kristofferson

I'd rather be sorry for something I've done, than for something that I didn't do.

Irving Kristol

Being frustrated is disagreeable, but the real disasters in life begin when you get what you want.

Louis Kronenberger

The trouble with us in America isn't that the poetry of life has turned into prose, but that it has turned into advertising copy.

Alan Krueger

You attribute perfect rationality to the whole of humanity, which has to be one of the most misguided assumptions ever.

Joseph Wood Krutch

Cats are rather delicate creatures and they are subject to a good many ailments, but I never heard of one who suffered from insomnia.

Cats seem to go on the principle that it never does any harm to ask for what you want.

[Man] is, perhaps, no more prone to war than he used to be and no more inclined to commit other evil deeds. But a given amount of ill will or folly will go further than it used to.

Larry Kubicz

There's a train leaving AFU in an hour. Be under it.

Geoff Kuenning

I tend to believe a theory that treats ordinary people as irrational. All of us are, at least occasionally.

Jerry Kuhn

I'll just never understand anyone who wants to become equal with crooks.

Milan Kundera

Anyone whose god is "something higher" must expect someday to suffer vertigo. Vertigo is something other than the fear of falling. It is the voice of the emptiness below us which tempts and lures us; it is the desire to fall.

Irv Kupcinet

What can you say about a society that says God is dead and Elvis is alive?

Vice Admiral Takeo Kurita

Would it not be shameful for the fleet to remain intact while our nation perishes? There are such things as miracles.
- Making his case for Japanese naval action to defend Leyte

~L~

Tony La Russa

People say I overthink. Bull. They think I overthink because they don't think that a lot of time I'm thinking. I deliberately underthink, so at game time, I can think regular and it looks like overthinking, but really, it's just thinking. I think.

John Laffin

A woman's place should be in the bed and not the battlefield, in crinoline or Terylene rather than in battledress, wheeling a pram rather than driving a tank. Furthermore, it should be the natural function of women to stop men from fighting rather than aiding and abetting them in pursuing it.
- Women in Battle

Charles Lamb

Lawyers, I suppose, were children once.

Richard Lamm

All we know about the new economic world tells us that nations which train engineers will prevail over those which train lawyers. No nation has ever sued its way to greatness.

Ann Landers

Class is an aura of confidence that is being sure without being cocky. Class has nothing to do with money. Class never runs scared. It is self-discipline and self-knowledge. It's the sure footedness that comes with having proved you can meet life.

Don't accept your dog's admiration as conclusive evidence that you are wonderful.

I don't have to have a computer to know what's out there [on the Internet].

This is a warning to all my readers. Do not believe everything you read on the Internet.

Lao Tzu

Govern a great nation as you would cook a small fish. Do not overdo it.

How did the great rivers and seas gain dominion over the hundred lesser streams? By being lower than they.

Stop thinking, and end your problems.

Mark Lappé

You can't expect physicians to be concerned about public health.

Larry the Cable Guy

I felt like I was poking a stick in to a bag of puppies.

Leonard Larsen

It's not true that cheaters never win and winners never cheat. Often as not, it's the other way around.

It's also not true the meek will inherit the earth or that virtue is its own reward. And I'm pretty sure it's not true that what goes around comes around, whatever that's supposed to mean.

Doug Larson

If people concentrated on the really important things of life, there'd be a shortage of fishing poles.

The cat could very well be man's best friend but would never stoop to admitting it.

Drew Larson

So, you've painted a scenario where a newcomer is taking medical advice from a complete stranger on Usenet.

That's also known as natural selection.

Tommy LaSorda

I've found that it's not good to talk about your troubles. Eighty percent of the people who hear them don't care and the other twenty percent are glad you're having trouble.

Latin Proverb

A well-beaten path does not always make the right road.

Vernon Law

If you don't play to win, why keep score?

D. H. Lawrence

I like to write when I feel spiteful; it's like having a good sneeze.

John Laws

It's true that there's a fool born every minute. It's also true that they don't die that fast.

Drew Lawson

If you put things in numbered lists, people sometimes believe that they are correct.

Mell Lazarus

The secret of dealing successfully with a child is not to be its parent.

Stephen Leacock

Advertising may be described as the science of arresting human intelligence long enough to get money from it.

Frank William Leahy

Egotism is the anesthetic that dulls the pain of stupidity.

Timothy Leary

There are three side effects of acid. Enhanced long term memory, decreased short term memory, and I forget the third.

We are dealing with the best-educated generation in history. But they've got a brain dressed up with nowhere to go.

Women who seek to be equal with men lack ambition

Joshua Lederberg

We're not alone at the top of the food chain.

Gypsy Rose Lee

I have everything now I had 20 years ago, except now it's all lower.

Nathaniel Lee

They called me mad, and I called them mad, and damn them, they outvoted me."

Robert E. Lee

Cupid is always busy when Mars is quiet and our young heroes think it is necessary to be killed in some way.

Duty is the sublimest word in our language. Do your duty in all things. You cannot do more. You should never do less.

I have great consideration for my African fellow citizens.

It is history that teaches us to hope.

It is well that war is so terrible; we should grow too fond of it.

To be a good soldier, you must love the army. But to be a good officer, you must be willing to order the death of the thing you love.

Gershon Legman

Murder is a crime. Describing murder is not. Sex is not a crime. Describing sex is.

John Lehman

Power corrupts. Absolute power is kind of neat.

Patricia Voichahoske Lehman

Both Barbie and Darth Vader perform a function in our society like secular gods Astarte and Lucifer didn't have nearly the audience they have. They are part of the language and part of the imagery of our daily lives.

Tom Lehrer

Another pervasive change in this country has been the decline of literacy. Admittedly, one always used to hear that a picture was worth a thousand words, but that was before they devalued the word.
- Lehrer, Tom. "In His Own Words: On Life, Lyrics and Liberals." Washington Post, Jan 3 1982: E1.

Base 8 is just like base 10, if you're missing two fingers.

I can't make references I could have made 20 years ago. Kids today are just as smart as ever but not well-read. They can tell you what happened on every episode of Gilligan's Island, but nothing about Shakespeare's plays.
- Spiller, Sandy. "A new Tom Lehrer surfaces." San Jose Mercury, Jan 29 1982: E3

If anyone objects to any statement I make, I am quite prepared not only to retract it, but also to deny under oath that I ever said it.

Life is like a sewer, what you get out of it depends on what you put into it.

Charles Godfrey Leland

Life is worth living for—or it would be—if it abounded more in such types as Mrs. General Custer and her husband. There was a bright and joyous chivalry in that man, and a noble refinement mingled with constant gaiety in the wife, such as I fear is passing from the earth.

Stanislaw Lem

The whole plan hinged upon the natural curiosity of potatoes.

Curtis LeMay

Killing Japanese didn't bother me very much at that time... I suppose if I had lost the war, I would have been tried as a war criminal.... Every soldier thinks something of the moral aspects of what he is doing. But all war is immoral and if you let that bother you, you're not a good soldier.

Jack Lemmon

Stay humble. Always answer the phone -- no matter who else is in the car.

Vladimir Ilyich Lenin

It is true that liberty is precious - so precious that it must be rationed.

People always have been the foolish victims of deception and self-deception in politics, and they always will be until they have learnt to seek out the INTERESTS of some class or other behind all moral, religious, political and social phrases, declarations and promises.
- "The Three Sources and Three Component Parts of Marxism"

The working class needs unity... Unity is... infinitely important to the working class. Disunited, the workers are nothing. United, they are everything.

War is war. Guns are not just for decoration.

We are dead men on furlough.

We shall be fighting the evils of bureaucracy for many years to come.

While the State exists, there is no freedom. When there is freedom, there is no State.

Hugh Leonard

The problem with Ireland is that it's a country full of genius, but with absolutely no talent.

Sergio Leone

I like Clint Eastwood because he has only two facial expressions: one with the hat, and one without it

Max Lerner

America is a passionate idea or it is nothing. America is a human brotherhood or it is a chaos.

Either men will learn to live like brothers, or they will die like beasts.

Just as men cannot now escape taking on collective responsibility for peace, neither can they escape taking on collective responsibility for economic plenty.

Oscar Levant

There's a fine line between genius and insanity. I have erased this line.

Sam Levenson

Any kid who has two parents who are interested in him and has a houseful of books isn't poor.

Primo Levi

If you wound the body of a dying man, the wound will begin to heal, even if the body dies within a day.
- Survival in Auschwitz

Anthony Lewis

A candidate has to be someone willing to spend hundreds of nights in motels and days repeating worn out phrases to the numbed faithful.

Barbara Lewis, Singer/Songwriter (barbaralewis.com)

You have the right to shape your future. Don't wait for someone else to do it for you. Speak up, Speak out. Design a world you want to live in. Don't wait for luck to create it... The world needs to see your works and to hear your voice.

C.S. Lewis

Of all tyrannies, a tyranny sincerely exercised for the good of its victims may be the most oppressive.

Paul Lewis

Remember, your basic assignment as a parent is to work yourself out of a job.

Sinclair Lewis

Advertising is a valuable economic factor because it is the cheapest way of selling goods, particularly if the goods are worthless.

Our American professors like their literature clear and cold and pure and very dead.

She did her work with the thoroughness of a mind that reveres details and never quite understands them.

When audiences come to see us authors lecture, it is largely in the hope that we'll be funnier to look at than read.

Georg Christoph Lichtenberg

Everyone is a genius at least once a year.

Sometimes men come by the name of genius in the same way that certain insects come by the name of centipede -- not because they have a hundred feet, but because most people can't count above fourteen.
- Reflections

Lin Yutang

What is patriotism but the love of the food one ate as a child?

Brad Linaweaver

Sometimes we cannot help staying alive. It is not that we choose these things. Life chooses us, or sometimes, it is a matter of death passing us by.
- "Red Clay, Crimson Clay"

Abraham Lincoln

Gentlemen, why don't you laugh? With the fearful strain that is upon me night and day, if I did not laugh, I should die.

He can compress the most words into the smallest idea of any man I know.

How many legs does a dog have if you call the tail a leg? Four. Calling a tail a leg doesn't make it a leg.

Human action can be modified to some extent, but human nature cannot be changed.

I am not bound to win, but I am bound to be true. I am not bound to succeed, but I am bound to live by the light that I have. I must stand with anybody that stands right, stand with him while he is right, and part with him when he goes wrong.

If I had two faces would I be wearing this one?

My concern is not whether God is on our side, but whether we are on God's side.

No matter how much cats fight, there always seems to be plenty of kittens.

The best way to destroy an enemy is to make him a friend.

Whenever I hear anyone arguing for slavery, I feel a strong impulse to see it tried on him personally.

With malice toward none, with charity for all, with firmness in the right, as God gives us to see the right, let us strive on to finish the work we are in...
- Second Inaugural

James Linn

And of course we all know that all Canadians are virtuous and never exaggerate for effect.

Mark Linton

I never thought of surgery as 'editing a person' before...

Mary Wilson Little

There is no pleasure in having nothing to do; the fun is in having lots to do and not doing it.

Joan Littlewood

Life is short. But there's more joy than we know, more brains than we know, more ability to learn. But learn for what? We learn quickly in times of war and disaster. But in life, there's a disaster all the time. The waste of human possibility. And we don't face it.

Livy

Men are least safe from what success induce them not to fear.

Llori

[My daughter's] teacher once told me that she knows more about the families of the children than she should know. In other words, the kids talk. My daughter would not think twice about telling her entire nursery school class that her mom was spanked and likes it <G>.

John Locke

It is one thing, to show a man that he is in an error, and another, to put him in possession of truth.

New opinions are always suspected, and usually opposed, without any other reason but because they are not common.

Vince Lombardi

If it doesn't matter who wins, then how come they keep score?

If you aren't fired with enthusiasm, you will be fired with enthusiasm.

It's not practice that makes perfect, it's perfect practice that makes perfect.

Henry Wadsworth Longfellow

We judge ourselves by what we feel capable of doing, while others judge us by what we have already done.

Alice Roosevelt Longworth

If you haven't got anything nice to say about anybody, come sit next to me.

Frank Looper

[O]ff topic cross-posting is bad ju-ju.

Konrad Lorenz

I believe I found the missing link between animal and civilized man. It is us.

Chuck Lorre

Sticks and stones may hurt our bones, but bones heal in a relatively short time, while one critical parent can cripple you forever.

Michael Lorton <mlorton@civetsystems.com>

But certainly, no show relies more on cultural knowledge than _The Simpsons_.

Has the sentence "My husband is normal" been uttered by any woman, ever?

Not all faith-based organizations are churches; sadly, not all churches are faith-based organizations.

[t]rying to find out what women want by asking individual women is like trying to teach yourself veterinary science by interviewing dogs -- in the unlikely event you learn anything, it is doubly unlikely that it will be anything helpful.

lothie@intercon.com

There's just something about pumping two hundred rounds of ammo into a defenseless piece of paper that makes me feel quite studly.....

Joe Louis

Everybody wants to go to heaven, but nobody wants to die.

You only live once, but if you do it right, once is enough.

Low Dog

This is a good day to die, follow me.
- June 25, 1876

James Russell Lowell

A sneer is the weapon of the weak.

Bruce Lowitt

If your favorite color is crimson and your kid is partial to, say, Auburn, you're probably asking yourself where you went wrong.

Sir J. Lubbock

Rest is not idleness, and to lie sometimes on the grass under the trees on a summer's day, listening to the murmur of water, or watching the clouds float across the sky, is by no means a waste of time.

Clare Boothe Luce

Because I am a woman, I must make unusual efforts to succeed. If I fail, no one will say, "She doesn't have what it takes". They will say, "Women don't have what it takes".

Censorship, like charity, should begin at home, but unlike charity, it should end there.

Ebbe Lundgaard, Danish Culture Minister

We can't guard ourselves against stupidity.

Eric Lundquist

You can't predict random events; you can only react to them in an intelligent manner.

Chief **Albert John Luthuli**, Nobel Laureate

The white is hit harder by apartheid than we are. It narrows his life. In not regarding us as human, he becomes less than human. I do pity him.

Unfortunately, human nature being what it is, the white man, when he settled here, concentrated on what he could get rather than on what he could give.

Carl Lydick (Speaker-to-Minerals)

Here's a clue, moron: If you brought more to the thread than projections of your own rather pathetic neuroses, you'd have a better chance.

How kind of you it was to delete the statement to which I was responding. That, you seem to believe, allows you to insert a strawman in its place and talk about that rather than what I was responding to. Have you not a shred of intellectual integrity?

If you throw a strawman into a heated debate, flames are likely to be the result.

Yet you never bother to tell us what you think the founding fathers DID mean. Your strategy is to keep bleating the above no matter what is posted in opposition to it, never providing a concrete claim of your own. Since you'll always be able to say that somebody's not addressing what you actually mean, you'll convince yourself that you've somehow supported your position. But you haven't.

Mary Lyon

If anyone thinks he has no responsibilities, it is because he has not sought them out.

Nine-tenths of our suffering is caused by others not thinking so much of us as we think they ought.

When you choose your fields of labor go where nobody else is willing to go.

Catra Yarrow Lyons

Willpower is for people who don't know what they want.

~M~

Dave Mabee

The difference between a used car salesman and a computer salesman is that a used car salesman knows when he's lying.

General **Douglas A. MacArthur, Jr.**

"Duty, Honor, Country" — those three hallowed words reverently dictate what you ought to be, what you can be, what you will be. They are your rallying point to build courage when courage seems to fail, to regain faith when there seems to be little cause for faith, to create hope when hope becomes forlorn.
- May 12, 1962

However horrible the incidents of war may be, the soldier who is called upon to offer and give his life for his country, is the noblest development of mankind.
- July 14, 1935

I know war as few other men now living know it, and nothing to me is more revolting. I have long advocated its complete abolition, as its very destructiveness on both friend and foe has rendered it useless as a means of settling international disputes.
- April 19, 1951

It is fatal to enter any war without the will to win it.

Men since the beginning of time have sought peace.... Military alliances, balances of power, leagues of nations, all in turn failed, leaving the only path to be by way of the crucible of war. We have had our last chance. If we do not now devise some greater and more equitable system, Armageddon will be at our door.
- September 2, 1945

Old soldiers never die; they just fade away. And like the old soldier in that ballad, I now close my military career and just fade away, an old soldier who tried to do his duty as God gave him the sight to see that duty.
- May 12, 1962

Rules are mostly made to be broken and are too often for the lazy to hide behind.

Talk of imminent threat to our national security through the application of external force is pure nonsense. Our threat is from the insidious forces working from within which have already so drastically altered the character of our free institutions — those institutions we proudly called the American way of life.
- May 15, 1951

That's the way it is in war. You win or lose, live or die—and the difference is just an eyelash.
- Reminiscences, page 145

The powers in charge keep us in a continuous stampede of patriotic fervor with the cry of national emergency. Always there has been some terrible evil to gobble us up if we did not furnish the exorbitant sums demanded. Yet, in retrospect, these disasters seem never to have been quite real.

The soldier, above all other people, prays for peace, for he must suffer and bear the deepest wounds and scars of war.
- May 12, 1962

There is no substitute for victory.
- March 20, 1951 [MacArthur re-iterated this theme on April 19, 1951 when, in a speech before Congress, he stated, "In war there can be no substitute for victory."]

Wall Street businessmen have no character. They never stand up for principle. They just support winners.

Thomas Babington Macaulay, 1st Baron Macaulay

The measure of a man's real character is what he would do if he knew he never would be found out.

Michael MacDonald

It is wrong to assume that because a computer can calculate PI to several thousand digits in a blink of an eye that it is any more intelligent than your average toaster.

Ross MacDonald

There's nothing wrong with Southern California that a rise in the ocean level wouldn't cure.

Pavel Machek

I think that more damage is done by people trying to remove virus than by viruses.

Niccolo Machiavelli

Among the other evils which being unarmed brings, it causes you to be despised.

Before all else, be armed.

For there is such a difference between the way men live and the way they ought to live, that anybody who abandons what is for what ought to be will learn something that will ruin rather than preserve him, because anyone who determines to act in all circumstances the part of a good man must come to ruin among so many who are not good.
- The Prince

God is merciful. He will not do everything and thus take away our free will and that share of glory that belongs to us.

It cannot be called ingenuity to kill one's fellow citizens, to betray friends, to be without faith, without mercy, without religion; by these means one can acquire power but not glory.

Put not your trust in princes, bureaucrats or generals, they will plead expedience while spilling your blood from a safe distance.
- The Prince

There is nothing more difficult to take in hand, more perilous to conduct, or more uncertain in its success, than to take the lead in the introduction of a new order to things.

Whoever desires to found a state and give it laws, must start with assuming that all men are bad and ever ready to display their vicious nature, whenever they may find occasion for it.
- "Discourse upon the First Ten Books of Livy "

Eric Mackay

Lightning is the shorthand of a storm, and tells of chaos.

Compton MacKenzie

The only mystery about the cat is why it ever decided to become a domestic animal.

Elle MacPherson

I was born nude, and I wish to be buried nude.

Lisa Madigan, Illinois Attorney General

The First Amendment protects not only a speaker's right to speak, but also a listener's right not to listen.

Madonna

I may be dressing like a traditional bimbo, whatever, but I am in charge...And isn't that what feminism is all about, you know, equality for men and women? And aren't I in charge of my life, doing the things I want to do?

Pattie Maes

The promise of Web personalization won't come about until privacy is respected by all participants, the value of collective participation won't happen until the current weight of information overload can be removed, and the hope that the Web can be a great equalizer won't occur until trust can be restored as a fundamental Internet underpinning.

Tom Magliozzi

Pick up a washing-machine-size subwoofer for the back seat. No Aspire owner should be without one of those.

So, you're a guinea pig, Rebecca. We're just glad to hear that you lived through the experiment.

Magyar Proverb

Beware of the bearded woman.

Gustav Mahler

I am a musician. That explains everything.

Rick Majerus

I microwave nachos. If it can't be done on a grill or a microwave, I won't do it.

Some guys smoke, some guys drink, some guys chase women. I'm a big barbecue sauce guy.

Allan Malamud

How can any team that plays in a conference that has 11 members and calls itself the Big Ten expect its players to be able to count the number of timeouts it has left in a game?

I respect Bo Jackson more for earning a bachelor's degree at Auburn 10 years after winning the Heisman Trophy than for anything he ever accomplished on a football or baseball field.

The investigation into the Texas Tech football and basketball programs includes allegations that athletes were given free bail-bonds services.

Purdue defeated Russia Siberia in an exhibition basketball game at West Lafayette, Ind., last month, but there are no plans for a home and home series.

Malayan Proverb

When elephants fight, the mousedeer between them is killed.

Thomas Malthus

The histories of mankind...are histories only of the higher classes.

Population, when unchecked, increases in geometrical progression of such a nature as to double itself every twenty-five years.

Subsistence increases only in an arithmetical ratio.

[Survival is] the perpetual struggle for room and food.

Sanford M. Manley

Trying to be right all the time is a very subtle way of being wrong.

Thomas Mann

War is only a cowardly escape from the problems of peace.

Katherine Mansfield

If you want to go to sleep, get a New Zealander to read to you.

Charles Manson

Living is what scares me. Dying is easy.

manx@netcom.com

Some kinds of madness are destructive. Still others are productive. I live somewhere in between.

Mao Tse Tung, Quotations from Chairman Mao Tsetung

An army without culture is a dull-witted army, and a dull-witted army cannot defeat the enemy.

Enable every woman who can work to take her place on the labour front, under the principle of equal pay for equal work.

If we have a correct theory but merely prate about it, pigeonhole it and do not put it into practice, then that theory, however good, is of no significance.

Modesty helps one to go forward, whereas conceit makes one lag behind.

Only a blockhead cudgels his brains on his own, or together with a group, to "find a solution" or "evolve and idea" without making any investigation...This cannot possibly lead to any effective solution or any good idea.

Political power grows from the barrel of a gun.

Two principles must be observed: (1) Say all you know and say it without reserve; (2) Don't blame the speaker but take his words as a warning.

War can only be abolished through war, and in order to get rid of the gun it is necessary to take up the gun.

Weapons are an important factor in war, but not the decisive one; it is the man and not the materials that counts.

When waking a sleeping tiger, use a long stick.

marcus@nando.net

When my wife and I were married this Spring, there were many, many Southern Baptists in attendance (she had worked in a church at one point in her life and had lots of SB friends) as were some of our kinky friends. Based on the comments at the reception, I've no doubt that when she promised to _obey_ me, that each set of friends heard and mentally saw something totally different.

Kurt W. Marek (C.W. Ceram)

The forces of the past still live on and exert their influence on us, though we may not be consciously aware of this. It is frightening to realize in full depth what it means to be a human being: that is, to realize that we are all imbedded in the flux of generations, whose legacy of thought and feeling we irrevocably carry along with us.
- Gods, Graves, and Scholars

Don Marquis

If you want to get rich from writing, write the sort of thing that's read by persons who move their lips when they're reading to themselves.

It is very insulting to attempt to reform people. When you behead a person you leave his soul as it is. But when you reform him you change his soul, and it is a dangerous thing to tamper with human souls.
- "The Almost Perfect State"

Publishing a volume of poetry is like dropping a rose-petal down the Grand Canyon and waiting for the echo.
- "The Sun Dial"

The chief obstacle to the progress of the human race is the human race.

S.L.A. Marshall

In the final and greatest reality...national strength lies only in the hearts and spirits of men.

We are reluctant to admit that essentially war is the business of killing.

Boris Marshalov

Congress is so strange. A man gets up to speak and says nothing. Nobody listens, then everybody disagrees.

Steve Martin

I like a woman with a head on her shoulders. I hate necks.

Groucho Marx

A hospital bed is a parked taxi with the meter running.

I find television very educational. The minute somebody turns it on, I go to the library and read a good book.

I wouldn't want to belong to any club that would have me as a member.

No one is completely unhappy at the failure of his best friend.

Outside of a dog, a book is man's best friend. Inside a dog, it's too dark to read.

Politics is the art of looking for trouble, finding it everywhere, diagnosing it incorrectly, and applying the wrong remedies.

Those are my principles. If you don't like them I have others.

Whatever it is, I'm against it!

Karl Marx

Capitalism will kill competition.

Go on, get out. Last words are for fools who haven't said enough.
- Last words (to housekeeper)

Money degrades all the gods of man and converts them into commodities.

The oppressed are allowed once every few years to decide which particular representatives of the oppressing class are to represent and repress them.

The philosophers have only interpreted the world, in various ways; the point, however, is to change it.
- "Thesis XI on Feuerbach"

There is only one way to kill capitalism - by taxes, taxes, and more taxes.

Glen Mason, Kansas University football coach

Grits aren't bad, but I'd rather eat Kansas beef...

Jackie Mason

Britain is the only country in the world where the food is more dangerous than the sex.

Cora Massingail, "The Hallelujah Trail"

Men are dirty boots at one end and a dirty mind at the other.

Tom Masson

'Be yourself' is the worst advice you can give to some people.

masterhyde@aol.com

Common sense and thoughtfulness is always in fashion, no matter where you are.

Hopefully, we would all have enough common sense to know what is going to shock people, and make intelligent decisions about how or when that is appropriate.

Jeckyll and Hyde are not opposing, but complementary forces

Remind me never to be right again. It makes you too easy a target around here.

Sam Masters

Feminism is the radical idea that women are people.

I love being scared, that's probably why I used to skydive.

Bat Masterson

There are many in this old world of ours who hold that things break about even for all of us. I have observed for example that we all get the same amount of ice. The rich get it in the summertime and the poor get it in the winter.

Emilie Mataja

Where do your wild thoughts come from?
- to Leopold von Sacher Masoch

W. Somerset Maugham

Excess on occasion is exhilarating. It prevents moderation from acquiring the deadening effect of a habit.

The ability to quote is a serviceable substitute for wit.

Tradition is a guide and not a jailer.

Guy de Maupassant

Patriotism is a kind of religion; it is the egg from which wars are hatched.
- "My Uncle Sosthenes"

Andre Maurois

Conversation would be vastly improved by the constant use of four simple words: I do not know.

We owe to the Middle Ages the two worst inventions of humanity -- gunpowder and romantic love.

Jack Mayberry

I voted for the Republicans because I didn't like the way the Democrats were running the country. Which is turning out to be like shooting yourself in the head to stop your headache.

John McCain

This is not about who they are. This is about who we are. We are Americans and we hold ourselves to a higher standard of conduct. And, no, the end does not justify the means. Not now. Not ever, when the means include torturing prisoners.

Charles McCabe

Any idiot can have the facts. Having opinions is an art.

Charlie McCarthy

Ambition is a poor excuse for not having sense enough to be lazy.

Eugene McCarthy

It is dangerous for a national candidate to say things that people might remember.

Mike McCarty

I think that it is a bit closer to reality to say that most postal employees are too busy to scrounge through mail, rather than too honest .

Will McCarty

I always say that planting cotton is the second-greatest urge known to man.

Matthew McConaughey

There's something really pure about ignorance.

Frank McCoy

Sometimes our enemies make us look better than our friends do.

James R. McDonough

[W]ar is not a series of case studies that can be scrutinized with objectivity...War is the suffering and death of people you know, set against a background of suffering and death of people you do not.
- Platoon Leader

Susan McDougal

I think if anyone believes that money does not play a part in the American justice system or the political system, they are very naïve. I never met a rich person in jail.

John McEnroe

Everybody loves success, but they hate successful people.

The important thing is to learn a lesson every time you lose. Life is a learning process and you have to try to learn what's best for you. Let me tell you, life is not fun when you're banging your head against a brick wall all the time.

This taught me a lesson, but I'm not sure what it is.

George McGovern

I'm fed up to the ears with old men dreaming up wars for young men to die in.

John McKay

If there was a contest and there were 97 prizes, the 98th would be a trip to Green Bay.

John "West" McKenna

Supercomputers solve supercomputer problems.

Mainframes solve mainframe problems.

PCs cause problems.

E.C. Mckenzie

Men's troubles are largely due to three things-women, money and both.

Rod McKuen

Cats have it all - admiration and an endless sleep and company only when they want it.

Mignon McLaughlin

Every society honors its live conformists and its dead troublemakers.

Marshall McLuhan

I don't necessarily agree with everything I say.

Paul McManus

I'm pretty sure you are wrong about the equator. I think that the water falls out of the bowl below the equator. If anyone from Antarctica or one of those below the equator countries is available, could you check to see if the ceiling in the toilet is wet.

William H. McNeill

Looked at from the point of view of other organisms, humankind... resembles an acute epidemic disease...
- Plagues and Peoples

The relation of purpose to process has always been puzzling to ordinary people.
- The Global Condition, Conquerors, Catastrophes, & Community, vii

We have to do the best we can with the language and concepts we inherit, and not worry about obtaining a truth that will satisfy everyone, everywhere, and for all time to come.
- Plagues and Peoples

Hal McRae

We didn't play one of our better games.
(After losing 13-0 against the NY Yankees)

Meguro Masahiko

A lot of university professors were connected with Unit 731. Especially upper level people...Those are the people who built the foundation of today's Japan.

James R. Mead

The beauties and blessings of civilization are very largely a myth.

Margaret Mead

I do not believe in using women in combat, because females are too fierce.

Never doubt that a small group of thoughtful committed citizens can change the world. Indeed, it is the only thing that ever has.

Thanks to television, for the first time the young are seeing history made before it is censored by their leaders.

Ülo Melton

Don't even get me started on lesbian thumb wars

Herman Melville

All wars are boyish and are fought by boys.

There are some enterprises in which a careful disorderliness is the true method.
- Moby Dick

Mencius

Truth is the way of the heaven, to believe in truth is the way of a man.

H.L. Mencken

A good politician is quite as unthinkable as an honest burglar.

A man may be a fool and not know it, but not if he is married.

As democracy is perfected, the office represents, more and more closely, the inner soul of the people. We move toward a lofty ideal. On some great and glorious day the plain folks of the land will reach their heart's desire at last, and the White House will be adorned by a downright moron.
- in the Baltimore Sun, July 26, 1920

Every failure teaches a man something; to wit, that he will probably fail again the next time.
- Sententiae

Every normal man must be tempted at times to spit on his hands, hoist the black flag, and begin slitting throats.

It is a sin to believe evil of others, but it is seldom a mistake.

It is hard to believe that a man is telling the truth when you know that you would lie if you were in his place.

No man, examining his marriage intelligently, can fail to observe that it is compounded, at least in part, of slavery, and that he is the slave.

No normal woman ever gives a hoot for law if law happens to stand the way of her private interest.

One cannot enter a State Legislature or a prison for felons without becoming, in some measure, a dubious character.

Texas is the place where there are the most cows and the least milk, and the most rivers and the least water in them, and where you can look the farthest and see the least.

The basic fact about human existence is not that it is a tragedy, but that it is a bore.

The opera...is to music what a bawdy house is to a cathedral.

The penalty for laughing in a courtroom is six months in jail; if it were not for this penalty, the jury would never hear the evidence.

There is only one honest impulse at the bottom of Puritanical religion, and that is the impulse to punish the man with a superior capacity for happiness.

Visitors are kindly requested to refrain from expectorating out of the windows.

When A annoys or injures B on the pretense of improving B, A is a scoundrel.
-- Newspaper Days

When you hear a man speak of his love for his country, it is a sign he expects to get paid for it.

[Women's] one comfort is the assurance that, even though it may be impossible to prevail against man, it is always possible to enslave and torture a man.

Susan Mengelkoch

Perception is everything. When perception sucks...eat chocolate.

Alex Mercer

Historically, financial advantage for a small minority has often been put before human health.
-- Disease Mortality and Population in Transition: Epidemiological-Demographic Change in England since the Eighteenth Century as part of a Global Phenomenon.

Merlin

For it is the doom of men that they forget.

Major General **John Meyer**

Reporters are like alligators. You don't have to love them, you don't necessarily have to like them. But you do have to feed them.

Michelangelo

Trifles make perfection and perfection is no trifle.

Lord, grant that I may always desire more than I accomplish.

Matt Midboe

If you didn't ridicule someone in public, did you REALLY ridicule them?

Don Middendorf

I for one would rather follow the interesting conversations of arrogant snobs than bask in the warm fuzzy glow of a throng of friendly morons.

Nevermind the fact that if the Phantom Menace turned out to be black&white, 8mm and about gay cowboys eating pudding, it would have still made a large fortune.

Amy Middon

I'm of the theory that alcohol doesn't relieve the pain, but if you drink enough you no longer care your mouth is on fire.

Barbara Mikkelson

Oh sure; get married and then everybody treats you like you're dead.

David Mikkelson, (snopes)

Despite the fact that I graduated from a Texas university, I happen to know that 1845 was not "after the Civil War".

I've found that rats are spontaneously created through the formula wife+rat=more rats.

It's a sad statement about the corruption of my innocence that since meeting Barbara, I have been to topless clubs more often than I have been to Disneyland.

You don't ever want to know about her cat-o'-nine-spoons.

John Stuart Mill

War is an ugly thing, but not the ugliest of things. The decayed and degraded state of moral and patriotic feeling which thinks that nothing is worth war is much worse. The person who has nothing for which he is willing to fight, nothing which is more important than his own personal safety, is a miserable creature, and has no chance of being free unless made or kept so by the exertions of better men than himself.

Edna St. Vincent Millay

My candle burns at both ends,

It will not last the night

But ah, my foes, and oh, my friends

It gives a lovely light.

Henry Miller

Every man with a belly full of the classics is an enemy of the human race.

How different the new order would be if we could consult the veteran instead of the politician. It's silly to go on pretending that under the skin we are all brothers. The truth is more likely that under the skin we are all cannibals, assassins, traitors, liars and hypocrites.

Jonathan Miller

Holidays are an expensive trial of strength. The only satisfaction comes from survival.

Olin Miller

You probably wouldn't worry about what people think of you if you could know how seldom they do.

Roger Miller

Some people walk in the rain, others just get wet.

Spike Milligan

I told you I was ill.
- Epitaph

If there was anybody in position of power with any semblance of mental health do you think the world would be in this bloody mess?

A. A. Milne

I am a Bear of very little brain, and long words bother me.
- Winnie the Pooh

One can't complain. I have my friends. Why, someone spoke to me only yesterday.
- Eeyore

One of the advantages to being disorganized is one is always making exciting discoveries.

No doubt Jack the Ripper excused himself on the grounds that it was human nature.

What I say is, if a fellow really likes potatoes, he must be a pretty decent sort of fellow.

Lou Minatti

Most of the soc.culture newsgroups are cesspools of vile, racist swill and off-topic nonsense.

Minnesota Fats

I wouldn't carry a golf bag if you put a machine gun in my mouth. Carry a golf bag, 100 pounds of clubs? You gotta put it in the car, take it outta the car...To me, it's the silliest thing on Earth.

Ninety nine out of 100 people think exercise is the greatest thing. I'll show you anybody who is an exercise nut, he's 50 60 years old - looks like he's 90.

Marvin Minsky

I bet the human brain is a kludge.

No computer has ever been designed that is ever aware of what it's doing; but most of the time, we aren't either.

Jeff Mintun

The update had the undocumented feature of turning my modem into a paperweight.

Ludwig von Mises

Modern government interference with business is a policy of protecting influential pressure groups from the effects of free competition in an unhampered market economy.

Missouri Supreme Court, 1918

We can imagine no reason why, with ordinary care, human toes could not be left out of chewing tobacco, and if toes are found in chewing tobacco, it seems to us that somebody has been very careless.

John N. Mitchell, US Attorney General

There are stupid students. I was one when I was in college.

You will be better advised to watch what we do instead of what we say.
- to a group of civil rights protestors on July 1, 1969 [See Daniel Moynihan for a statement about this.]

Robin Mitchell

At first I was amazed that anyone would make up such a transparent falsehood. Now I'm even more amazed that people are not only falling for it but actually defending it...

Mary Modahl

The idea that you can construct an electronic microcosm that is safe from human nature is misguided.

Mohammed

The ink of the scholar is more sacred than the blood of the martyr.

Moliere

Here they hang a man first, and try him afterwards.

It is not only for what we do that we are held responsible, but also for what we do not do.

Writing is like prostitution. First, you do it for the love of it, then you do it for a few friends, and finally you do it for the money.

Count **Helmuth von Moltke**

An enemy will usually have three courses open to him. Of these he will select the fourth

The Stock Exchange has acquired such an influence that it is able, in order to protect its interests, to launch armies into war.

John Molony (Mayor of Mount Isa, Australia)

May I suggest if there are five blokes to every girl, we should find out where there are beauty-disadvantaged women and ask them to proceed to Mount Isa.

Jacques Monod

[A] curious aspect of the theory of evolution is that everybody thinks he understands it.
- "On the Molecular Theory of Evolution"

Ashley Monroe

No, life isn't fair... Why do you think bras come in different sizes? :)

Marilyn Monroe

Hollywood is a place where they'll pay you a thousand dollars for a kiss and fifty cents for your soul.

I don't mind living in a man's world as long as I can be a woman in it.

C. E. Montague

War hath no fury like a non-combatant.

Lady **M. W. Montague**

No entertainment is so cheap as reading, nor any pleasure so lasting.

Michel Eyquem de Montaigne

I prefer the company of peasants because they have not been educated sufficiently to reason incorrectly.

There is no man so good that if he placed all his actions and thoughts under the scrutiny of the laws, he would not deserve hanging ten times in his life.

When I play with my cat, who knows whether she isn't amusing herself with me more than I am with her?

Charles-Louis de Secondat, baron de La Brède et de Montesquieu

A rational army would run away.

If one only wished to be happy, this could be easily accomplished; but we wish to be happier than other people, and this is always difficult, for we believe others to be happier than they are.

Useless laws weaken the necessary laws.

What the orators lack in depth, they give you in length.

Jordan Montgomery

Ahh, the soothing o' the Pipes...Whenever I find myself missing its melodious sounds, I just toss the cat in the dryer on low heat.

<monunk@sna.com>

I have been a vegetarian for 30 years and I won't accept violence. If someone tries to get violent with me, I'll kick the shit out of them.

Demi Moore

It all comes down to two things - love and fear. I prefer to operate more out of love and less out of fear. To live in fear is like being in a prison.

Charles Wilson, 1st Baron Moran

Courage is will-power, whereof no man has an unlimited stock; and when in war it is used up, he is finished. A man's courage is his capital and he is always spending.

[W]ar is a cruel and wasteful holocaust, though a necessary evil if men are to live in freedom.

Jeanne Moreau

Age does not protect you from love, but love, to some extent, protects you from age.

Success is like a liberation or the first phrase of a love story . . .

Some people are addicts. If they don't act, they don't exist.

Cynthia Morgan

Exchanging your tin fork for an electric one doesn't make the soup any easier to eat.

Sen. **John A. Tyler Morgan** (Alabama)

A lie is an abomination unto the lord and an everpresent help in time of need.

Christopher Morley

Life is a foreign language; all men mispronounce it.

My theology, briefly, is that the universe was dictated, but never signed.

No one appreciates the very special genius of your conversation as a dog does.

Read every day something no one else is reading. Think every day something no one else is thinking. It is bad for the mind to be always part of unanimity.

The real purpose of books is to trap the mind into doing its own thinking.

The unluckiest insolvent in the world is the man whose expenditure of speech is too great for his income of ideas.

Toni Morrison (Chloe Anthony Wofford), Nobel Laureate

Bryn Mawr had done what a four-year dose of liberal education was designed to do: unfit her for eighty per cent of useful work of the world.

The ability of writers to imagine what is not the self, to familiarize the strange and mystify the familiar, is the test of their power.

And like any artist with no art form, she became dangerous.

Mitchell Moss, Professor of Urban Policy and Planning at NYU

If you want to improve the mental health of New Yorkers, get a good bullpen for the Yankees.

Helge Moulding

I think, therefore I look things up

Daniel P. Moynihan

Few grasped that Nixon was putting forth a set of administrative and legislative proposals designed fundamentally – and deliberately – to fulfill the promises of the 1960s.
[speaking about John Mitchell's comments to protestors]

No one is innocent after the experience of governing. But not everyone is guilty.

There are some mistakes only someone with a Ph.D. can make.

<mrf@kalypso.cybercom.net>

It is common courtesy to warn people around you when you're about to do something they might think strange or bizarre, and it's only wise to refrain from displays of behavior that people without any context of understanding will probably take to mean that you're an abusive twit and need to be locked up.

<mrskin@mindspring.com>

The goal of censorship is thought control, and fear is its most effective tool. If arbitrary rules and/or enforcement makes more people fear to communicate about the Forbidden Topic, well, all the better, from the viewpoint of censors.

Hierarchical systems such as Germany and Japan employed tended to produce distorted information that led leaders to make mistakes. The Japanese were particularly bad in this respect - making apologies with a knife to the stomach DOES tend to lead one to give rosy reports to one's superiors.

Robert Mueller

I asked a Burmese why women, after centuries of following their men, now walk ahead. He said there were many unexploded land mines since the war.

Baron **von Münchhausen**

If anyone doubts my veracity, I can only say that I pity his lack of faith.

David Muhlenfeld

Repetition alone will make something stick in a listener's head. The question is, once your song is in their head, will they want to stick that head in an oven?

Martin Mull

Having a family is like having a bowling alley installed in your brain.

H.H. Munro

Confront a child, a puppy and a kitten with a sudden danger; the child will turn instinctively for assistance, the puppy will grovel in abject submission, the kitten will brace its tiny body for a frantic resistance.

Iris Murdoch

The absolute yearning of one human body for another particular body and its indifference to substitutes is one of life's major mysteries.

Benito Mussolini

War alone brings up to its highest tension all human energy and puts the stamp of nobility upon the peoples who have the courage to face it.

War is to men what maternity is to women.

Chuck Muth

I now know what Osama bin Laden's appropriate punishment should be: Life sitting in the audience of non-stop political speeches by people who don't know how to give political speeches.

It was a failure, but it was not a mistake

quoted by **Doug Muth**

Privacy is a basic human right, not a government granted privilege!

Mike Muth

A movie can rarely do justice to the book, but some books need mercy rather than justice.

A picture is worth a thousand lies.

Accept all people as the individuals they are, and treat them as they wish to be treated - just as you would have them do for you.

All mechanical devices break. The more complex the device, the more quickly it is likely to break.

All things are neither good nor evil. They simply are. It is the intent with which they are used which may be characterized as good or evil.

Although it is manifestly the right thing to do, it is difficult to accept that our own actions have consequences which we must bear. It is much easier to point fingers at others.

Among men, discussion of sports has become like unto an arcane secret jargon which causes women's eyes to glaze over as they desperately hunt for someone who's talking sense.

An important rule of thumb: When visiting another culture, learn the customs and conform to them or at least don't violate any tabus.

Any human organization tends, over time, toward mediocrity. Whatever brilliance may occur is due to individuals and their efforts rather than any aspect of the organization. Organizations with less formal structure and less constrained by bureaucratic concerns tend to give individuals a little more leeway and thus tend to less mediocrity.

Any system which gives people authority over others contains within it the seeds of oppression.

Ask not what you can do for your country; ask what your government is doing to you and how much they are making you pay for it.

Behind every successful man there stands a woman - with a cattle prod.

Bigger is better. If you don't believe me, just ask the guy selling popcorn at the movie theater.

Civil discourse is a fine thing. I would certainly like to see more people try it.

"Cops" appeals to the average TV viewer because they see such pathetic people that they can feel smug about their own tawdry lives.

Crunchy coffee is just not my thing.

Dealing with these guys is like shooting fish in a barrel with a rocket launcher. You can do it, but it makes a mess, the satisfaction is fleeting, and it tends to annoy bystanders.

Deliberately omitting pertinent material in order to present a different view of facts or to twist another person's statements' apparent meaning is just as dishonest as blatantly telling an untruth.

Disraeli had it almost right. There are four kinds of lies: lies, damned lies, statistics, and history.

Education is not a spectator sport.

Either sophisticated language is not a defining characteristic of humanity or quite a large number of posters on Usenet and in blogs are not human.

Even if all a person does is personally show kindness to others and refrain from hostility, they make this world a little better. We don't all have to be doctors toiling away in the third world. We just have to overcome a bit of our selfish nature and turn outward in constructive ways.

Every mentally competent adult is responsible for their own actions. If they take actions (such as doing drugs or drinking) which render them more liable to break the law, then they should be held accountable for that as well.

Every time one of us helps another, s/he helps all of us. Even if all you do is smile and say "Hello" when you encounter people on the street, you are helping to make the world a better place. We can't all be Mother Theresa.

Everyone is entitled to their own opinions, likes and dislikes. I don't even care if folks disagree with me. However, that does not create in me any requirement to agree with them or remain silent in the face of argument and/or accusation. Anytime someone presents an opinion, each of us should feel free to ignore it or to discuss it without unpleasantness or ridicule.

Everyone knows that the social function of marriage is to keep you from spending your Saturday nights alone at the Phoenix public library.

Everything you post to Usenet can come back to haunt you.

Facts are inconvenient things which refuse to bend themselves to fit one's arguments.

Faith is a matter of personal choice and we don't have the right to impose it upon others. On the other hand, we don't have the right to deny it to others either.

Faith is not something you have, it is a part of what you are.

Freedom of choice is a terrible thing for it allows us to become our own worst enemies.

Going to church and shouting out that "I am a Christian" no more makes me a Christian than going to a car lot and shouting "I am a Chrysler" would make me a minivan.

Hate is like drinking poison and waiting for the other person to die.

Having seen the elephant, I know that I don't want to ever see a movie which does a good job of depicting the war.

He's self aware. Unfortunately, that seems to be the extent of his awareness.

Here's a big clue: the world is not out to get you. However, when you kick the rest of the world in the shins, don't expect folks to stand around with embarrassed smiles on their faces.

I believe that the Truth is. It doesn't matter how I feel about it, I can't change it. What I can do, is to examine what others claim to be the facts and subject them to analysis. This goes double for the Fourth Estate.

I do not want the government imposing religious rules on anyone, not even if they are the rules to which I adhere.

I figure I have more chances of winning the lottery if I don't play.

I'm not into exercising. My thought is: No pain, no pain.

I need either more sleep or more caffeine.

I used to wish that stupidity were painful. One day, I thought about it for a while and realized that I would never be able to stand all the screaming and moaning.

I'll wager there's a pot of something at the end of that rainbow.

I would not like to see religion taught in the schools. That's a matter for parents and church and does not belong in the hands of the state.

If all men were truly equal, who would get the best parking places?

If all you want from life is the assurance you will always have a roof over your head, a bed in which to sleep, and three squares a day, knock off a bank or two.

If hard work is so good for you, why don't the rich don't keep it all to themselves?

If I put a cow into a sheep pen, is it a sheep? If I don the trappings of a faith but not the substance, am I truly of that faith?

If it even looks like I might sing, mothers pull their children indoors, dogs howl, grown men weep, and the SWAT team surrounds my house.

If it is not against the law, it is not a crime - no matter how morally or ethically repugnant it might be.

If someone addresses an apology to you when they *know* you are not there to hear it, have they really made an apology? Or, have they just made a public statement so they look better in others' eyes?

If we could convert cluelessness to electricity, you could well be the key to resolving the world energy crisis.

If you stop excluding your nightmares, the person of your dreams is within easy reach.

In a "good" discussion, there are no winners and losers. Rather, everyone benefits from the give and take. In this environment, ego has no place. Ego-less discussion hopefully leads to a friendly consensus. The feeling that someone must win or lose a disagreement leads only to rancor, increased tension, and disharmony - and rarely leads to consensus.

In my experience, the folks who use religion as an excuse to impose their standards upon others are usually doing exactly that: using religion as an excuse. "God wants you to..." is a marvelous argument which is difficult to refute - even when the person shouting it is seven kinds of wrong.

In my youth, I wore the uniform of this country. I followed the flag where it led me and I served it well. I have blood on my hands. Trust me. You don't want that.

Insult is not a valid argumentative technique unless you're a child on the playground - and then it only gets you a beating.

Installing Microsoft Windows is not magic. There are sound technical reasons why one must first sacrifice a young goat by the light of the new moon.

It is difficult to kill another human being. One of the time-honored methods of enabling this behavior is to indoctrinate your soldiers to hate or despise the enemy.

It is harder to justify conquest and killing when you regard the enemy as your equal. Contempt for your enemy also makes atrocity so much easier.

It's only a short goosestep from "They're not like us" to concentration camps.

It's time to grow up and take responsibility for your own actions and stop whining "they made me do it."

It takes something special to be a ranger. Sometimes that something is just the sheer determination to push through to the end, despite what your body is telling you. When you are most fatigued, at your weakest - that's when you need to suck it up and get the mission done. Excuses won't get you far when you or your mates are lying in their own blood because your feet hurt or you were tired.

Just because you can sing "Amazing Grace" to the melody of "Gilligan's Island" doesn't mean you should.

Lawyers are simply highly educated mechanics who use words and the provisions of law to repair or build things. Just as we pay mechanics to exercise their particular skills and knowledge for us, we pay lawyers to exercise their skills for us. I find lawyers, as a class, to be no more reprehensible than tradesmen who provide their skills for hire.

Lies do not become more true when you shout them more often. Truth is - and you can't change it by lying.

Lord, save me from those who would save me.

Many of us rush blindly down the pathways of life, hurtling toward the end we fear and wish to avoid.

Many people profess to be of whatever religion but have an imperfect idea of what that means. This creates a problem of identification. Am I a Christian if I obey *some* of the NT teachings? Or, am I something else. If I own a farm but plant no crops and raise no animals, am I a farmer? Does it change things if I say I'm a farmer? How about if I till the fields but plant no seed?

Military service is only one of a multitude of ways to serve. Moreover, those who do things at the local level also serve their country. Our country is not just in Washington or the military bases overseas. It is every person, every square inch of ground. If I do something to make life better for others, that can be seen as service to country, even if that was not my intent.

Not all "highway robbery" occurs on the road.

Not everything which is wrong is illegal and not everything which is legal is right.

Only three things in life are certain: Death, Taxes, and Microsoft.

Oppression takes many forms. You can annihilate a people without using violence.

Peace on Earth, good will toward men is not such a bad idea, no matter what your religion. I just wish we could all practice that the year-round.

People and organizations frequently do the wrong things. People act from habit or instinct more often than from consciously reasoned decisions. A quick look at headlines, history, and generally the world around us shows that large organizations tend to mediocrity. This is because organizations rely as much on custom (the way it's done, TWID) as anything else for day to day decisions. Risk takers will either more quickly ascend the corporate ladder or find themselves on the street. It is fear of the latter which induces individuals to not buck the system - which is nothing more than accumulated safe decisions.

People are free to be stupid all they like.

People have the right to spout whatever nonsense they wish (provided it's not incitement to criminal activity). That right, however, engenders in no one any obligation to listen. You can climb on your soapbox whenever they like, and I can listen, disagree, or walk away if I choose. Indeed, walking away would in this case be a form of expression. Thus, I have a right to walk away from such unwanted sermons. Moreover, their right to freedom of expression does not entitle anyone to use my commercial location to express themselves.

People who are really serious about their Harley(s) don't mind a little puddled blood.

People who can't stand disagreement should not argue.

Politicians appear to have the ethics and morals of a cat in heat.

Racism and stupidity know no national borders.

Schools can correct ignorance. Unfortunately, there is no cure for stupidity.

"Soldier" is a state of being, not a job description

Some articles of faith are not matters of religion.

Sometimes I think the only way to remove old software from a system is to use liberal amounts of plastique and the occasional nuclear weapon.

Sometimes, the only fights you win are the ones you stay out of.

Stupidity has no beginning and no end. It simply is.

Stupidity is its own reward.

The fact that you are not prohibited from doing a thing does not make it right or appropriate. You are allowed to be stupid, but that doesn't mean stupidity is a good thing.

The major food groups are Caffeine, Chocolate, Chips, Candy, Beer, and Pizza. Foods of the gods, they are.

The job of a soldier is the controlled application of deadly force to support national aims as directed by his/her chain of command. Very often, that includes the taking of human life. It very frequently requires that soldiers place their lives in each others' hands.

The mere existence of legal system with police powers does not ensure that the populace will act in a lawful manner. The need for courts and police argues strongly that people act with disregard to the law. It is an interesting contradiction that more police usually means that crime is more commonplace.

The person who does a payroll deduction or writes a check every now and again is still doing a service. On the other hand, I like to think that giving of oneself rather than of one's bank account is an act of true charity. Each time we engage in such an act, we grow and we help others in ways which touch them, sometimes profoundly. Yes, without the money, the food doesn't get to the soup kitchen. But, without the volunteer, it doesn't get from the package to the person who needs it. The friendly smile and perhaps a kind word from the person who dishes out the food is of more value than that one meal.

The person who said, "Swallow a live frog in the morning and nothing worse will happen to you all day," obviously never worked for the government.

The person who will benefit the most from forgiving is the one who forgives. You can't harbor/nurture a grudge without resenting/hating all men (including yourself) to some extent. Allowing the hurt to fester is a bit like picking at a scab. You can't really heal until you stop.

The reason for going fishing is not to catch fish. It is to *be fishing*.

The state in which a person may exist is a result of how they react to the world around them. Certainly life often gives us rotten choices. People can't be held accountable for those external factors, only for how they react to them.

The truth is that, regardless of nationality, some people are jerks and the rest of us have to deal with them more than we like.

There are few problems which cannot be resolved through the proper application of plastic explosives.

There are people who *can* say that I must listen to them, such as judges and policemen in the execution of their office. Others can obtain my voluntary cooperation or pay cash.

There is no grander scale than a human life.

There is no justice in this world - only the law and those who enforce it.

There were three loathsome things in Florida which I don't miss: Fire ants, cockroaches, and tourists.

Upgrading is a way of life for Microsoft Windows users.

Very few people want justice for anyone. Usually they just want vengeance.

Virtually all traffic accidents happen because someone made a bad decision. Traffic laws and the rules of the road provide the parameters which help us to make better decisions. Generally, they are there because other people made bad decisions and someone learned from them and passed on those bits of wisdom. Anyone who disregards the rules puts themselves and others at greater risk.

Warfare is a ghastly business and it's all to easy to descend to depths better left unexplored. It's even easier when you don't have to look your victims in the eyes.

Watching Benny Hill once is okay. Twice is less so. Three times is the sign of psychological disorder...

We can't make things safe without limiting someone's freedom to choose for themself. Any choice for greater safety means less freedom. True freedom means the freedom to starve or to go to Hell in a handbasket if one so chooses.

We all have an inalienable right to make fools of ourselves in public. Whether anyone chooses to watch is up to them.

We are a nation of law. When we discard law for expedience, we cease to be that which has allowed this nation to prosper and our people to live in freedom.

We should not assume they were not heroes just because they did not do the things claimed and did not get a basket full of medals. Heroes come in all shapes and forms and many never pick up a rifle.

What most people would consider freedom is an illusion everywhere. A truly free state would be intolerable to the vast majority of people. If one wishes to accrue the benefits from living within a society, one must adhere to that society's laws and customs. Nothing in life is without a price.

What people really need to learn in school (and usually don't) is how to reason and how to separate good data from the noise.

When oil prices go up, gasoline prices go up. When oil prices go down, gas prices go up.

When you read "Playboy" magazine for the articles, *then* you know you've grown up.

"Why am I so stuck up about the truth?" Perhaps because,"The truth shall set you free." Perhaps because I was brought up to believe that honesty was good and that good people were honest with one another. Perhaps because the truth is a precious thing worth protecting while lies are despicable and unworthy of existence. Perhaps because people who value truth are not racists while racists base their existence on self-serving lies. Perhaps because the truth is of God. Perhaps all those things and more.

Why do we call merchant vessels "merchantmen" but refer to each of those ships as "she"?

World War II was a massive, violent upheaval which rent the very fabric of society. Men descended to incredible depths of behavior. Members of every combatant nation committed crimes. In some military forces, the criminality was intentional and widespread, in others, it was prohibited but too often unpunished.

You cannot hate another without hating yourself.

Your opinion is not proof of anything except that it's your opinion. Even then, you could be lying about that.

Joe Myers

We don't hate the Mormons because of caffeine, we hate the Mormons because of the Osmonds.

~N~

Nakagawa Yonezo, Professor Emeritus, Osaka University

Some of the experiments [performed by Unit 731] had nothing to do with advancing the capability of germ warfare, or of medicine. There is such a thing as professional curiosity: "What would happen if we did such and such?" What medical purpose would be served by performing and studying beheadings? None at all. That was just playing around. Professional people, too, like to play.

Joe Namath

When you have confidence, you can have a lot of fun. And when you have fun, you can do amazing things.

When you win, nothing hurts.

Nansen

The whole world can tell a snake from a dragon, but you cannot fool a Zen monk.

Napoleon

A man will fight harder for his interests than his rights.
- Maxims

A wise general always has a line of retreat planned, from which to launch the hammer blow of victory.

Ability is nothing without opportunity.

Give me enough medals and I'll win any war.

Glory is fleeting but obscurity is forever.

History is a set of lies agreed upon.

If they want peace, nations should avoid the pin-pricks that precede cannon shots.

In politics an absurdity is not a handicap.

Men, in general, are but great children.

Never ascribe to malice that which is adequately explained by stupidity.
(N'attribuez jamais a la malice ce que l'incompetence Explique)

The tools belong to the man who can use them.

Ogden Nash

Any dish that has either a taste or an appearance that can be improved by parsley is ipso facto a dish unfit for human consumption.

People who have what they want are fond of telling people who haven't what they want that they really don't want it.

Gamal Abdel Nasser

People do not want words -- they want the sound of battle...the battle of destiny.

The genius of you Americans is that you never make clear cut stupid moves, only complicated stupid moves which make us wonder at the possibility that there may be something to them which we are missing.

George Jean Nathan

An optimist is a fellow who believes a housefly is looking for a way to get out.

Athletic sports, save in the case of young boys, are designed for idiots.

I drink to make other people interesting.

Patriotism is often an arbitrary veneration of real estate above principles.

The test of a real comedian is whether you laugh at him before he opens his mouth.

What passes for woman's intuition is often nothing more than man's transparency.

Carrie Nation

Men are nicotine soaked, beer besmirched, whiskey greased, red eyed devils.

National Review

The Lord's Prayer is 66 words, the Gettysburg Address is 286 words, there are 1,322 words in the Declaration of Independence, but government regulations on the sale of cabbage total 26,911 words.

Joseph Nebus

I'd needed to buy a shirt and things kind of spiralled out of control from there.

Smileys are the worst threat to literacy since the sacking of the library at Alexandria.

While my father is in every other way the superior handyman in every other regard, when he starts spackling the walls the room ends up significantly smaller.

Mohammed Neguib

Religion is a candle inside a multi-colored lantern. Everyone looks through a particular color but the candle is always there.

A.S. Neill

I'd rather see a contented dustman than a neurotic Ph.D.

Michael H. Neill

You try to eat lasagna with a plastic fork. Lasagna cries out for steel.
- http://bmj.bmjjournals.com/cgi/eletters/331/7531/1498#124832

Don Nelson

Coaching is a lot like raising kids. I have to yell at the young ones. They don't know what they're doing.

Rick Nelson

You see, ya can't please everyone, so ya got to please yourself
- "Garden Party"

Ted Nelson

Any nitwit can understand computers. Many do.

I'm all for people doing exactly what they want to do no matter how stupid.

I think that the greatest rule of the computer field is that nothing ever goes away anywhere near as quickly as people expect them to.

Most people do not dare to challenge the prevailing constructs, to consider ideas that are so different. They take the present world as given.

Software is best understood as a branch of movie making.

Graig Nettles

When I was a little boy, I wanted to be a baseball player, and join the circus. With the Yankees, I've accomplished both.

John von Neumann

Anyone who attempts to generate random numbers by deterministic means is, of course, living in a state of sin.

It would appear that we have reached the limits of what it is possible to achieve with computer technology, although one should be careful with such statements, as they tend to sound pretty silly in 5 years.

There's no sense in being precise when you don't even know what you're talking about.

Alan Nevins

On the granite of hard fact grows the moss of legend, and even pure myth contains its grains of stony reality.

Maggie Newman

Remember that poodles come in different sizes. I couldn't fit a standard poodle in my freezer, but I think I could cram a miniature one in there and I could definitely squeeze in one of those little Toys.

Sir **Isaac Newton**

I do not know what I may appear to the world, but to myself I seem to have been only a boy playing on the seashore, and diverting myself in now and then finding a smoother pebble or a prettier shell than ordinary. Whilst the great ocean of truth lay all undiscovered before me.

Non-Famous Lauren <nflauren@netcom.com>

Some things are just good for their own sakes, beyond analysis and thought.

John S. Nichols

Cats aren't clean, they're just covered with cat spit.

Eric Nicol

Very little is known about the War of 1812 because the Americans lost it.

Nicole

I think what all parents should learn to accept is that there is no guarantee that children will become what we want them to be...but it is guaranteed that if we love them, instead of "feeding off of them" they will know what love is...and hopefully, spread it around

Terry Nielsen

By the way, under our current [Canadian] justice system, looters aren't shot but they are given Air Miles for whatever they have taken.

Friedrich Nietzsche

A casual stroll through the lunatic asylum shows that faith does not prove anything.

Against war it may be said that it makes the victor stupid and the vanquished revengeful.

Convictions are more dangerous enemies of truth than lies.

Do you believe then that the sciences would ever have arisen and become great if there had not before hand been magicians, alchemists, astrologers and wizards, who thirsted and hungered after abscondite and forbidden powers?

God created woman. And boredom did indeed cease from that moment – but many other things ceased as well! Woman was God's second mistake.

Hope in reality is the worst of all evils, because it prolongs the torments of man.

How good bad music and bad reasons sound when one marches against an enemy!

If you fight dragons long enough, you become a dragon; if you stare into the Abyss, the Abyss will stare back into you.

In heaven all the interesting people are missing.

In individuals, insanity is rare; but in groups, parties, nations, and epochs it is the rule.

- Beyond Good and Evil

Morality is the herd-instinct in the individual.

People who have given us their complete confidence believe that they have a right to ours. The inference is false; a gift confers no rights.

The concept of 'greatness' entails being noble, wanting to be by oneself, being capable of being different, standing alone...

The irrationality of a thing is no argument against its existence, rather a condition of it.

The most quiet words are the ones that bring the storms. Thoughts that come on pigeon's feet rule the world.

Chester Nimitz

Among the Americans who served on Iwo Jima, uncommon valor was a common virtue.

Anais Nin

We don't see things as they are, we see them as we are.

Richard M. Nixon

Always remember, others may hate you, but those who hate you don't win unless you hate them back, and then you destroy yourself.

Any change is resisted because bureaucrats have a vested interest in the chaos in which they exist.

Defeat doesn't finish a man -- quit does. A man is not finished when he's defeated. He's finished when he quits.

Enemies can be personal, professional, political, or ideological. Two people can be personal friends and yet enemies in one or more of the other three categories.

Every politician's promise has a price--the taxpayer pays the bill.
- Aug 23, 1972

I am not a crook.

I have often thought that if there had been a good rap group around in those days I might have chosen a career in music instead of politics.

I think I've got a lousy personality, and I'm not a personality kid.

I was not lying. I said things that later on seemed to be untrue.

I would have made a good Pope.

Let us begin by committing ourselves to the truth -- to see it like it is, and tell it like it is -- to find the truth, to speak the truth, and to live the truth.

Life is a roller coaster, exhilarating on the way up and breathtaking on the way down.
-- In the Arena

Parents are always special people. It's hard to let them go no matter when.

Sure there are dishonest men in local government. But there are dishonest men in national government too.

The next President must take an activist view of his office. He must articulate the nation's values, define its goals, and marshal its will.

Today, China's economic power makes U.S. lectures about human rights imprudent. Within a decade, it will make them irrelevant. Within two decades, it will make them laughable. By then, the Chinese may threaten to withhold MFN (Most-Favored-Nation) status from the U.S. unless we do more to improve living conditions in Detroit, Harlem and South-Central Los Angeles.

What Indo-China proves is that where the will to resist does not exist it is not possible to save the people from coming under Communist domination. In other words, military strength, mutual-defense treaties, military assistance operating together will not do the job alone unless the people are on your side.
- 1954

Louis Nizer

A graceful taunt is worth a thousand insults.

Kimani Njogu

Ethnicity is just one of the many identities we possess as human beings. We are farmers, teachers, doctors, welders, artists, men, women, parents, students. We can invoke these other identities and de-emphasize the ethnic identity, when necessary. Wise governments allow citizens to move in and out of these identities freely.

It is unfortunate that the primary objective of most political leaders in the world continues to be personal gain and individual preservation as well as financial advantage.

Lord Northcliffe

News is what somebody, somewhere wants to suppress. All the rest is advertising.

Nostradamus <n...@example.com (actually at nostradamus.net)>

Supermarkets lose a little money on every sale, they just make it up on volume.

<Nuclear2@ix.netcom.com>

When I was a young athlete (as opposed to the old beer drinking sofa stud I am now)...

Naomi Shihab Nye

I want to be famous in the way a pulley is famous, or a buttonhole, not because it did anything spectacular, but because it never forgot what it could do.

~O~

Edna O'Brien

The vote, I thought, means nothing to women. We should be armed.

Sean O'Casey

All the world's a stage and most of us are desperately unrehearsed.

Flannery O'Connor

Everywhere I go, I'm asked if the universities stifle writers. My opinion is that they don't stifle enough of them.

Lona O'Connor

If this has been a rotten day, do one thing to turn it around without using alcohol, potato chips, [caffeine], or chocolate.

O'Henry

A straw vote only shows which way the hot air blows.

Richard A. O'Keefe

Students will copy whatever you write. This even applies to things labelled "Bad example. Don't do this."

Mark O'Meara

I've been on a winning, losing, and tying team and to tell the truth, I didn't have fun on any of them.

Eugene O'Neill

There is no present or future, only the past, happening over and over again, now.

Kevin S. O'Neill

Blowing a bunch of algebra past people is not an argument.

Dr Phil said I can't change if I don't want to change, and I've had the same underwear on ever since.

I think what I think, but I think I'm wrong in thinking it, actually.

Rob O'Regan

The great thing about making predictions is that if they come true, you take credit for being a genius. If they don't, you simply hope no one remembers the inane things you said were going to happen.

PJ O'Rourke

Anyway, no drug, not even alcohol, causes the fundamental ills of society. If we're looking for the source of our troubles, we shouldn't test people for drugs, we should test them for stupidity, ignorance, greed and love of power.

Even very young children need to be informed about dying. Explain the concept of death very carefully to your child. This will make threatening him with it much more effective.

Giving money and power to Government is like giving whiskey and car keys to teenage boys.

There are a number of mechanical devices which increase sexual arousal, particularly in women. Chief among them is the Mercedes Benz 380SL convertible.

Barack H. Obama

I believe deeply that we cannot solve the challenges of our time unless we solve them together.

Loving your country shouldn't just mean watching fireworks on the Fourth of July; loving your country must mean accepting your responsibility to do your part to change it.

Teodoro Obian Nguema

There is no poverty in Guinea. . .The people are used to living in a different way.

Ochs

For it's only love that frees the fire for burning.

Tom M. Oliver from the escarpment overlooking the Valley of the three Bosques

Ask not what your government can do for you, but how to get out of the way when it does!

...better for all of us, especially today's high school students, it would be to comprehend that all of them, from the unwise at Lexington Common, to the unwitting euchered into service on both sides of the drystone walls and split rail fences of Virginia or into the cavalry of the 1870s to all of those, willing and unwilling, dispatched to France, the Pacific Islands, Korea or Viet Nam, are our brothers, fathers, sons and cousins (and now a few sisters and daughters). They are we, and we they, and when we cannot or will not accept that, it's time to turn in the franchise.

Two large Jackalope breeding operations in Eastern Colorado were shifted to the cross-breeding of "'roos", a quaint genetic steroid-pumped dehorned misfortune of the mating of a jackalope with a possum.

Ken Olson, CEO DEC

Trouble isn't when your stock price goes down; trouble is when your kids take dope.

OMM

If the Mexican Roman Catholic archdiocese came out against running your tongue across the floors of gas station restrooms, there'd still be some kind of bitchy outcry.

Robert Orben

Illegal aliens have always been a problem in this country. Ask any native Indian.

Daniel Ortega

I continue being a revolutionary who pursues ideals, growing in the understanding and learning that what is desired is not always possible.

William A. Orton

If you keep your mind sufficiently open, people will throw a lot of rubbish into it.

George Orwell

Advertising is the rattling of a stick inside a swill bucket.

In our time, political speech and writing are largely the defense of the indefensible.
- "Politics and the English Language"

International sport is war without shooting.

[Kipling] sees clearly that men can only be highly civilized while other men, inevitably less civilised, are there to guard and feed them.

Most people get a fair amount of fun out of their lives, but on balance life is suffering, and only the very young or very foolish imagine otherwise.

On the whole, human beings want to be good, but not too good and not quite all the time.

Political language. . . is designed to make lies sound truthful and murder respectable, and to give an appearance of solidity to pure wind.

Serious sport has nothing to do with fair play. It is bound up with hatred, jealousy, boastfulness, disregard of all rules, and sadistic pleasure in witnessing violence: in other words, it is war minus the shooting.
- "Shooting an Elephant"

The nationalist not only does not disapprove of atrocities committed by his own side, but he has a remarkable capacity for not even hearing about them.

Those who "abjure" violence can only do so because others are committing violence on their behalf.

Brad Osberg

As I arrived home from work, I could hear the sounds of maniacal laughter and terrified goats coming from within the house. As I put my key in the door, I couldn't help but think, "Here we go again."

Alexander Osborne

The one certain thing, is that if 'they' don't like it, they'll get you for it somehow, given a chance. A great amount of harassment by agencies of the state in any country is just that harassment, without prosecution, because you don't fit the norm.

Personally, I set a high value on courtesy as the lubricant by which unwelcome ideas and criticism may be more easily shoved up the asshole of an opponent's consciousness.

Charles Osgood

Being Politically Correct means always having to say you're sorry.

Scott Ostler, San Francisco Chronicle

It would appear that the [Dallas] Cowboys have a very effective drug program. However, the team's anti drug program is another story.

James Otis

It is a clear truth that those who every day barter away other men's liberty will soon care little for their own.

- "The Rights of the British Colonies Asserted and Proved"

Otter <otter@nada.net>

If I hear Brown Eyed Girl one more time I'm stabbing screwdrivers in my ears.

Ovid

A woman is always buying something.

Few people want the pleasures they are free to take.

I must confess, I do not love well unless I am ill used.

Oxford Union Society, London, Rule 46

Any member introducing a dog into the Society's premises shall be liable to a fine of one pound. Any animal leading a blind person shall be deemed to be a cat.

(Back To Table of Contents)

~P~

Pierre Pachet, Professor of Physiology at Toulouse, 1872

Louis Pasteur's theory of germs is ridiculous fiction.

General **S. Padmanabhan**, Indian Army

If we have to go to war, jolly good.
- Discussing the possibility of war with Pakistan

Clarence Page

The difference between Colin Powell and Jesse Jackson is the difference between riding tall in the saddle and being a burr under the saddle.

Since my spouse does not take kindly to my lustfully staring at other women, we do not dine at Hooters.

There is a limit to how much someone can apologize for something they didn't do.

Camille Paglia

Cats are autocrats of naked self- interest. They are both amoral and immoral, consciously breaking rules. Their "evil" look at such times is no human projection: the cat may be the only animal who savors the perverse or reflects upon it.

Identity is shaped through conflict and opposition.

Madeleine Page

Just a friendly warning, dear. If you ooze that sort of ingratiating oily charm, I shall hurt you.

Please understand that we are considerably less interested in you than you are.

What separates MAN from the rest of the animal kingdom is his ability to trim headers.

Satchel Paige

How old would you be if you didn't know how old you was?

Thomas Paine

A long habit of not thinking a thing wrong, gives it a superficial appearance of being right, and raises at first a formidable outcry in defence of custom.
- Common Sense

Give to every other human being every right that you claim for yourself – that is my doctrine.

He who is the author of a war lets loose the whole contagion of hell and opens a vein that bleeds a nation to death.

He who would make his own liberty secure must guard even his enemy from opposition.
- Common Sense

Society is produced by our wants and government by our wickedness.
- Common Sense

The more simple any thing is, the less liable it is to be disordered, and the easier repaired when disordered...
- Common Sense

War involves in its progress such a train of unforeseen and unsupposed circumstances that no human wisdom can calculate the end. It has but one thing certain, and that is to increase taxes.

When we are planning for posterity, we ought to remember that virtue is not hereditary.

Bob Paisley

If you're in the penalty area and don't know what to do with the ball, put it in the net and we'll discuss the options later.

David Palmer

Unfortunately, Microsoft has fallen on hard times recently, and can no longer afford to hire a college student to come in and tune the code for greater speed.

John Palmer, on uncertainty

[I]f all are seeking friendship and understanding, and want to do what is right, there will be a lot of common ground. Differences can be learned about, and perhaps even celebrated; points of agreement can be solidified. Fear of differences can become fascination, and what seems to be an ugly mark might end up being part of a beautiful mosaic.

Mike Palmer

You need two pretty incalcitrant sides to let home-schooling escalate into a shoot-out,

Spokesman for Paris Chamber of Commerce

The overall impression from the British and the Germans is that they love France itself but would rather that the French didn't live there.

Dorothy Parker

Age before beauty; and pearls before swine.

I might repeat to myself, slowly and soothingly, a list of quotations beautiful from minds profound; if I can remember any of the damn things.
-- "The Portable"

If all the girls who attended the Harvard-Yale game were laid end to end, I wouldn't be surprised.

Love is like quicksilver in the hand. Leave the fingers open and it stays. Clutch it, and it darts away.

Money cannot buy health, but I'd settle for a diamond studded wheelchair.

The best way to keep children at home is to make the home atmosphere pleasant and let the air out of the tires.

The cure for boredom is curiosity. There is no cure for curiosity.

This is not a novel to be tossed aside lightly. It should be thrown with great force.

Kathleen Parker

Forgive me for being a mother, but if MTV really wants to help kids deal with healthy sex, it might set a new standard. Insist that people in music videos put on some clothes and stop behaving like animals in rut.

Tom Parkins

Anything that happens enough times to irritate you will happen at least once more.

Jack Parr

I have never seen a bad television program, because I refuse to. God gave me a mind, and a wrist that turns things off.

Poor people have more fun than rich people, they say; and I notice it's the rich people who keep saying it.

Tom Parsons

The trouble with political circuses is that you never know who are going to turn out to be the clowns.

Dolly Parton

In the end, gravity wins.

You would be surprised how much it costs to look this cheap.

Blaise Pascal

If all men knew what others say of them, there would not be four friends in the world.

Love demands all and has a right to it.

Men are so necessarily mad, that not to be mad would amount to another form of madness.
- "Pensees"

Steve Patlan

It's kind of like being a ref at an Arkansas Razorback basketball game: you can't call everything. No Blood, No Foul.

Troy Patterson

If there exist venues where men give scads of cash and pledges of ardor to female performers who do not remove their brassieres, then I would like to know where they are, so as not to lurch erroneously into one.
- "The Lifetime Original Movie 2.0"

Jackie Patti (http://www.ornery-geeks.org/)

I have PRECISELY the same obligation to be polite as everyone else in society does, and that obligation rapidly evaporates when someone makes rude comments about which civil rights they think I don't have a 'special' right to.

Someone made the interesting observation that so many parents are worried about their kids hearing them have sex, but few worry about the kids hearing them fight.

PattyMaci

And though unexpected results might sometimes get you a Nobel Prize, usually you just get stretch marks.

George S. Patton, Jr.

A pint of sweat will save a gallon of blood.

An army is like a piece of spaghetti. You can't stand behind and push, you have to get out in front and pull.

If everyone is thinking alike then somebody isn't thinking.

In war death is incidental. Loss of time is criminal.

Never tell people how to do things. Tell them what to do and they will surprise you with their ingenuity.

Wars may be fought by weapons, but they are won by men. It is the spirit of the men who follow and of the man who leads that gains the victory.

Paul

For why should my freedom be judged by another's conscience?
- I Corinthians 10:29

Jane Pauley

You can't look at a sleeping cat and be tense.

Wolfgang Pauli

No, no, you're not thinking, you're just being logical.

This isn't right. This isn't even wrong.

<paussav@sc.lafb.af.mil>

Note that corporations formulate their response based on actuarial risk. If the person complaining does not affect the corporation's bottom line then that person will be ignored. If the complainer can act to reduce the corporation's profit then those concerns are accommodated.

PauSto <pausto@erols.com>

The most adamantly enforced rules are the rules that cover the butts of and benefit the promotion of "The people who enforce the rules"!

Tom Paxton

Well, the years have gone by too quickly, it seems,
- "Marvelous Toy"

Gordon W Paynter

Paynter's "clueless newbie correlation": If you don't post you are not observed to be clueless.

Subjects new to usenet are reluctant to post until such a time as they feel sure that many others are as clueless as they.

Charles Peguy

It is better to have a war for justice than peace in injustice.

Eva Peron

Charity separates the rich from the poor; aid raises the needy and sets him on the same level with the rich.

Mike W. Perry

Even jerks can have high IQs. Intelligence isn't virtue.

It's silly to run around trying to promote nonsense merely because that nonsense exhaults [sic] a particular race, sex or whatever.

Michael D. Persin

She must be two people. One person could never make me feel this good.

Eddy Peters

Not only does the English Language borrow words from other languages, it sometimes chases them down dark alleys, hits them over the head, and goes through their pockets.

Norm Peterson ("Cheers")

I cannot be bought. And, I cannot be threatened. But you put the two together and I'm your man.

It's a dog eat dog world out there and I'm wearing Milkbone underwear.

Most people don't know this, but I'm pretty famous.

Never been better. Just once I'd like to be better.

Once the trust goes out of relationship, it's really no fun to tell lies.

A. Padgett Peterson

Virus writers remind me of a litter of puppies, investigating everything without really understanding it. Eventually they grow up if they stay out of real danger but meanwhile someone else has to clean up their messes.

James L. Petigru

South Carolina is too small to be a republic and too large to be an insane asylum.

John Petit-Senn

It requires less character to discover the faults of others than is does to tolerate them.

Let us believe neither half of the good people tell us of ourselves, nor half the evil they say of others.

The hatred we bear our enemies injures their happiness less than our own.

Beryl Pfizer

If you treat children like grown-ups, they'll probably behave just as badly as the rest of us.

William Lyon Phelps

Nature makes boys and girls lovely to look upon so they can be tolerated until they acquire some sense.

If happiness truly consisted in physical ease and freedom from care, then the happiest individual would not be either a man or a woman; but an American cow.

Philip the Foole (ptf@ix.netcom.com)

Don't get me wrong. I'm a sensitive, steeped in feminist consciousness, 90's kind of guy. I would never reduce a woman to a pair of shapely legs in skin tight shiny black leather high heeled fetish boots and a whip. I just want to find who the boot maker was. For a friend.

I am a genuine Foole. Accept no substitutes.

If people want to be part of an "Inner Circle" the polite thing to do is to form a ring around them.

If you want to attempt to e flirt with someone, first read their stuff to see if their sig line includes "E flirters will be killed." This is not a good sign.

If you want to find where your armor is weak, check your bruised spots.

It would have been impolite to get the host's carpet all blood-stained.

If one person calls you an ass, laugh it off. If a dozen people who seem to be reasonably sound thinkers on most other subjects call you an ass, get fitted for a saddle.

No matter how spicy you like your food, someone will tell you that it is too hot and someone else will tell you that it is too bland. Season to your own taste.

The old Druids went into battle wearing nothing but blue paint. OK, so they were slaughtered by the Romans, but at least they _looked_ cool.

People who engage in religious persecution never call it religious persecution.

The secret of success is to hire people who are smarter than oneself. That has always been easy for me to achieve...

They offered to pay me what I'm worth, but I don't work that cheap.

While not uniformly a fan of American law enforcement efforts, [I favor] issuing bazookas to the Highway Patrol for use when they see a driver weaving down the road. Sure, you'd get the occasional person with mechanical problems in their steering wheel, but that would be a small price to pay.

Eden Phillips

The world is full of magical things, patiently waiting for our wits to grow sharper.

Emo Phillips

I like to think as my body as a temple, or at least as a relatively well-managed Presbyterian youth center.

Some mornings, it's just not worth chewing through the leather straps.

Gene Phillips

When I read letters attacking religions and attributing America's greatness to a religious heritage, I reflect on the fact that our great nation was founded by pious Christians who cleared out the Indians so they could have enough land for their slaves to raise cotton on.

Wendell Phillips

The community which does not protect its humblest and most hated member in the free utterance of his opinions, no matter how false or hateful, is only a gang of slaves. If there is anything in the universe that can't stand discussion, let it crack.

Philo

People have been known to learn to fly these machines with no assistance from commercial airlines, and could in fact fly a cooler of motel chitlin's anywhere in the country.

Master Sergeant **Donald Phinney**

A mine is the cheapest soldier you can get because you don't have to feed it and you don't have to take care of it. But then, the other thing is: You sign a peace treaty and it doesn't know that either.

Jean Piaget

The principle goal of education is to create men who are capable of doing new things, not simply of repeating what other generations have done -- men who are creative, inventive and discoverers.

Pablo Picasso

Computers are useless. They can only give you answers.

There are only two kinds of women goddesses and doormats.

George E. Pickett, Major General, CSA

Up men, up, and to your posts. Let no man forget this day that he is from Old Virginia!
- July 3rd 1863

Jozef Pilsudski

Irrespective of what her government will be, Russia is terribly imperialistic.

Scottie Pippen

I put my suitcase down, looked up at the Sears Tower, and said "Chicago, here I am and I'm gonna conquer you." Then I looked down and my suitcase was gone.

Luigi Priandello

Life is little more than a loan shark: it exacts a very high rate of interest for the few pleasures it concedes.

David Pischke

Engineering is the art of moulding materials we do not fully understand into shapes we cannot fully analyse and preventing the public from realising the full extent of our ignorance.

William Pitt

Necessity is the excuse for every infringement of human freedom. It is the argument of the tyrant and the creed of the slave.

Leonard Pitts

Age ravages only flesh. But the spirit, defiant, endures.

I can't believe God requires ignorance, that He gave us brains he doesn't want us to use, or that intelligence and faith are mutually exclusive.

Never satisfy a short-term impulse at the expense of a long-term goal. Never do what feels good in the moment if it's going to cost you something that matters a whole lot more in the end. The trade is never worth it.

The new bigotry has learned to hide itself among the babble of legitimate discourse by forgoing the obviousness of a John Rocker and calling itself by different, less inflammatory names.

To love somebody is to make yourself hostage to the fortunes of others.

We cling to the rules, cling to order—or just the illusion thereof—because without that, we stand defenseless before the worst in ourselves.

Where once there were mom and pop stores and people serving people, now there are superstores and self-serve checkouts and press one for more options. Where once there were institutions whose names reflected civic pride or noteworthy citizens, now there are institutions branded like cattle by corporate America. This is not progress, it's pollution.

Words and images that might seem innocuous to some are viewed entirely differently by those who remember when similar words and images were used in the service of quite intentional insults.

Max Planck

A new scientific truth does not triumph by convincing its opponents and making them see the light, but rather because its opponents eventually die, and a new generation grows up that is familiar with it.

Plato

All in all, nothing human is worth taking very seriously...

As empty vessels make the loudest sound, so they that have the least wit are the greatest blabbers.

Astronomy compels the soul to look upwards and leads us from this world to another.
- The Republic

I have hardly ever known a mathematician who was capable of reasoning.

Love is a serious mental disease.

No one has ever died an atheist.

Only the dead have seen the end of war.

Those who are too smart to engage in politics are punished by being governed by those who are dumber.

We can easily forgive a child who is afraid of the dark; the real tragedy of life is when men are afraid of the light.

Ernst Jan Plugge

The day Microsoft makes something that doesn't suck is probably the day they start making vacuum cleaners.

Plutarch

We ought not to treat living creatures like shoes or household belongings, which when worn with use we throw away.

Edgar Allan Poe

Those who dream by day are cognizant of many things which escape those who dream only by night.

Henri Poincare'

To doubt everything or to believe everything are two equally convenient solutions; both dispense with the necessity of reflection.

Carmen Policy

San Franciscans consider themselves to be stable, solid articulate, classy and substantive people. Whereas L.A. is viewed to be tinsel, pizzazz, Hollywood, trendy, and less real.

Polybius

For it is history, and history alone, which, without involving us in actual danger, will mature our judgment and prepare us to take right views, whatever may be the crisis or the posture of affairs.
- The Histories of Polybius

Alexander Pope

Blessed is he who expects nothing, for he shall never be disappointed.
- Letter to John Gay, Oct. 6, 1727

Do good by stealth, and blush to find it fame.

Sir **Karl Popper**

Our knowledge can only be finite, while our ignorance must necessarily be infinite.

Popular Mechanics, March 1949

Where a calculator on the ENIAC is equipped with 18,000 vacuum tubes and weighs 30 tons, computers in the future may have only 1,000 vacuum tubes and perhaps weigh 1 1/2 tons.

Joe Posnanski

Florida's defensive players seemed stunned that Nebraska was running the option, though the Cornhuskers started running that offense before Nebraska officially became a state.

Scott Post, <spost@netusa1.net>

Consumer Reports had a web page, but it was recalled after it rolled over on a fast turn and killed a waiting NBC news crew.

Pournelle, Jerry (J.E. Pournelle, Ph.D.)

A nation which despises its soldiers will all too soon have a despicable army.

Anyone who loses work because it wasn't backed up deserves what happened.

Despite the silly sayings about violence never settling anything, history IS changed on the battlefield...

For those who can lead men to Hell, there is the vision that they might lead them to Paradise...but history records few instances of success.

It's the nature of government, to build enduring institutions, structures that stay long after their purpose is over. If you pay people to help the poor, you have people who won't be paid if there aren't any poor, so they'll be sure to find some.
- Prince of Sparta

That's the thing about people who think they hate computers. What they really hate is lazy programmers.
- Oath of Fealty

The enemy of every free man is a real greedy successful one. [The] Biggest enemies of capitalism are successful capitalists.
- Prince of Sparta

The trend in the United States has been to cut all ties, so that individuals are alone. The citizen against the bureaucracy, against 'them,' only nobody is really in control and you can't say who 'they' are.

To stand on the firing parapet and expose yourself to danger; to stand and fight a thousand miles from home when you're all alone and outnumbered and probably beaten, to spit on your hands and lower the pike; to stand fast over the body of Leonidas the King; to be rear guard at Kunu ri; to stand and be still to the Birkenhead drill; these are not rational acts.

Colin Powell

Don't give up on the political process. Fix it.

I can never forgive a [political] leadership that said, in effect: These young men—poor, educated, less privileged—are expendable...but the rest are too good to risk...Of the many tragedies of Vietnam, this raw class discrimination strikes me as the most damaging to the ideal that all Americans are created equal.
- My American Journey

There are no secrets to success. It is the result of preparation, hard work, learning from failure.

We have a value system and a culture system within the armed forces of the United States. We have this mission: to fight and win this nation's wars.

Enoch Powell

History is littered with wars which everybody knew would never happen.

Lewis Power, US Supreme Court Justice

Fourth Amendment freedoms cannot properly be guaranteed if domestic security surveillances may be conducted solely within the discretion of the Executive Branch.

Lisa Power

People would rather be told pretty lies about sex rather than the truth - it's messy, sometimes frustrating, often deeply silly and still one of the most enjoyable sports around...

Sir Terry Pratchett

Give a man a fire and he's warm for a day, but set fire to him and he's warm for the rest of his life.

It is better to light a flamethrower than to curse the darkness.
- Men at Arms

Look into the face of a man who will kill you for a belief and your nostrils will snuff up the scent of abomination. Hear a speech declaring a holy war and, I assure you, your ears should catch the clink of evil's scales and the dragging of its monstrous tail over the purity of the language.
- Pyramids

Of course it's daft, it's traditional.

One reason for the bustle was that over large parts of the continent other people preferred to make money without working at all, and since the Disc had yet to develop a music recording industry they were forced to fall back on older, more traditional forms of banditry.
- Equal Rites

SOME SHADOWS ARE SO LONG THEY ARRIVE BEFORE THE LIGHT.
- Death, Soul Music

Time is a drug. Too much of it kills you.
- Small Gods

George D. Prentice

A word of kindness is seldom spoken in vain, while witty sayings are as easily lost as the pearls slipping from a broken string.

William Prescott

Don't one of you fire until you see the whites of their eyes.
- June 17, 1775, Breed's Hill

Elvis Presley

I don't know anything about music. In my line you don't have to.

I have no use for bodyguards, but I have a very special use for two highly trained certified public accountants.

J. B. Priestley

Like its politicians and its war, society has the teenagers it deserves.

Brian Proffit

Brian Proffit is an author and speaker on topics as diverse as technology (he was director of PC Week Corporate Labs and contributing editor to PC Magazine) and theology (he has also been a pastor).

You can't always judge the best product by the number of copies in use. Look how many people are using Windows.

Providence (RI) Journal Bulletin

Neanderthals are not really extinct...sightings allegedly have been made, among other places, in the cloakrooms of the U.S. Senate and on the playing fields of the National Football League.

PS Magazine, (Army preventive maintenance magazine) August 1993

A slipping sear could let your M203 grenade launcher fire when you least expect it. That would make you quite unpopular in what's left of your unit.

Publius Syrius

The greater a man is in power above others, the more he ought to excel them in virtue. None ought to govern who is not better than the governed.

Pyrrhus

Another such victory over the Romans, and we are undone.
-- in Plutarch's Lives

~Q~

Dave Quackenbush

Lying is not illegal and in most cases not even reprehensible.

Paul Quantrill

Seven days in [Las Vegas] is a dangerous thing. I did OK myself, but a lot of guys didn't. The ATM machines were pretty busy.

Dan Quayle

[It's] time for the human race to enter the Solar System.

Queenie

I think the laws of ethics are mutable when it comes to marriage. Sometimes, the laws of physics, too.

Queenie
[No, not that Queenie. This is another one...]

You know your cat is wise. In fact they are so wise, they have you fooled into thinking they can't be trained to do anything.

Gloria Quinn (Boron Elgar)

In a very different way, carbs are my specialty. Just ask my thighs.

This is something I know to be true because I saw it on TV & it was a documentary because part of it was in black & white. Black and white stuff is like, historical and everything.

Dan Quisenberry

I have seen the future, and it's very much like the present, only longer.

Kevin D. Quitt

My wife explained to me that "debriefing" is the same thing as interrogation, but with sandwiches.

~R~

Ronald Radosh

There are, as has been said, some arguments so stupid that only an intellectual could be counted on to make them.
- http://historynewsnetwork.org/articles/article.html?id=173

Ayn Rand

Contradictions do not exist. Whenever you think that you are facing a contradiction, check your premises. You will find that one of them is wrong.

Every major horror of history was committed in the name of altruistic motive.

Unjust laws have to be fought ideologically; they cannot be fought or corrected by means of mere disobedience and futile martyrdom.

Ranger School slogan

Hope is NOT a method unless you are the chaplain!

Mich Ratcliffe

A computer lets you make more mistakes faster than any invention in human history -- with the possible exceptions of handguns and tequila.
- "Technology Review", April 1992

<rch@lanminds.com>

Its not easy shaving a hamster, they're very sensitive to most shaving creams and will only use Calvin Klein's 'Obsession' <TM> aftershave; but the results are sensational (or Sinsational!)

Ronald Reagan

Facts are stupid things.

Government is like a baby. An alimentary canal with a big appetite at one end, and no sense of responsibility at the other.

Politics is supposed to be the second oldest profession. I have come to realize that it bears a very close resemblance to the first.

The best view of government is in the rearview mirror as you're driving away from it.

There are no such things as limits to growth, because there are no limits on the human capacity for intelligence, imagination and wonder.

Why should we subsidize intellectual curiosity?

You can tell a lot about a fellow's character by his way of eating jellybeans.

Daniel L. Reardon

The pessimist may turn out to be right, but the optimist has a better time on the trip.

Red Dog, Oglala chief

My friend, this is the way we have been raised. Do not think us strange. All men are different.

Ambrose Redmoon (James Neil Hollingworth)

Courage is not the absence of fear, but the judgment that something else is more important than fear.

Mark Reichert

Not that I expect you to have stunning moment of clarity and realize your errors. I expect you to go pigheadedly, laying waste to all around you, until reality smacks you upside the head hard. I have no idea what you will do then.

Dr. **Allan L. Reiss**

It doesn't take a lot of analytical machinery to think someone getting poked in the eye is funny.

Jules Renard

At the bottom of all patriotism is war: that is why I am no patriot.

Laziness is nothing more than the habit of resting before you get tired.

Major **Marcus A. Reno**

The harrowing sight of the dead bodies crowning the height on which Custer fell, and which will remain vividly in my memory until death, is too recent for me not to ask the good people of this country whether a policy that sets opposing parties in the field armed, clothed, and equipped by one and the same government should not be abolished.
- July 5, 1876

Faith Resnick

People that hate cats will come back as mice in their next life.

James Reston

A government is the only known vessel that leaks from the top.

All politics are based on the indifference of the majority.

Dusty Rhoades

Bungee jumping and skydiving are for wimps. If you want to experience true gut-wrenching terror, have children.

Grantland Rice

For when the One Great Scorer comes to write against your name, He marks -- not that you won or lost -- but how you played the game.

Outlined against a blue-gray October sky the Four Horsemen rode again. In dramatic lore they are known as Famine, Pestilence, Destruction and Death. These are only aliases. Their real names are: Stuhldreher, Miller, Crowley and Layden. They formed the crest of South Bend cyclone before another fighting army team was swept over the precipice at the Polo grounds this afternoon as 55,000 spectators peered down upon the bewildering panorama spread out on the green plain below.
-- "New York Herald Tribune", October 19, 1924

Richard

I can picture in my mind a world without war, a world without hate. And I can picture us attacking that world, because they'd never expect it.

Beah Richards

Both class and race survive education, and neither should. What is education then? If it doesn't help a human being to recognize that humanity is humanity, what is it for? So you can make a bigger salary than other people?

Keith Richards

I was No. 1 on the `who's likely to die' list for 10 years. I mean, I was really disappointed when I fell off the list,

Major General **Frank Richardson**

It is a touching fact that men, dying in battle, often call upon their mothers. I have heard them do so in five languages.

General **Matthew B. Ridgway**

Professional soldiers are sentimental men, for all the harsh realities of their calling. In their wallets and in their memories they carry bits of philosophy, fragments of poetry, quotations from the scriptures, which, in times of stress and danger, speak to them with quiet meaning.

Rivarol

Cats don't caress us - they caress themselves on us.

Frank Rizzo

The streets are safe in Philadelphia. It's only the people who make them unsafe.

Bob Roberds

Anyhow, studies have proved conclusively that *all* women are sexually insatiable / very promiscuous, except when they're with me.

Dave Roberts

You never break the law in order to make the law.

Chief Justice **John G. Roberts, Jr.**

Where the First Amendment is implicated, the tie goes to the speaker, not the censor.

Maximilien François Marie Isidore de Robespierre

Terror is nothing more than justice, prompt, secure, and inflexible.

Michael Robinson

In the good old days of Zen training, it was traditional to thwack the student in the head with a stick when he said something like that.

John D. Rockefeller

I know of nothing more despicable and pathetic than a man who devotes all of the hours of the waking day to the making of money for money's sake.

Knute Rockne

One man practicing sportsmanship is far better than 50 preaching it.

Carl Rogers

The only person who is educated is the one who has learned how to learn and change.

Jim Rogers

Lots of things are right there in front of our faces, including noses, which would be far more effective instruments to make decisions with than planetary positions (useful for, say, discerning sh** from shinola).

John Rogers (Kung Fu Monkey)

There are two novels that can change a bookish fourteen-year old's life: The Lord of the Rings and Atlas Shrugged. One is a childish fantasy that often engenders a lifelong obsession with its unbelievable heroes, leading to an emotionally stunted, socially crippled adulthood, unable to deal with the real world. The other, of course, involves orcs.

Will Rogers

Everybody is ignorant, only on different subjects.

Government investigations have always contributed more to our amusement than they have to our knowledge.

Lead your life so you wouldn't be ashamed to sell the family parrot to the town gossip.

Liberty doesn't work as well in practice as it does in speeches.

The more you observe politics, the more you've go to admit that each party is worse than the other.

Stupidity got us into this mess; why can't it get us out?

There's no trick to being a humorist when you have the whole government working for you.

Roman Rollard

A hero is a man who does what he can.

Bill Romanowski

When emotions get high, logic is low...A lot of times, you do things you're not crazy about.
(on being asked about spitting in JJ Stokes' face)

Erwin Rommel

Fortune favors the bold.

Mortal danger is an effective antidote for fixed ideas.

Manfred Rommel

Competition creates high efficiency but it doesn't create moral goals. Survival of the fittest cannot be the goal - competition should be the servant and not the master.

Some [German wine] has such a close relation to vinegar that it takes a lot of patriotism to drink it. Today we call it "dry wine."

Eleanor Roosevelt

No one can make you feel inferior without your consent.

You must do the thing you think you cannot do.

Franklin D. Roosevelt

In every battle there comes a time when one group of warriors must be sacrificed for the benefit of the whole...
- March 1942, writing off the defenders in the Philippines

More than an end to war, we want an end to the beginning of all wars--yes, an end to this brutal, inhuman and thoroughly impractical method of settling the differences between governments.

Peace, like charity, begins at home.

Peace, like war, can succeed only where there is a will to enforce it, and where there is available power to enforce it.

The truth is found when men are free to pursue it.

The motto of war is: "Let the strong survive; let the weak die." The motto of peace is: "Let the strong help the weak to survive."

We, and all others who believe in freedom as deeply as we do, would rather die on our feet than live on our knees.

We have always known that heedless self-interest was bad morals; we know now that it is bad economics.

When you come to the end of your rope, tie a knot and hang on.

Theodore Roosevelt

A man who has never gone to school may steal from a freight car; but if he has a university education, he may steal the whole railroad.

Do not hit at all if it can be avoided, but never hit softly.

Far and away the best prize that life offers is the chance to work hard at work worth doing.

In any moment of decision, the best thing you can do is the right thing. The worst thing you can do is nothing.

In doing your work in the great world, it is a safe plan to follow a rule I once heard on the football field: Don't flinch, don't fall; hit the line hard.

No man is above the law and no man below it.

No man is justified in doing evil on the grounds of expedience.

The best executive is one who has sense enough to pick good people to do what he wants them to do, and self-restraint enough to keep from meddling with them while they do it.

The man who loves other countries as much as his own stands on a level with the man who loves other women as much as he loves his own wife.

The nation behaves well if it treats the natural resources as assets which it must turn over to the next generation increased, and not impaired, in value.
-- speech before the Colorado Live Stock Association, Denver, August 29, 1910, The New Nationalism

The poorest way to face life is with a sneer.

The surest sign of ignorance is to call your detractors ignorant.

The things that will destroy America are prosperity at any price, peace at any price, safety first instead of duty first, the love of soft living and the get rich quick theory of life.

There is a homely adage which runs, "Speak softly and carry a big stick: you will go far." If the American nation will speak softly and yet build and keep at a pitch of highest training a thoroughly efficient navy, the Monroe Doctrine will go far.

To waste, to destroy our natural resources, to skin and exhaust the land instead of using it so as to increase its usefulness, will result in undermining in the days of our children the very prosperity which we ought by right to hand down to them amplified and developed.

We cannot meet the future either by mere gross materialism or by mere silly sentimentalism; above all, we cannot meet it if we attempt to balance gross materialism in action by silly sentimentalism in words.

Billy Rose

Never invest in anything that needs feeding or painting.

Lloyd Rose

The Romantics had sex and drugs, but lacking rock-and-roll they made do with Switzerland.

Pete Rose

I'd walk through hell in a gasoline suit to keep playing baseball.

Dr. **Isadore Rosenfeld**

If you're habitually flatulent, get a dog, have it lie nearby and blame it when necessary.

John Ross

Underground nuclear testing, defoliation of the rain forests, toxic waste ... Let's put it this way: if the world were a big apartment, we wouldn't get our deposit back.

Gioacchino Antonio Rossini

Give me a laundry list and I'll set it to music.

Clinton Rossiter

Since Congress is no longer minded or organized to guide itself, the refusal or inability of the President to serve as a leader results in weak and disorganized government.

Jean Jacques Rousseau

Whether strength of body or of mind, or wisdom, or virtue, are found in proportion to the power or wealth of a man is a question fit perhaps to be discussed by slaves in the hearing of their masters, but highly unbecoming to reasonable and free men in search of the truth.

Helen Rowland

A husband is what's left of the lover once the nerve has been extracted.

Roy@NET1Plus.com

I'd take on that entire group of screaming idiots with one U.S. Army M1A2 Abrams anyday. I'd show them the true meaning of infantry being called 'Crunchies.'

Darrell Royal, University of Texas football coach

As long as a person doesn't admit he is defeated, he is not defeated -- he's just a little behind and isn't through fighting.

Reverend **Charles Royden**

The greater a person's sense of guilt, the greater their need to cast blame on others.

Mike Royko

As hard as I try to be sensitive and politically correct, I can't avoid bumping my way into boorish opinions, thus offending those who are truly enlightened.

It's unnatural for people to run around city streets unless they are thieves or victims. It makes people nervous to see someone running. I know that when I see someone running on my street, my instincts tell me to let the dog out after him.

Lee Rudolph

No one wants a good education. Everyone wants a good degree.

Arthur C. Ruger

Personal piety does not automatically equate to possession of the highest wisdom. Someone of greater piety than your own does not mean that that someone has more wisdom than you.

Damon Runyon

It may be that the race is not always to the swift, nor the battle to the strong but that is the way to bet.

John Ruskin

The distinguishing sign of slavery is to have a price, and to be bought for it.
- The Crown of Wild Olive

In order that people may be happy in their work, these three things are needed: they must be fit for it; they must not do too much of it; and they must have a sense of success in it.

Bertrand Russell

Change is indubitable, whereas progress is a matter of controversy.

Men are born ignorant, not stupid; they are made stupid by education.

Most people would die sooner than think; in fact, they do so.

One of the symptoms of an approaching nervous breakdown is the belief that one's work is terribly important.

[O]ne man can be right and most can be wrong. All advances that have been made of any importance have been started initially by a very small minority, often only one. This man has always been ridiculed and persecuted by humanity. It's a law of history.

One should respect public opinion insofar as is necessary to avoid starvation and keep out of prison, but anything that goes beyond this is voluntary submission to an unnecessary tyranny.

Orthodoxy is the grave of intelligence

So far as I can remember, there is not one word in the Gospels in praise of intelligence.

The time you enjoy wasting is not wasted time.

The trouble with the world is that the stupid are cocksure and the intelligent are full of doubt.

There is much pleasure gained from useless knowledge.

We have two kinds of morality side by side: one which we preach but do not practice. And the other which we practice but seldom preach.
- Sceptical Essays

Jami JoAnne Russell

So I'm right. Period. Anyone who believes different is retarded.

John Russell

If peace cannot be maintained with honor, it is no longer peace.

Sanity calms, but madness is more interesting.

Stephen W. Russell

You know, you can go to jail for promoting a bullfight, a dog fight or even a chicken fight but not a people fight! Go figure.

Russian Proverb

German: a good fellow maybe, but it is better to hang him.

The hammer shatters glass but forges steel.

The tallest blade of grass is the first to be cut down.

With lies you may go ahead in the world, but you can never go back.

You cannot drive straight on a twisting lane.

Rusty the Bookman

Just because one side of an argument is flamingly silly, does not mean that the other side is not just as bad.

~**S**~

Leopold von Sacher-Masoch, Venus in Furs

Love knows no virtue, no profit; it loves and forgives and suffers everything, because it must.

Never feel secure with the woman you love, for there are more dangers in woman's nature than you can imagine.

Power makes people over-bearing.

Woman's character is characterlessness.

Carl Sagan

A celibate clergy is an especially good idea, because it tends to suppress any hereditary propensity toward fanaticism.

Françoise Sagan

A dress makes no sense unless it inspires men to want to take it off you.

I like men to behave like men - strong and childish.

Antoine de Saint-Exupery

A single event can awaken within us a stranger totally unknown to us. To live is to be slowly born.

It is the savor of bread broken with comrades that makes us accept the values of war.

David St. Hubbins

It's such a fine line between stupid, and clever.

J.D. Salinger

Life is a game, boy. Life is a game that one plays according to the rules...
- Mr. Spencer to Holden Caulfield, Catcher in the Rye

Luke Salisbury
[Author of The Answer is Baseball, The Cleveland Indian, Blue Eden, Hollywood and Sunset.]

Baseball is green and safe. It has neither the street intimidation of basketball nor the controlled Armageddon of football. . .Baseball is a green dream that happens on summer nights in safe places in unsafe cities.

The novel is no longer the main event under the cultural bigtop. Like baseball, God, New York City, it doesn't go away, it just reappears in less attractive form.

Writers write about their families. We invent, explain, recreate, escape them. Imagine how they might have been different.

Paul M. Sander

If all it took to fix something were a few dirty words, then between the two of us, we could fix anything.

George Santayana

Fashion is something barbarous, for it produces innovation without reason and imitation without benefit.

Men have feverishly conceived a heaven only to find it insipid, and a hell to find it ridiculous.

To call war the soil of courage and virtue is like calling debauchery the soil of love.

To delight in war is a merit in a soldier, a dangerous quality in the captain, and a positive crime in the statesman.

To me, it seems a dreadful indignity to have a soul controlled by geography.

Susan Sarandon

I think it's very hard to be naked in a scene and not be upstaged by your nipples.

Claire Sargent

I think it's about time we voted for senators with breasts. After all, we've been voting for boobs long enough.

Jean Paul Sartre

Hell is other people

Man is condemned to be free; because once thrown into the world, he is responsible for everything he does.

Three o'clock is always too late or too early for anything you want to do.

When the rich wage war it's the poor who die.

Satank

The red and white man; the broad plains seem now to contract, and the white man grows jealous of his red brother. He once came to trade; he now comes to fight...He now covers his face with the cloud of jealousy and anger and tells us to be gone, as the offended master speaks to his dog....We once gave you our hearts; you have them now.

Virginia Satir

Since we are totally unique, there are no grounds for competition.

Graydon Saunders

Just remember wild hostility is 100% good birth control.

Robert C. Savage

Most people are willing to pay more to be amused than to be educated.

Antonin Scalia, Supreme Court Justice

Faith with no rational thought is false. What is irrational is to reject (without question) the possibility of miracles,

Scarecrow

Some people without brains do an awful lot of talking.
- "Wizard of Oz"

Maggie Scarf

Getting angry can sometimes be like leaping into a wonderfully responsive sports car, gunning the motor, taking off at high speed and then discovering the brakes are out of order.

Arno Schaefer

The nice thing about Windows is It does not just crash, it displays a dialog box and lets you press 'OK' first.

Tom Schaefer

At some point, most of us will bump up against an uncomfortable truth: We have too much, and our lives are not fulfilled. The newest gadgets and appliances, closets crammed with clothes, dwellings more expansive than our daily needs do not enrich our lives.
- "Wichita Eagle", May 19, 2001

Roger C. Schank

Questions are the important thing. Answers are less important. Learning to ask good questions is the heart of intelligence.

We can tell people abstract rules of thumb which we have derived from prior experiences, but it is very difficult for other people to learn from these. We have difficulty remembering such abstractions, but we can more easily remember a good story. Stories give life to past experience. Stories make the events in memory memorable to others and to ourselves. This is one of the reasons why people like to tell stories.
- Tell Me a Story

Friedrich von Schiller

Against stupidity the very gods themselves contend in vain.

Mike Schilling

If Sean Connery walked into a white tie dinner in nothing but boxers with valentine hearts on them, every other male would strip down to his shorts and feel uncomfortable about wearing the wrong ones.

Lyle Schjodt

You can tell when farmers are doing well because they go out and buy a new truck.

Arthur M. Schlesinger, Jr.

For most Americans, the Constitution had become a hazy document, cited like the Bible on ceremonial occasions but forgotten in the daily transactions of life.

JoAnne Schmitz

A guy who married a dead woman just ain't normal. No offense intended.

It is the nature of the addict to think about most things in limited terms. It worked yesterday, it worked today, it will work tomorrow.

You cannot explain human nature unless you abandon rationality. Fortunately, if you abandon rationality, you can explain anything.

Carl Schurz

If you want to be free, there is but one way; it is to guarantee an equally full measure of liberty to all your neighbors. There is no other.

They will not fail to recognize that our dignity, our free institutions and the peace and welfare of this and coming generations of Americans will be secure only as we cling to the watchword of true patriotism: "Our country--when right to be kept right; when wrong to be put right."

Debbie Schwartz

Back in *my* day, we didn't have handy dandy power cords and electrical outlets to plug them in to. We had to hand crank our computers to start them up. Lots of times the crank would stick, so you'd have to give it a good kick to get it loose. That's why, to this day, it's still called "booting" a computer.

Delmore Schwartz

Existentialism means that no one else can take a bath for you.

Albert Schweitzer

Man is a clever animal who behaves like an imbecile.

One other thing stirs me when I look back at my youthful days, the fact that so many people gave me something or were something to me without knowing it.
- "Memories of Childhood and Youth"

There are two means of refuge from the miseries of life: music and cats.

Andrew Scott

You've met people who can't think or speak? Most people either do one or the other.

Duncan Campbell Scott, Canadian Deputy Superintendent of Indian Affairs

I want to get rid of the Indian problem. . . Our objective is to continue until there is not a single Indian in Canada that has not been absorbed into the body politic.

Kill the Indian in the child.

Raymond S. Scott

American soldiers. . .can be trusted to decide when to shoot to kill in combat, but cannot be trusted with photographs of naked people. Huh?

Sir Walter Scott

One hour of life, crowded to the full with glorious action, and filled with noble risks, is worth whole years of those mean observances of paltry decorum.

Madeleine Scuderi

Men should keep their eyes wide open before marriage, and half shut afterward.

Nigel Scullion, Australian Senator

Always wear clean underwear.

Paul Seabury and Angelo Codevilla

Military goods are valuable not for the materials and labor that go into them, but for the strategic gains that can be got out of using them. No one in wartime has ever been struck by a piece of gross national product.
- WAR: Ends and Means

Consumer's Guide, Sears, Roebuck and Co. (1987)

If you don't find it in the Index, look very carefully through the entire catalogue.

Steve Sebelius

Chuck Muth? You can't handle the Muth!

Peter Seebach

Which is not to say that I have strong opinions about [programming] code style; why, just the other day I saw someone put "sz" in front of the name of a string, and I didn't raze his house to the ground and salt the earth he had lived on. In point of fact, I haven't even mutilated his pets.

<selk@midway.uchicago.edu>

There's a non zero chance that all of the particles in my body may decide to jump to Pluto any moment now.

Amartya Sen

India is catching up with other sexist, modern societies like South Korea and China in sex-selective abortions. It's a technological revolution of a reactionary kind.

Seneca

A quarrel is quickly settled when deserted by one party: there is no battle unless there be two.

It is expedient for the victor to wish for peace restored; for the vanquished it is necessary.

Laws do not persuade just because they threaten.

Let tears flow of their own accord: their flowing is not inconsistent with inward peace and harmony.

Nothing is more common than for great thieves to ride in triumph when small ones are punished.

Of war men ask the outcome, not the cause.

Successful and fortunate crime is called virtue.

Richard Sexton

This article was made from the finest quality words and sentances. Minor imperfections in syntax, like the grain in fine leather, serve to enhance it's beauty.

Mary Shafer

Give a man a fish and you feed him for a day. Introduce him to the Internet and you won't see him again for at least a week.

We didn't just do weird stuff at Dryden, we wrote reports about it.

William Shakespeare

And Caesar's spirit, ranging for revenge,
With Ate by his side come hot from hell,
Shall in these confines with a monarch's voice
Cry' Havoc!' and let slip the dogs of war;
That this foul deed shall smell above the earth
With carrion men, groaning for burial.
- Julius Caesar, Act III Scene I

Maids want nothing but husbands, and when they have them, they want everything.

This above all, to thine own self be true, and it must follow, as the night the day, thou canst not then be false to any man.

Use every man after his desert, and who should 'scape whipping?

Alan Shapiro

Firing a 57mm at a Tiger [tank] is like hitting the Empire State Building with a golf club.

George Bernard Shaw

A pessimist thinks everybody is as nasty as himself, and hates them for it.

Chess is a foolish expedient for making idle people believe they are doing something very clever when they are only wasting their time.

Do not do unto others as you would they should do unto you. Their tastes may not be the same.

I often quote myself; it adds spice to my conversation.

I showed my appreciation of my native land in the usual Irish way by getting out of it as soon as I possibly could.

It is dangerous to be sincere unless you are also stupid.

Let a short Act of Parliament be passed, placing all street musicians outside the protection of the law, so that any citizen may assail them with stones, sticks, knives, pistols, or bombs without incurring any penalties.

Liberty means responsibility; that is why most men dread it.

Martyrdom is the only way in which a man can become famous without ability.

Never wrestle with a pig. You both get dirty, and the pig likes it.

Nothing ever is done in this world until men are prepared to kill one another if it is not done.

Peace is not only better than war, but infinitely more arduous.

Reasonable people adapt themselves to the world. Unreasonable people attempt to adapt the world to themselves. All progress, therefore, depends on unreasonable people.

Take the utmost trouble to find the right thing to say, and then say it with the utmost levity.

The more things a man is ashamed of, the more respectable he is.

The substitution of election by the incompetent many for appointment by the corrupt few properly describes the institution of Democracy.

The world is populated in the main by people who should not exist.

There is no satisfaction in hanging a man who does not object to it.

When two people are under the influence of the most violent, most insane, most delusive, and most transient of passions, they are required to swear that they will remain in that excited, abnormal and exhausting condition until death do them part.

When we want to read of the deeds that are done for love, whither do we turn? To the murder column.

Why should we take advice on sex from the Pope. If he knows anything, he shouldn't

You'll never have a quiet world till you knock the patriotism out of the human race.

Petr Shelokhonov

Small minds talk about people; average minds talk about events; great minds talk about ideas, a genius doesn't need to talk.

Gary Shelton, St. Petersburg Times

Actually, it is widely known that the safest way to get through the [Miami] Dolphin locker room is to tell the safeties you're a [San Diego] Charger.

Alan Shepard

It's a very sobering feeling to be up in space and realize that one's safety factor was determined by the lowest bidder on a government contract.

Philip H. Sheridan

I have the greatest horror of popular demonstrations [for] those very men who deafen you with their cheers today are capable tomorrow of throwing stones and mud at you.

If I owned hell and Texas, I would rent Texas out and live in hell!

The power to command men, and give vehement impulse to their joint action, is something which cannot be defined by words, but is plain and manifest in battles, and whoever commands an army in chief must choose his subordinates by reason of qualities which can alone be tested in actual conflict.

There is one thing that you should appreciate, and that is that the improvement in guns and in the material of war, in dynamite and other explosives, and in breech-loading guns, is rapidly bringing us to a period when war will eliminate itself; when we can no longer stand up and fight each other in battle, and when we will have to resort to something else.

This you know is a free country and people have the lawful right to misrepresent as much as they please. . .

Blackie Sherrod

Is there a parable here? Fellow in Gilbert, Ariz., won two Super Bowl tickets by diving headfirst in 2,000 pounds of cow manure.

William T. Sherman

I am tired and sick of war. Its glory is all moonshine. It is only those who have neither fired a shot, nor heard the shrieks and groans of the wounded who cry aloud for more blood, more vengeance, more desolation. War is hell.

I took care of Grant when he was drunk, and he took care of me when I was crazy.

The legitimate object of war is a more perfect peace.

War is cruelty, and you cannot refine it.

War is simply power unrestrained by constitution or compact.

Joe Shimkus

C++ is a superset of C but gives you even more ways to have your name cursed by the person who has to fix your code.

Dinah Shore

Trouble is part of your life, and if you don't share it, you don't give the person who loves you a chance to love you enough.

Toby Silver

Do you not remember that our tradition indicates it is better to kill a man than to slander him?

I also think that driving a car is a dangerous undertaking. Not because I might do something wrong, but because the road is full of stupid drivers.

<simmons@hobbes.gtlug.org>

Logic, common sense, fairness and objective analysis do NOT belong on USENET and your Rude and Boorish attempts to treat its citizens as thinking, civilized beings is simply not appreciated here!

John Simon

Democracy encourages the majority to decide things about which the majority is blissfully ignorant.

Paul Simon

Man hears what he wants to hear, and disregards the rest.
- "The Boxer"

Leo G Simonetta

I have been told that afu [alt.folklore.urban] now prefers a M107 Long-Range Sniper Rifle when reaching out to touch someone.

I like the black helicopters but I am just an old fashioned kind of guy.

Minot Simons

No pleasure philosophy, no sensuality, no place nor power, no material success can for a moment give such inner satisfaction as the sense of living for good purposes, for maintenance of integrity, for the preservation of self-approval.

Isaac Bashevis Singer

Doubt is part of all religion. All the religious thinkers were doubters.

Life is God's novel. Let him write it.

You must believe in free-will; there is no choice.

Charan Singh

Even for our enemies in misery--there should be tears in our eyes.

Jaswant Singh, Indian Minister of External Affairs

I am extremely hesitant to contradict generals and what they have to say.

- News conference, Jan 13, 2002

Edith Sitwell

A great many people now reading and writing would be better employed keeping rabbits.

Simon Slavin

For myself, life [is] quite complicated and scary enough.

I'm stunned at how Microsoft's marketing people allow them to have a Windows mode called 'safe'. It raises the question of what the normal [mode] is called.

Leslie Small

I am not being willfully stupid, just responding from ignorance.

I love being an evil influence.

Many years ago, my boyfriend's brother went to England. He saw Stonehenge. And this was before they fenced it off and you could walk around. When I asked him how Stonehenge was...he informed me that the bathrooms had blue crepe toilet paper.

Adam Smith

It is the maxim of every prudent master of a family, never to make at home what it will cost more to make than to buy

It is not from the benevolence of the butcher, the brewer, or the baker, that we expect our dinner, but from their regard to their own self-interest. We address ourselves, not to their humanity but to their self-love, and never talk to them of our own necessities but of their advantages.

Alan Smith

If Lesbian seagulls can pairbond for years, surely that doesn't prove that they are creatures of Satan, does it?

Ask me that again the next time they fly over your car.

Alexander Smith

Love is but the discovery of ourselves in others, and the delight in the recognition.

To be occasionally quoted is the only fame I care for.

Daniel P. B. Smith

Oh, relax. Nobody reads Gibran any more anyway. Gone, gone, gone...along with Rod McKuen, and Maxwell Anderson, and the use of the words "ambience" and "charisma," and pop art, and twelve-tone music.

H. Allen Smith

When there are two conflicting versions of the story, the wise course is to believe the one in which people appear at their worst.

Brigadier General **Jacob H. Smith**

I want no prisoners. I wish you to burn and kill; the more you burn and kill, the better it will please me.
- to Major Littleton Waller on Samar, 1901

Logan Pearsall Smith

All reformers, however strict their social conscience, live in houses just as big as they can pay for.

Married women are kept women, and they are beginning to find it out.

Otis Smith

I don't believe I said that. If I said that, I misquoted myself.

Sydney Smith

Do not assume that because I am frivolous I am shallow; I don't assume that because you are grave you are profound.

Marriage resembles a pair of shears, so joined that they cannot be separated, often moving in opposite directions, yet always punishing anyone who comes in between them.

There is one piece of advice, in a life of study, which I think no one will object to; and that is, every now and then to be completely idle - to do nothing at all.

Tobias George Smolett

Some folks are wise and some are otherwise.

Jan L.A. van de Snepscheut

In theory, there is no difference between theory and practice, but, in practice, there is.

J Sobenson

The tossing of a cat is much recommended before cooking it.

Socrates

By all means marry; if you get a good wife, you'll be happy. If you get a bad one, you'll become a philosopher.

Children today are tyrants. They contradict their parents, gobble their food, and tyrannize their teachers.

Once made equal to man, woman becomes his superior.

Our posterity will wonder about our ignorance of things so plain.

The hottest love has the coldest end.

Wisdom begins in wonder.

Gary D. Solis, Son Thang: An American War Crime

As long as nations give weapons to very young men there will be war crimes. We must train our warriors as best we can, not only in the use of arms, but in the morality of their use. That training cannot be accomplished by the military alone.

[H]ell hath no fury like a noncombatant.

On the other hand, many judge advocates, in Vietnam and elsewhere, also had the pleasant experience of meeting supercilious civilian attorneys in trial and quietly kicking their legal asses.

The civilian grand jury, the creature of the prosecution, would indict a ham sandwich, if the prosecutor vigorously proposed it.

Brad Solomon

There's no dealing with a cat who knows you're awake.

Alexander Solzhenitsyn

Patriotism means unqualified and unwavering love for the nation, which implies not uncritical eagerness to serve, not support for unjust claims, but frank assessment of its vices and sins, and penitence for them.
- "From Under the Rubble"

Reporters can be worse than the KGB.

You only have power over people so long as you don't take everything away from them. But when you've robbed a man of everything, he's no longer in your power - he's free again.

Jacob Sommer

But if you only look at past wrongs you'll never see future rights.

S.P. Somtow, (Somtow Papinian Sucharitkul)

It's usually only us poor folks which gets killed in battle.
- Darker Angels

Sophocles

Truly, to tell lies is not honorable, but when the truth entails tremendous ruin, to speak dishonorably is pardonable.

Theodore Sorensen

Nixon was more popular than his party and more able and likeable than his enemies portrayed him.

Thomas Sowell

Slavery's most important legacy may be a painful insight into human nature and into the terrible consequences of unbridled power.
- Race and Culture: A world view

J. Duncan Spaeth

I know why the sun never sets on the British Empire: God wouldn't trust an Englishman in the dark.

Gene Spafford <spaf@cs.purdue.edu>

People rail about their "rights" without understanding that every right carries responsibilities that need to be observed too, not least of which is to respect others' rights as you would have them respect your own.

Usenet is like a herd of performing elephants with diarrhea massive, difficult to redirect, awe inspiring, entertaining, and a source of mind boggling amounts of excrement when you least expect it.

Spanish Proverb

It is better to weep with wise men than to laugh with fools.

Let him who does not know what war is go to war.

Live with wolves, and you learn to howl.

Love is like war: you begin when you like and leave off when you can.

More grows in the garden than the gardener knows he has sown.

One drink is just right, two are too many, three are too few.

Since we cannot get what we like, let us like what we can get.

Tell me who you live with and I will tell you who you are.

War, hunting, and love have a thousand pains for one pleasure.

spectrum@magenta.com

Unlike modern languages that attempt to enforce good programming practices, you can lie, cheat, and steal in Fortran.<G>

Herbert Spencer

How often misused words generate misleading thoughts.

The ultimate result of shielding men from the effects of folly is to fill the world with fools.

Volumes might be written upon the impiety of the pious.

Oswald Spengler

Socialism is nothing but the capitalism of the lower classes.

Everything that is called duty, the prerequisite for all genuine law and the substance of every noble custom, can be traced back to honor. If one has to think about it, one is already without honor.

Ownership is not only a right, it is a duty. Ownership obligates. Use your property as if it had been entrusted to you by the people.

Garrison Spik

You talk about a breeding ground for bad writing, academia is where it's at.

Norman Spinrad

We have met the Devil and he is us.
- Deus X

Eliot Spitzer

Driven by hubris, we become blind to our own fallibility and make terrible mistakes.

Dr. Benjamin Spock

All the time a person is a child he is both a child and learning to be a parent. After he becomes a parent he becomes predominantly a parent reliving childhood.

The more people have studied different methods of bringing up children the more they have come to the conclusion that what good mothers and fathers instinctively feel like doing for their babies is best after all.

Judy Sproles

If there is a opinion, facts will be found to support it.

Josef Stalin

A single death is a tragedy, a million deaths are a statistic.

Ideas are more powerful than guns. We would not let our enemies have guns, why should we let them have ideas.

Sincere diplomacy is no more possible than dry water or wooden iron.

You cannot make a revolution with silk gloves.

Lisa Ann Stalnaker

I'm already half-crazy, do I really need to take a pill that will give me vivid and disturbing dreams?

I've just learned to smile and nod my head, usually with my mouth full.

I can also touch my tongue to my nose.

I learned the hard way in college to never, ever do that at a table full of lesbians.

I couldn't say anything nasty because she was holding a staple gun.

If you're going to insist on using logic and facts, you will be an utter failure at conspiracy theories.

It's always wise to stand a safe distance away from distraught women wielding hammers.

Of course Dave doesn't understand how to integrate the two processes. He's a Southerner. Southerners have *never* understood integration.

She gave him that disgusted look that women give to men who have utterly failed in their gossip responsibilities.

What is wrong with me that I can't even find a decent psycho?

Mark Stalzer

To really blow up an investment house requires a human being.
- Risks Digest, volume 19, # 1

Jenny Stamatakos

It is impossible to remain seriously upset when waggling a rubber fish in your hand.

Dan Stanford

Experience is what you get when you don't get what you want.

starchsr@icubed.net

I've always felt that there were a lot of silent letters not shown in the phrase 'Extreme sports' or 'extreme' anything...the missing letters are 'ly stupid', right after the first word.

Starhawk

Perhaps we can practice some compassion toward each other, judging people not by what they profess to believe but by their actions, and not blaming other religions for the transgressions of their imperfect followers.

Gary Stark

Symphony orchestra?? CALIFORNIA ??? Sounds like a contradiction in terms!!

Lonny Starr

No matter what happens, there's always somebody who knew it would.

Ervin Staub

Evil that arises out of ordinary thinking and is committed by ordinary people is the norm, not the exception.
- The roots of Evil: The origins of Genocide and Other Group Violence

Justice **Robert W. Steele**, Colorado Supreme Court

When we deny to one, however wicked, a right plainly guaranteed by the constitution, we take that same right from everyone. When we say to Moyer, "You must stay in prison because if we discharge you, you may commit a crime," we say that to every other citizen.

Mark Steese

Certain species of bats are about the only mammals that truly freak me out. But then they'd probably say the same about me. In their freaky little bat voices.

Trying to make Ronald [McDonald] 'sexy' would be wrong in every way imaginable and in many ways that have yet to be imagined.

Vilhjalmur Stefansson

What is the difference between unethical and ethical advertising? Unethical advertising uses falsehoods to deceive the public; ethical advertising uses truth to deceive the public.

John Steinbeck

I've seen a look in dogs' eyes, a quickly vanishing look of amazed contempt, and I am convinced that basically dogs think humans are nuts.

The profession of book writing makes horse racing seem like a solid business.

George Steinbrenner

I'll always return your calls, but don't phone me again.

If you can't laugh at yourself and have others laughing at you, it's pretty sad. Now that doesn't apply to my players. They are not allowed to laugh at me.

Gloria Steinem

I have yet to hear a man ask for advice on how to combine marriage and a career.

One day, an army of gray-haired women may quietly take over the earth.

Some of us are becoming the men we wanted to marry.

We can tell our values by looking at our checkbook stubs.

Jim Steinman

You can't run away forever; but there's nothing wrong with getting a good head start.

Casey Stengel

Everybody line up alphabetically according to your height.

Fellers, I don't want you to feel bad about this [loss]. This has been a team effort. No one or two guys could have done all this.

The secret of managing is to keep the guys who hate you away from the ones who are undecided.

George Stephanopolous

I didn't think I was a hypocrite because my defense of Clinton against past bimbo eruptions had been predicated on my belief that he wouldn't create new ones, but maybe I was complicit because when I worked for Clinton I had been willing to suspend my disbelief about some of his more suspect denials.
- All Too Human

The President has kept all of the promises he intended to keep.
- on "Larry King Live," 2/16/96

Gil Stern

Man is a complex being; he makes the deserts bloom and lakes die.

Elf Sternberg

The mistake frequently made by less schooled feminists lies in the belief that power is somehow wrong. Power is neither wrong nor right. It is the application of power, and inability to properly choose what power to submit too, that gives power such a bad reputation.

E.R. Stettinius, Jr.

Happiness has many roots, but none more important than security.

Adlai Stevenson

A free society is a place where it's safe to be unpopular.

In America any boy may become President and I suppose it's just one of the risks he takes.

Man does not live by words alone, despite the fact that sometimes he has to eat them

On this shrunken globe, men can no longer live as strangers.

Robert Louis Stevenson

Marriage is one long conversation, checkered by disputes.

Jeff Stilson

I had a linguistics professor who said that it's man's ability to use language that makes him the dominant species on the planet. That may be. But I think there's one other thing that separates us from animals. We aren't afraid of vacuum cleaners.

Joseph Stilwell

The higher a monkey climbs, the more you see of its behind.

Mike Stone

History is not "written by the victors". It is written (all too often) by sentimental twits.

Sharon Stone

Someone once told me I have a mind that's like a bad neighborhood; I shouldn't go in there alone.

Paul Stookey

What's happening here is everything sounds fine to you, but our existential reality is all messed up.

Lon Stowell

The AWD of SUV's is kinda handy in urban vehicles, it allows one to get over hapless pedestrians without high-centering or getting stuck on the gooey bits.

Paul Strassmann

I believe the fog of war is not necessarily created by the enemy.

Igor Stravinsky

A good composer does not imitate; he steals.

I have learned throughout my life as a composer chiefly through my mistakes and pursuits of false assumptions, not by my exposure to founts of wisdom and knowledge.

August Strindberg

I loathe people who keep dogs. They are cowards who haven't got the guts to bite people themselves.

Theodore Sturgeon

There is really only one sense and that is touch; all the other senses are only other ways of touching. But if you can't touch with touch, you can't touch with much.

Andre Suares

Just as war is waged with the blood of others, fortunes are made with other people's money.

Satguru Sivaya Subramuniyaswami

People who swear, even if it is just under their breath, are cursing themselves.

Harry G. Summers

Money too often speaks much louder than logic.

The more lurid the war story, the more likely it is a bald-faced lie.

Baroness Edith Summerskill

Nagging is the repetition of unpalatable truths.

Noel Susskind

Do not waste your time trying to point out the wrongs and weaknesses in others before you look into your own heart and find the serenity to accept what God has given all of us here.

S. Andrew Swann, (Steven Swiniarski), Profiteer

A criminal is a revolutionary without the pretense.

All revolutionaries are criminals meeting in secret.

Justice in government is as rare as a rich [man] in prison.

True enemies are as rare as true friends.

Jonathan Swift

It is again objected, as a very absurd, ridiculous custom, that a set of men should be suffered, much less employed and hired, to bawl one day in seven against the lawfulness of those methods most in use, toward the pursuit of greatness, riches, and pleasure, which are the constant practice of all men alive on the other six.
- "Argument Against Abolishing Christianity in England"

We have just enough religion to make us hate, but not enough to make us love, one another.

When a true genius appears in the world you may know him by this sign: that all the duces are in confederacy against him.

Pope **Sylvester II** (Gerbert of Aurillac)

Italy may produce crops, but Gaul and Germany breed soldiers.

Publius Syrus

Some remedies are worse than the disease.

Leo Szilard

I'm all in favor of the democratic principle that one idiot is as good as one genius, but I draw the line when someone takes the next step and concludes that two idiots are better than one genius.

Pronouncement of experts to the effect that something cannot be done has always irritated me.

~T~

Tacitus

Anything little known is assumed to be wonderful.

It is a sin peculiar to man to hate his victim.

The desire for safety stands against every great and noble enterprise.

The more corrupt the state, the more numerous the laws.

Things forbidden have a secret charm.

Hippolyte Taine

I have studied many philosophers and many cats. The wisdom of cats is infinitely superior.

Joseph Takagi, "Die Hard"

Hey, we're flexible. Pearl Harbor didn't work out so we got you with tape decks.

Charles Maurice de Talleyrand-Périgord, 1st Sovereign Prince de Bénévent

Language exists to conceal true thought.

Phil Talmadge

I wouldn't say voters are stupid. But the same voter who wants unlimited services also does not want to pay for it. There's a disconnect.

Captain **Tameichi Hara**

The beatings will continue until the morale improves.

Andrew S. Tanenbaum

However, as every parent of a small child knows, converting a large object into small fragments is considerably easier than the reverse process.

Never underestimate the bandwidth of a station wagon full of tapes hurtling down the highway.

Lieutenant Commander **Lori Tanner**

When you have a leader who exhibits what a leader should...then people follow.

Christine Tannis

I'm into both S&M. If I beat myself, I get the best of both worlds!

Tasha Star

It makes sense when one wants acceptance, to be tolerant and accepting of others.

Chip Taylor

God, grant me the Senility to forget the people I never liked anyway, the good fortune to run into the ones I do, and the eyesight to tell the difference.

Elizabeth Taylor

I feel very adventurous. There are so many doors to be opened, and I'm not afraid to look behind them.

I've always admitted that I'm ruled by my passions.

I've still got a lot of living left to do. It's not over. The fat lady has not sung.

It is strange...that the years teach us patience; that the shorter our time, the greater our capacity for waiting.

Success is a great deodorant. It takes away all your past smells.

Alfred, Lord Tennyson

I am a part of all that I have met.

Sheri S. Tepper

Ignorance may be bliss, but it's poor life insurance.

Mother Teresa

If you judge people, you have no time to love them.

St. Teresa of Avila

I do not fear Satan half so much as I fear those who fear him.

I had a vision of a smiling angel, who pierced my heart again and again with a golden arrow, producing a pain so sweet that I screamed aloud; but simultaneously I felt such infinite sweetness that I wished the pain to last eternally.

Studs Terkel

Had my luck been better, I might have become a first-rate pimp. Or a candidate for public office. Or even an advisor to presidents.

Wisdom, to paraphrase Stephen Vincent Benet, is a hard bought thing.

Linda Terrell

I eat vegetarians regularly...cows are vegetarians, aren't they?

Tertullian

He who lives only to benefit himself confers on the world a benefit when he dies.

Nothing that is evil is necessary.

Of little worth is the recommendation which has for its prop the defamation of another.

Reason without goodness is not reason, and goodness without reason is not goodness.

There is no public entertainment which does not inflict spiritual damage.

Tev, <tvyse@mcs.com>

I had a life. I prefer the Internet.

Dave Tewksbury

Bodies in motion tend to remain in motion. Bodies at rest tend to remain in bed.

<tgpollma@uoknor.edu>

When I bite into a York Peppermint Patty, I get the sensation that I'm floating on a bowl of tangerine Jell O, as marsupial nymphs cleanse my soul with moist towelettes.

Margaret Thatcher

I owe nothing to Women's Lib.

In politics, if you want anything said, ask a man; if you want anything done, ask a woman.

You don't tell deliberate lies, but sometimes you have to be evasive.

Bob Thaves

Remember Ginger Rogers did everything Fred Astaire did, but she did it backwards and in high heels.
(Often misattributed to Faith Whittlesey)

Joe Theisman

The word "genius" isn't applicable in football. A genius is a guy like Norman Einstein.

Clarence Thomas

Government cannot make us equal; it can only recognize, respect and protect us as equal under the law.

We are not beggars or objects of charity. We don't get smarter just because we sit next to white people in class, and we don't progress just because society is ready with handouts.

Dylan Thomas

Do not go gentle into that good night

Old age should burn and rave at close of day;

Rage, rage against the dying of the light

Hunter S. Thompson

Myths and legends die hard in America. We love them for the extra dimension they provide, the illusion of near infinite possibility to erase the narrow confines of most men's reality. Weird heroes and mould breaking champions exist as living proof to those who need it that the tyranny of "the rat race" is not yet final.

They don't hardly make 'em like him any more - but just to be on the safe side, he should be castrated anyway.

When the going gets weird, the weird turn pro.

Tracy Thompson

Reality is rarely what we imagine. Great and noble things do not always happen for great and noble reasons.

Thorazine Bob

My new medication has given me a whole new set of career opportunities

Henry David Thoreau

A government in which the majority rule in all cases cannot be based on justice, even as far as men understand it. - "On the Duty of Civil Disobedience"

Beware of all enterprises that require new clothes.

If a man does not keep pace with his companions, perhaps it is because he hears a different drummer. Let him step to the music which he hears, however measured or far away.

It is a characteristic of wisdom not to do desperate things.

Men have become the tools of their tools.

David H. Thornley

Understanding somebody doesn't necessarily mean liking them, cooperating with them, or giving them a break when they're down.

Jeremy Thorpe

Greater love hath no man than this, to lay down his friends for his life.

Garth Thornton

The universe is not in the habit of giving up explanations to cursory examinations.

Thucydides

The Nation that makes a great distinction between its scholars and its warriors will have its thinking done by cowards and its fighting done by fools.

<Tiger@deltanet.com>

I get so tired of the public debate on so many issues being dominated by those who want all sorts of activities banned, restricted, avoided, outlawed, etc. on the grounds that there is risk involved. Life is full of all sorts of risks and it is up to each of us to be informed as to what they are and to decide which are worth the rewards and which are not.

Henrik Tikkanen

Truly great madness cannot be achieved without significant intelligence.

Krista Tippett

Outward glory does not equal, and may in fact thwart, personal happiness.

Josip Broz Tito

Any movement in history which attempts to perpetuate itself, becomes reactionary.

Chris Titus

Everybody wants a normal life and a cool car; most people settle for the car

Alexis de Tocqueville

No protracted war can fail to endanger the freedom of a democratic country.

One of the most ordinary weaknesses of the human intellect is to seek to reconcile contrary principles, and to purchase peace at the expense of logic.

Jesse E. Todd, Jr.

The average person. . .knows about as much about how computers work as the average person in the Middle Ages knew about the solar system.

J.R. Tolkein

I have no use for adventures. They're nasty disturbing things that make you late for dinner.
- Bilbo Baggins

Leo Tolstoy

Government is an association of men who do violence to the rest of us.

What a strange illusion it is to believe that beauty is goodness.

Tomioka Heihachiro

Humans and animals are the same. If you hit them, they learn to obey.

Lily Tomlin

If truth is beauty, how come no one has their hair done in a library?

Man invented language to satisfy his deep need to complain.

No matter how cynical you get, it is impossible to keep up.

The trouble with the rat race is that even if you win, you're still a rat.

Paul Tomblin

Renting airplanes is like renting sex: It's difficult to arrange on short notice on Saturday, the fun things always cost more, and someone's always looking at their watch.

Sergeant **Bede Tongs**

What do you day to a dying man,
Do you call him Bob, or Digger, or Mate?
- "What do you say to a dying man?"

Enzo Torresi

The reason that God was able to create the world in seven days is that he didn't have to worry about the existing configuration.

Linus Torvalds

...the Linux philosophy is 'laugh in the face of danger'. Oops. Wrong one. 'Do it yourself'. That's it.

I'm always right. This time I'm just even more right than usual.

Let's put it this way: if you need to ask a lawyer whether what you do is "right" or not, you are morally corrupt. Let's not go there. We don't base our morality on law.

Alfred Toscanini

When I was young, I kissed my first woman, and smoked my first cigarette on the same day. Believe me, never since have I wasted any more time on tobacco.

Toynbee

Civilization is a movement, not a condition; it is a voyage, not a harbour.

Major **Wilhelm Trapp**

If this Jewish business is ever avenged on earth, then have mercy on us Germans.

Trevanian (Rodney Whitaker), Shibumi

It is a truism of American politics that no man who can win an election deserves to.

It is an ironic fiction that strategic (i.e., anti-civilian) bombing can break a nation's will to fight. In Germany, Britain, and Japan, the effect of strategic bombing was to give the people a common cause, to harden their will to resist in the crucible of shared difficulties.

Recall also that the old must make much of their experience. It is all they have left.
- Otake-san

The concept of fair play is totally alien to the mentality of the French, a people who have produced generations of aristocrats, but not a single gentleman; a culture in which the legal substitutes for the fair; a language in which the only word for fair play is the borrowed English.

Where is the fiber in a people whose best-selling poet is Rod McKuen, the Howard Cosell of verse?

Lee Trevino

Pressure is when you've got 35 bucks riding on a four foot putt and you've only got five dollars.

Calvin Trillin

English people apparently queue up as a sort of hobby. A family man might pass a mild autumn evening by taking the wife and kids to stand in the cinema queue for a while and then leading them over for a few minutes in the sweetshop queue and then, as a special treat for the kids, saying "Perhaps we've time to have a look at the Number Thirty-One bus queue before we turn in."

I suppose the odd jogger looks normal, but runners...just look pathetic to me...They look like those people in the health food store: gray pallor, stringy little beards, sunken chests. They make you want to call 911.

If law school is so hard to get through...how come there are so many lawyers?

The price of purity is purists.

There's a theory that almost anything that's fun is going to be ruined sooner or later by people from California.

Tedi Trindle

[A]dvertisers need you to want to be something other than what you are in order to sell you their product.

Leon Trotsky

In a country where the sole employer is the State, opposition means death by slow starvation. The old principle: who does not work does not eat, has been replaced by a new one: who does not obey shall not eat.

Captain **Thomas Troubridge**, Royal Navy

Whenever I see a fellow look as if he was thinking, I say that is mutiny.
- after hanging five crewmen in 1795

Harry S. Truman

I come to the office each morning and stay for long hours doing what has to be done to the best of my ability. And when you've done the best you can you can't do any better.

I knew what I was doing when I stopped the war that would have killed half a million youngsters on both sides if those bombs had not been dropped. I have no regrets and, under the same circumstances, I would do it again.
- Aug 5, 1963

If you want a friend in this town, buy a dog.

It is amazing what you can accomplish if you do not care who gets the credit.

The buck stops here.

We shall never be able to remove suspicion and fear as potential causes of war until communication is permitted to flow, free and open, across international boundaries.

Major General **Lucian Truscott**

The time to cry over your soldiers is after the battle is won.

Konstantin Tsiolkovsky, 1899

The Earth is the cradle of humanity, but one cannot live in the cradle forever.

TSM

His job is to make you look stupid, and if I were his boss I'd give him a fat raise and a promotion.
- to a hapless trollee, 04/28/99

Paul E. Tsongas

No one on his deathbed ever said, I wish I had spent more time on my business.

Gideon J. Tucker

Every man's life, liberty, and property are in danger when the Legislature is in session.

John Tudor

Technology makes it possible for people to gain control over everything, except over technology.

Edward Tufte

An ill specified or preposterous model or a puny data set cannot be rescued by a graphic, no matter how clever.

Marshal **Mikhail Tukhachevski**, USSR

The path of the world conflagration passes over the corpse of Poland.

Coffee should be black as hell, strong as death, and sweet as love.

Bill Turlock

I like a good suicide bombing where the suicidee is the only one getting killed.

I remember hearing it too, so it must be true!

The only thing pennies are good for is to stop people from giving you more of them.

There are so many ways to mis-interpret that statement I'm not even going to begin to try to figure a way to make it less ambiguous

We admire most those who dissemble for a living--actors and politicians.

Bishop **Desmond Tutu**

God has an incredible sense of humour.

Mark Twain (Samuel Clemens)

All people are liars from the cradle onward, without exception, and...they begin to lie as soon as they wake in the morning, and keep it up without rest or refreshment until they go to sleep at night.
- "My First Lie, and How I got out of it"

All you need in this life is ignorance and confidence -- and then success is sure.

Always do right. It will gratify some people and amaze the rest.

Clothes make the man. Naked people have little or no influence in society.

Courage is resistance to fear, mastery of fear--not absence of fear.
- The Tragedy of Pudd'nhead Wilson

Don't believe anything you read and only half of what you see.

Facts, or what a man believes to be facts, are delightful... Get your facts first, and then you can distort them as much as you please.
- "Science and Religion"

Few things are harder to put up with than the annoyance of a good example.
- The Tragedy of Pudd'nhead Wilson

God made the Idiot for practice, and then He made the School Board

God only made man because he was disappointed with the monkey.

Heaven goes by favor. If it went by merit, you would stay out and your dog would go in.

I do not like work even when someone else does it.

I have never let schooling interfere with my education.

I never was so scared before and survived it.

If you pick up a starving dog and make him prosperous, he will not bite you. This is the principal difference between man and his dog.
- The Tragedy of Pudd'nhead Wilson

In our country we have those three unspeakably precious things: freedom of speech, freedom of conscience, and the prudence never to practice either.

It could probably be shown by facts and figures that there is no distinctively native American criminal class except Congress.

It is a worthy thing to fight for one's freedom; it is another sight finer to fight for another man's.
- In an 1898 letter to the Reverend Joseph Twichell

It is better to deserve honours and not have them than to have them and not to deserve them.

It was against my principles, but I find that principles have no real force except when one is well fed.
- "The Diary of Adam and Eve"

Let us so endeavor to live, that when we come to die, even the undertaker will be sorry.
- The Tragedy of Pudd'nhead Wilson

Lying is universal we all do it; we all must do it. Therefore, the wise thing is for us diligently to train ourselves to lie thoughtfully.

Never put off until tomorrow what you can do the day after tomorrow.

Talking of patriotism, what humbug it is; it is a word which always commemorates a robbery. There isn't a foot of land in the world which doesn't represent the ousting and re-ousting of a long line of successive owners.
- A Connecticut Yankee in King Arthur's Court

The man who does not read good books has no advantage over the man who cannot read them.

Virtue has never been as respectable as money.

When angry, count to four; when very angry, swear.
- The Tragedy of Pudd'nhead Wilson

When I was a boy of 14, my father was so ignorant I could hardly stand to have the old man around. But when I got to be 21, I was astonished at how much the old man had learned in seven years.

Boss Tweed

I don't care who does the electing as long as I get to do the nominating.

Rick Tyler

I crisped ants with a magnifying class when I was 10 or 11, but have been kind ever since, and hardly ever kill anyone.

I would rather be with the people on this mailing list than with the finest people in the world

In Alaska, where men outnumber women, the women say that the odds are good, but the goods are odd

I've probably been [to Chicago] 20 times. The weather was nice once. Why do people live there?

TyMeDwn1st

[I marvel] at the chutzpah of folks who only drop in to tell us what we're doing wrong.

Tanith Tyrr

Everyone consensually chooses their own degree of risk. If you choose to take drugs, alone or with a consenting partner or partners, that's one thing. I have nothing to say about that, except please don't do it in my house. I'd actually prefer that drugs be legalized, for various reasons which I won't go into here; but I don't advocate their use under any circumstances where it might threaten the health of others.

Home Depot is an enthusiastic bondager's best friend...

People's *lives* are more important than my personal amusement, or even my financial solvency when it comes right down to it.

The truth is, we are *all* in a position to learn from one another, and the moment we stop recognizing this is the moment our brains start fossilizing into a closed pit of mush.

Don Tyson, Tyson Foods

Politics is a series of unsentimental transactions between those who need votes and those who have money.

Sun Tzu

Therefore the considerations of the intelligent always include both benefit and harm.

What is of extreme importance in war is to attack the enemy's strategy.

~U~

Stewart L. Udall

America today stands poised on a pinnacle of wealth and power, yet we live in a land of vanishing beauty, of increasing ugliness, of shrinking open space, and of an over-all environment that is diminished daily by pollution and noise and blight.

Ukrainian Proverb

The church is near but the roads are icy. The tavern is far but I will walk carefully.

Miguel de Unamuno

Sometimes to remain silent is to lie.

U.S. Armed Forces Survival Manual

A hand grenade exploded in a school of fish will supply food for days.

U.S. Navy

By using the deck striping as a guide, you will avoid the embarrassing experience of taxiing a plane right over the side into all of that water. It is pretty generally agreed that a plane parked under several hundred feet of water is improperly parked.
-- Taxi Sense, Aviation Training Division, Office of the Chief of Naval Operations, U.S. Government Printing Office 1944, NAVAER 00-80Q-20 OPNAV 33-5

US Supreme Court

If there is a bedrock principle underlying the First Amendment, it is that the Government may not prohibit the expression of an idea simply because society finds the idea itself offensive or disagreeable.
- Justice William J. Brennan, writing for the majority in "Texas v. Johnson" 491 U.S. 397 (1989)

In the Armed Forces, as everywhere else, there are good men and rascals, courageous men and cowards, honest men and cheats.
-- Ball et al. v. U.S.

The Constitution grants Congress and the President the power to acquire, dispose of, and govern territory, not the power to decide when and where its terms apply...

Security depends upon a sophisticated intelligence apparatus and the ability of our Armed Forces to act and to interdict. There are further considerations, however. Security subsists, too, in fidelity to freedom's first principles...

Liberty and security can be reconciled; and in our system they are reconciled within the framework of the law...

The laws and Constitution are designed to survive, and remain in force, in extraordinary times.
- Justice Anthony M. Kennedy, writing for the majority in "Boumediene et al. v. Bush, President of the United States, et al." 553 U. S. ____ (2008)

The jury has the right to judge both the law as well as the fact in controversy.
- Chief Justice John Jay, Georgia vs. Brailsford, 1794

The price of lawful public dissent must not be a dread of subjection to an unchecked surveillance power. Nor must the fear of unauthorized official eavesdropping deter vigorous citizen dissent and discussion of Government action in private conversation. For private dissent, no less than open public discourse, is essential to our free society...

Official surveillance, whether its purpose be criminal investigation or ongoing intelligence gathering, risks infringement of constitutionally protected privacy of speech. Security surveillances are especially sensitive because of the inherent vagueness of the domestic security concept, the necessarily broad and continuing nature of intelligence gathering, and the temptation to utilize such surveillances to oversee political dissent. We recognize, as we have before, the constitutional basis of the President's domestic security role, but we think it must be exercised in a manner compatible with the Fourth Amendment. In this case we hold that this requires an appropriate prior warrant procedure.
-- United States v. United States District Court, 407 U.S. 297 (1972)

US Third Circuit Court of Appeals

As the most participatory form of mass speech yet developed, the Internet deserves the highest protection from government intrusion.

Just as the strength of the Internet is chaos, so the strength of our liberty depends upon the chaos and cacophony of the unfettered speech the First Amendment protects.

US v Dougherty, 1972

The jury has unreviewable and irreversible power to acquit in disregard of the instruction given by the trial judge.

US Lawn Mower Racing Association

Being on national television takes lawn mower racing to a new level.

~V~

Jeff Valdez

Cats are smarter than dogs. You can't get eight cats to pull a sled through snow.

Paul Valery

A man who is 'of sound mind' is one who keeps the inner madman under lock and key.

There could be real peace only if everyone were satisfied. That means there is not often a real peace. There are only actual states of peace which, like wars, are mere expedients.

Bill Van

Accusing the people you are debating of making irrational accusations they haven't made and would never make is not the true path to harmony.

Martin Van Buren

Railroad carriages are pulled at the enormous speed of fifteen miles per hour by engines which, in addition to endangering life and limb of passengers, roar and snort their way through the countryside, setting fire to the crops, scaring the livestock, and frightening women and children. The Almighty certainly never intended that people should travel at such break-neck speed.

Tom Vanderbilt

The more time spent in assembling a toy, the less it will actually be used. (A corollary: The packaging is inevitably more interesting than what's inside.)

Bill Vaughan

A citizen of America will cross the ocean to fight for democracy, but won't cross the street to vote in a national election.

If there is anything the nonconformist hates worse than a conformist, it's another nonconformist who doesn't conform to the prevailing standard of nonconformity.

Thorstein Veblen

The Dog...commends himself to our favour by affording play to our propensity for mastery and as he is also an item of expense, and commonly serves no industrial purpose, he holds a well-assured place in men's regard as a thing of good repute.

Juha Veijalainen

This must be true. It was on the major national newspaper, on three TV channels and on two tabloids.

Veronique Chez Sheep

As an adult, I only know what I read on the internet.

Don't use superglue on the condom next time.

I admit, it hadn't occurred to me that either of them looked fat, just that they had great sheep.

I'm hoping the mountain lion population will increase and keep the coyote and mountain biker population in check.

I've known a few middle-aged guys who smoke pot regularly, and a 'permanent state of duh-ness' is an eloquent descriptor.

Nothing on earth would make me do more research on this.

Soccer is a game of finesse and beauty and sexy knees. Which are unpadded and shown in all their glory.

Some days there isn't enough herring in the world to give you the smack you're asking for.

Thank heavens I'm atheist, otherwise I'd be in fear of going to hell.

Gore Vidal

Half of the American people have never read a newspaper. Half never voted for President. One hopes it is the same half.

It is not enough to succeed; others must fail.

It makes no difference who you vote for--the two parties are really one party representing four percent of the people.

On the whole history tends to be rather poor fiction - except at its best.

Viet Tam Luu

There's no such thing as a setback, only progress in another direction.

Elaine Viets

Snake removal is a man's job...Personally, I think it's ridiculous. Everyone knows men have a God-given mission to remove big, hairy spiders.

Kevin Vigor

I came in late on this thread, which of course grants me license to make wild unsubstantiated claims based on utter ignorance.
- March 28, 1997 in alt.folklore.urban

Viking proverb

A man should be wise, but not overly wise, lest he know his fate in advance.

Praise not the day until evening has come; a woman until she is burnt; a sword until it is tried; a maiden until she is married; ice until it has been crossed; beer until it has been drunk.

Pancho Villa

Don't let it end like this. Tell them I said something.
- last words

Judith Viorst

Love is the same as like except you feel sexier.

You end up as you deserve. In old age you must put up with the face, the friends, the health, and the children you have earned.

Rick Vizachero

Once again, somebody had taken a fast, reliable, easy, useful program and turned it to gooey mud in the pursuit of the GUI like interface.

They call it a 24 hour support line because it takes 24 hours for anybody to answer the phone.

Voltaire (François-Marie Arouet)

A witty saying proves nothing.

"Alas!" said Candide, "I have known this love...all it has ever brought me was one kiss and twenty kicks in the ass."
- Candide

All the persecutors declare against each other mortal war, while the philosopher, oppressed by them all, contents himself with pitying them.

Appreciation is a wonderful thing; it makes what is excellent in others belong to us as well.

God created sex. Priests created marriage.

In fact natural law teaches us to kill our neighbor, and this is how people behave all over the world. If we do not exercise our right to eat him, that is because we have other ingredients for a good meal..."
- Candide

In general, the art of government consists in taking as much money as possible from one class of the citizens to give to the other.

In this country we find it pays to shoot an admiral from time to time to encourage the others.
- Candide

It is dangerous to be right in matters on which the established authorities are wrong.

It is said that God is always on the side of the heaviest battalions.

Marriage is the only adventure open to the cowardly.

"My fair lady," replied Candide, "when a man is in love, jealous, and whipped by the Inquisition, he is out of his mind."
- Candide

Originality is nothing but judicious imitation.

Since the whole affair had become one of religion, the vanquished were of course exterminated.

The public is a ferocious beast: one must either chain it up or flee from it.

Those who can make you believe absurdities, can make you commit atrocities.

To succeed in this world it is not enough to be stupid, you must also be well-mannered.

When it is a question of money, everybody is of the same religion.

Work keeps away three great evils: boredom, vice and need.

Kurt Vonnegut

All of the true things I am about to tell you are shameless lies.

Make love when you can. It's good for you.

Nothing compares to the complicated futility of ignorance.
- Hocus Pocus

We are what we pretend to be, so we must be careful about what we pretend to be.

Where's evil? It's that large part of every man that wants to hate without limit, that wants to hate with god on its side...

It's that part of an imbecile...that punishes and vilifies and makes war gladly.
-- Howard W. Campbell, Jr, Mother Night

~W~

Don Wade, "Evansville Courier"
[Author of Always Alabama: The History of Crimson Tide Football]

To be an NFL running back is to always be running through a busy intersection with huge trucks in impassioned pursuit.

Tom Waits

The large print giveth, and the small print taketh away.

Lieutenant Commander **John C. Waldron**, Torpedo 8, USS Hornet

God must look after drunks and marines.

David Wall

If you expect tender loving from a taser you're in for a shock.

It's easy to resist temptation when it comes in the form of Budweiser.

David Glenn Walker

Your most sacred possession is your integrity.

George Wallace

I look like a white man. But my heart's as black as anyone's.

Horace Walpole

Life is a comedy for those who think and a tragedy for those who feel.

Andy Walton

I am a descendant of Florida, Florida State and Univ of Georgia grads. This goes a long way toward explaining why I went to a school with no football team.

Joe Waltz, Jr, DA for Houma, LA

It's our job to prosecute criminals, not barbers

Bob Ward

A 16 pound sledgehammer is not always better than a 16 oz ball peen hammer

Give a man a fish, feed him for a day. Teach a man to fish, and he'll want to come along and drink all your beer.

I've got a black belt in buffet, but I still don't like the Jell-o oozing over the crab legs.

knowing the sekret buzzwords and formulae no more makes you an economist than owning a pencil makes you a poet.

Life's too short for food that doesn't taste good.

The fact that I read most of the threads here in no way obligates me to share my opinion (if any) of the subject under discussion.

When I was a yoot, the Southern Baptist church I attended had no pews - they had folding chairs bolted together in racks of five. I can testify that, if one is napping in the back row, tipping the whole row back on the back legs, the noise when gravity wins out is enough to wake the entire congregation.

Peter Ward

I didn't get where I am today by over-exerting myself.

To be a good mathematician, you have to learn the expression "and so, trivially", and the best times to use it so you can leave a large chunk out of your working.

Andrew Warinner

I don't know why you set up this particular straw man but somewhere there is a pig unable to build his house.

John Warren, Ph.D. (www.lovingdominant.org)

The level of misinformation on the net can be truly shocking.

Shared learning is often the best learning.

If eccentric people are stupid, they tend to be classified as "just plain crazy." Unless, of course, if they are stupid and have money which returns them to the "eccentric" classification. <grin>

Patricia J. Washburn

If I did kill someone, it would probably be anyone who ever said to me, "You could be so pretty if you'd just lose a few pounds."

Booker T. Washington

No race can prosper till it learns that there is as much dignity in tilling a field as in writing a poem

You can't hold a man down without staying down with him.

Government is not reason; it is not eloquence; it is force! Like fire, it is a dangerous servant and a fearful master.

George Washington

Few men have virtue to withstand the highest bidder.

Observe good faith and justice toward all nations. Cultivate peace and harmony with all.

The immediate objectives are the total destruction and devastation of [Indian] settlements. It will be essential to ruin their crops in the ground and prevent their planting more.

Laurence Watkins (http://www.brainsurgery.co.uk/watkins/)

There are lots of good reasons for making a hole in someone's head, and in a neurosurgeon's hands it is not a risky procedure, but for someone doing it themselves the risks are huge.

J.D. Watson

One could not be a successful scientist without realizing that, in contrast to the popular conception supported by newspapers and mothers of scientists, a goodly number of scientists are not only narrow-minded and dull, but also just stupid.
- The Double Helix

J.C. Watts

What good does it do to hook kids up to computers if it merely speeds up the process by which they receive bad ideas.

Evelyn Waugh

I was driven into writing because I found it was the only way a lazy and ill-educated man could make a decent living.

John Wayne

A friend told me to shoot first and ask questions later. I was going to ask him why, but I had to shoot him.
- on Rowan & Martin's Laugh-In

I can't be in this picture ["Blazing Saddles"], it's too dirty...but I'll be the first in line to see it.

Earl Weaver

Are you going to get any better or is this it?

Bob Webster

When you drill a hole in your skull, or even if someone else drills it for you, some fairly major side effects can creep up.

Charlie Weis

Everybody knows how prestigious the Notre Dame quarterback is. There's one thing everybody in the country is going to know, they're going to know who the president of the United States is and they're going to know who the quarterback of Notre Dame is.

Orson Welles

I hate television. I hate it as much as peanuts. But I can't stop eating peanuts.

My doctor told me to stop having intimate dinners for four. Unless there are three other people.

We began to realize, as we plowed on with the destruction of New Jersey, that the extent of our American lunatic fringe had been underestimated.
- on the reaction to the "War Of The Worlds" broadcast.

Arthur Wellesley, Duke of Wellington

I am one of those who think it very desirable to have no reform. I told you years ago that the people are rotten to the core.

Nothing except a battle lost can be half so melancholy as a battle won.

There are no manifestos like cannon and musketry.

They came on in the same old way, and we sent them back in the same old way.

H. G. Wells

Advertising is legalized lying.

John Wesley

Hence even the children of God are not agreed as to the interpretation of many places in holy writ; nor is their difference of opinion any proof that they are not the children of God.

Jassamyn West

We want the facts to fit the preconceptions. When they don't, it is easier to ignore the facts than to change the preconceptions.

Mae West

A man in the house is worth two on the street

Give a man a free hand and he will run it all over you.
- "Klondike Annie"

I only like two kinds of men: foreign and domestic.

When women go wrong, men go right after them.

Rebecca West

All our Western thought is founded on this repulsive pretence that pain is the proper price of any good thing

Before a war military science seems a real science, like astronomy; but after a war it seems more like astrology.

I myself have never been able to find out what feminism is; I only know that people call me a feminist whenever I express sentiments that differentiate me from a doormat or a prostitute.

It is sometimes very hard to tell the difference between history and the smell of skunk.

Dr. **Ruth Westheimer**

We have two hands. What's wrong with having one of them on the mouse?

Edith Wharton

An unalterable and unquestioned law of the musical world required that the German text of French operas sung by Swedish artists should be translated into Italian for the clearer understanding of English speaking audiences.

Specialist **Michael Wheeler**, US Army

Sadomasochism has gotten a bad rap.

E. B. White

Democracy is the recurrent suspicion that more than half of the people are right more than half of the time.

The time not to become a father is eighteen years before a world war.

To perceive Christmas through its wrapping becomes more difficult with every year.

Theodore White

The magic Camelot of John F. Kennedy never existed.

William Allen White

Go east and you hear them laugh at Kansas; go west and they sneer at her; go south and they cuss her; go north and they have forgotten her. Go into any crowd of intelligent people gathered anywhere on the globe, and you will find the Kansas man on the defensive
- "What's the Matter with Kansas?"

Alfred North Whitehead

Knowledge does not keep any better than fish.
- "The Aims of Education"

The great advances in civilization are processes that all but wreck societies in which they occur.

Katherine Whitehorn

A food is not necessarily essential just because your child hates it.

Outside every thin woman is a fat man trying to get in.

Mr. Whitekeys

We all want to bribe a politician. We all thought it'd take a Mercedes or a Porsche. Nobody knew you could buy a politician for the cost of a used riding lawn mower.

Charlotte Whitton

Whatever women do they must do twice as well as men to be thought half as good. Luckily this is not difficult.

Doctor Who

Gosh that takes me back...or is it forward? That's the trouble with time travel, you never can tell.
- "Androids of Tara"

The very powerful and the very stupid have one thing in common; they don't alter their views to fit the facts. They alter the facts to fit their views.

Wibble

I prefer Yorkshire terriers myself, deep fried in a good beer batter.
- December 12, 1998 in alt.folklore.urban

Every dark cloud has a silver lining. Lightning kills most of those who look for it.

Oscar Wilde

A gentleman is one who never hurts anyone's feelings unintentionally.

Always forgive your enemies nothing annoys them so much.

An idea that is not dangerous is unworthy of being called an idea at all.

As long as war is looked upon as wicked, it will always have its fascination. When it is looked upon as vulgar, it will cease to be popular.

Bachelors should be heavily taxed. It's not fair that some men should be happier than others.

Bigamy is having one wife too many. Monogamy is the same.

Consistency is the last refuge of the unimaginative.

Don't you realize that missionaries are the divinely provided food for destitute and underfed cannibals? Whenever they are on the brink of starvation, Heaven in its infinite mercy sends them a nice plump missionary.

I am not young enough to know everything.

I don't like principles. I prefer prejudices. They are more honest.

I like persons better than principles and I like persons with no principles better than anything else in the world.

It is a very sad thing that nowadays there is so little useless information.

Men marry because they are tired; women because they are curious. Both are disappointed.
- "A Woman of No Importance"

Moderation is a fatal thing. Nothing succeeds like excess.

Patriotism is the virtue of the vicious.

Philosophy teaches us to bear with equanimity the misfortunes of others.

The only way to get rid of temptation is to yield to it.

The pure and simple truth is rarely pure and never simple.

There is much to be said in favor of modern journalism. By giving us the opinions of the uneducated, it keeps us in touch with the ignorance of the community.

There is nothing in the world like the devotion of a married woman. It is a thing no married man knows anything about.

Wickedness is a myth invented by good people to account for the curious attractiveness of others.

Work is the curse of the drinking class.

Billy Wilder

France is the only country where the money falls apart and you can't tear the toilet paper.

Eric Williams

Slavery was not born of racism: rather, racism was the consequence of slavery.

Robin Williams

[Living in Los Angeles is] like being a hemophiliac in a razor factory.

The main difference between cats and dogs is you'll never see a cat running around a park going, "Let's Chase Frisbees!"

You imagine purgatory is something like [Los Angeles] except not such good parking. It's always 'How am I doing? Where am I on the food chain?'

Charles V. Willie, Sociologist and Professor Emeritus, Harvard Graduate School of Education.

Both conflict and cooperation are essential in community life. Like pain in the human body, conflict in the community indicates that something is wrong and needs to change.

By idolizing those whom we honor, we do a disservice both to them and to ourselves... we fail to recognize that we could go and do likewise.

Teachers cannot educate students in whom they have no confidence and students cannot learn from teachers whom they do not trust. These reciprocal beliefs when implemented together result as esteem for teachers by students and esteem for students by teachers.

Theresa Willis

Using a light pole in lieu of brakes is not the best way to stop a car.

Earl Wilson

If you think nobody cares if you're alive, try missing a couple of car payments.

Woodrow Wilson

If a dog will not come to you after having looked you in the face, you should go home and examine your conscience.

If you want to make enemies, try to change something.

No man can sit down and withhold his hands from the warfare against wrong and get peace from his acquiescence.

No one who has read official documents needs to be told how easy it is to conceal the essential truth under the apparently candid and all-disclosing phrases of a voluminous and particularizing report.

Once lead this people into war and they will forget there ever was such a thing as tolerance.

Only a peace between equals can last.

The chief embarrassment in discussing the office [of Vice President] is that in explaining how little there is to say about it one has evidently said all there is to say.

The freedom of the seas is the sine qua non of peace, equality and co-operation.

The right is more precious than peace.

The world must be made safe for democracy. Its peace must be planted on the tested foundations of political liberty.

There must be, not a balance of power, but a community of power; not organized rivalries, but an organized peace.

Erastus Wiman

Nothing is ever lost by courtesy. It is the cheapest of pleasures, costs nothing, and conveys much.

"Winchester Evening Star"

Nixon, probably, is basically a moderate conservative, though with some liberal tendencies. Kennedy is basically a moderate liberal, but with many conservative leanings.
- February 1958

Katarina Witt

My photos have some kind of innocence to them--as innocent as you can be when you are naked.

George Witton, Lieutenant, Bushveldt Carbineers

War is calculated to make men's natures both callous and vengeful, and when civilised rules and customs are departed from on one side, reprisals are sure to follow on the other
-- Scapegoats of the Empire: The True Story of Breaker Morant's Bushveldt Carbineers

P. G. Wodehouse

He spoke with a certain what-is-it in his voice, and I could see that, if not actually disgruntled, he was far from being gruntled.
- The Code of the Woosters

Judges, as a class, display, in the matter of arranging alimony, that reckless generosity which is found only in men who are giving away someone else's cash.

The fascination of shooting as a sport depends almost wholly on whether you are at the right or wrong end of the gun.

Gene Wolfe

There is no limit to stupidity. Space itself is said to be bounded by its own curvature, but stupidity continues beyond infinity.

John Wooden

Off the court, we disagreed, but I always taught we can disagree but we don't have to be disagreeable.

There's no progress without change. However, all change isn't progress.

Wooden Leg

I do not know where [Sitting Bull was during the battle]. I had not thought about trying to find out. I suppose he was helping the women and children and old people, where he belonged. He had a son in the fight. Any man having a son serving as a warrior was expected to stay out of battles and give the son his chance to get warrior honors.

Harriet Woods

You can stand tall without standing on someone. You can be a victor without having victims.

Virginia Woolf

On the outskirts of every agony sits some observant fellow who points.

For most of history, Anonymous was a woman.

Frank Lloyd Wright

A doctor can bury his mistakes but an architect can only advise his clients to plant vines.

Early in life I had to choose between honest arrogance and hypocritical humility. I chose the former and have seen no reason to change.

Television is chewing gum for the eyes.

Many wealthy people are little more than janitors of their possessions.

Tim Wright

Good gravy is it's own food group.

I used to blame our kids behavior on my wife's mis-spent youth, till she reminded me she mis-spent her youth with me.

Re-orgs are excellent means for taking happy employees, slamming them into a crappy organization and crushing their spirit. At the same time they take the spiritually precrushed and put them into a warm, nurturing, fulfilling group just long enough to give them a brief glimmer of hope and happiness before slamming them back into hell on the next re-org.

~X~

Malcolm X

Education is our key to the future. For, tomorrow belongs to those who prepare for it today.

You can't separate peace from freedom because no one can be at peace unless he has his freedom.

The X Files

Life is like a box of chocolates. A cheap, thoughtless, perfunctory gift that nobody ever asks for. Unreturnable, because all you get back is another box of chocolates. You're stuck with this undefinable whipped-mint crap that you mindlessly wolf down when there's nothing else left to eat. Sure, once in a while, there's a peanut butter cup, or an English toffee. But they're gone too fast, the taste is fleeting. So you end up with nothing but broken bits, filled with hardened jelly and teeth-crunching nuts, and if you're desperate enough to eat those, all you've got left is an empty box filled with useless, brown paper wrappers.

Ninety nine percent of the people of this world are fools, and the rest of us are in great danger of contagion.

Xho

It is hard to be proactively retrospective, so I'll just have to wait.

Your feelings of self-certainty are poor replacements for truth.

~Y~

Chuck Yeager

Never wait for trouble.

Rules are made for people who aren't willing to make up their own.

You do what you can for as long as you can, and when you finally can't, you do the next best thing. You back up but you don't give up.

You don't concentrate on risks. You concentrate on results. No risk is too great to prevent the necessary job from getting done.

Boris Yeltsin

You can build a throne with bayonets, but you can't sit on it for long.

Anne C. Young

Never underestimate the power of brains and a push up bra.

Bill Young, POW

Sometimes, when crimes have been committed it is necessary to go back and mark the spot.

Brigham Young

I love the Constitution and government of this land, but I hate the damned rascals that administer the government.

Edward Young

We are all born originals why is it so many of us die copies?

Lin Yutang

Besides the noble art of getting things done, there is the noble art of leaving things undone. The wisdom of life consists in the elimination of non-essentials.

If you can spend a perfectly useless afternoon in a perfectly useless manner, you have learned how to live.

~Z~

Jeff Zahn

[It] contains "vegetable stabilizer" which sounds ominous. How unstable are vegetables?

Israel Zangwill

The Jews are a frightened people. Twenty centuries of Christian love have broken down their nerves.

Darryl F. Zanuck

If two men on the same job agree all the time, then one is useless. If they disagree all the time, then both are useless.

Emiliano Zapata

It is better to die on your feet than to live on your knees.

<zaphkiel@ix.netcom.com>

Fear not the flames of your fellow man. Think of it as an opportunity to learn, or, as I have found out, as an opportunity to giggle. :)

Heck, accurate untruths is first year law school stuff. It's considered a cake course.

In Sanskrit, they have a beautiful word for suffering. They call it veydana. It has two meanings. Suffering is one, and knowledge is the other. Vedana comes from the root veda. Veda is the source of knowledge. Suffering is knowledge. Ignorance is bliss.

Oh, sure, they SAY 'blessed are the peacemakers', but the next thing you know it's another crusade or jihad. Even Buddhists, who are about as peaceful as you can get, occasionally get out the old lighter fluid and set themselves on fire.

The power of love. Apparently you aren't familiar with it? It's most intoxicating, and must be freely offered.

Frank Zappa

Everything you know is wrong.

If your children ever find out how lame you really are, they're gonna murder you in your sleep.

In the fight between you and the world, back the world.

Most rock journalism is people who can't write interviewing people who can't talk for people who can't read.

You can't be a Real Country unless you have A BEER and an airline. It helps if you have some kind of a football team, or some nuclear weapons, but at the very least you need a BEER.

David Zeiger

Whenever I find myself in a difficult situation, I ask myself "What Would Jesus Do?" The mental image of my opposition being cast into pits of hellfire for all eternity *is* comforting, but probably not what the inventors of the phrase had in mind.

Zen Saying

Anything one cannot bear to give up is not owned, but is in fact the owner.

Before the enlightenment, I chopped wood and carried water. After the enlightenment, I chopped wood and carried water.

Adolf Ziegler, President of the Reich Culture Chamber, 1937

Our patience with all those who have not been able to fall in line is at an end... What you are seeing here are the crippled products of madness, impertinence, and lack of talent... I would need several freight trains to clear our galleries of this rubbish...This will happen soon.

Stephan Zielinski

Don't get angry at the New Agers. Sell them something.

Zig Ziglar

Kids go where there is excitement. They stay where there is love.

Fuzzy Zoeller

The fact I've seen guys stone-cold drunk beat guys stone-cold sober tells you what kind of game golf is.

Carl Zwanzig

Duct tape is like the force. It has a light side, and a dark side, and it holds the universe together.

"You're still here? It's over! Go Home"
- Ferris Bueller

Appendix 1 – GNU Free Documentation License

0. PREAMBLE

The purpose of this License is to make a manual, textbook, or other functional and useful document "free" in the sense of freedom: to assure everyone the effective freedom to copy and redistribute it, with or without modifying it, either commercially or noncommercially. Secondarily, this License preserves for the author and publisher a way to get credit for their work, while not being considered responsible for modifications made by others.

This License is a kind of "copyleft", which means that derivative works of the document must themselves be free in the same sense. It complements the GNU General Public License, which is a copyleft license designed for free software.

We have designed this License in order to use it for manuals for free software, because free software needs free documentation: a free program should come with manuals providing the same freedoms that the software does. But this License is not limited to software manuals; it can be used for any textual work, regardless of subject matter or whether it is published as a printed book. We recommend this License principally for works whose purpose is instruction or reference.

1. APPLICABILITY AND DEFINITIONS

This License applies to any manual or other work, in any medium, that contains a notice placed by the copyright holder saying it can be distributed under the terms of this License. Such a notice grants a world-wide, royalty-free license, unlimited in duration, to use that work under the conditions stated herein. The "Document", below, refers to any such manual or work. Any member of the public is a licensee, and is addressed as "you". You accept the license if you copy, modify or distribute the work in a way requiring permission under copyright law.

A "Modified Version" of the Document means any work containing the Document or a portion of it, either copied verbatim, or with modifications and/or translated into another language.

A "Secondary Section" is a named appendix or a front-matter section of the Document that deals exclusively with the relationship of the publishers or authors of the Document to the Document's overall subject (or to related matters) and contains nothing that could fall directly within that overall subject. (Thus, if the Document is in part a textbook of mathematics, a Secondary Section may not explain any mathematics.) The relationship could be a matter of historical connection with the subject or with related matters, or of legal, commercial, philosophical, ethical or political position regarding them.

The "Invariant Sections" are certain Secondary Sections whose titles are designated, as being those of Invariant Sections, in the notice that says that the Document is released under this License. If a section does not fit the above definition of Secondary then it is not allowed to be designated as Invariant. The Document may contain zero Invariant Sections. If the Document does not identify any Invariant Sections then there are none.

The "Cover Texts" are certain short passages of text that are listed, as Front-Cover Texts or Back-Cover Texts, in the notice that says that the Document is released under this License. A Front-Cover Text may be at most 5 words, and a Back-Cover Text may be at most 25 words.

A "Transparent" copy of the Document means a machine-readable copy, represented in a format whose specification is available to the general public, that is suitable for revising the document straightforwardly with generic text editors or (for images composed of pixels) generic paint programs or (for drawings) some widely available drawing editor, and that is suitable for input to text formatters or for automatic translation to a variety of formats suitable for input to text formatters. A copy made in an otherwise Transparent file format whose markup, or absence of markup, has been arranged to thwart or discourage subsequent modification by readers is not Transparent. An image format is not Transparent if used for any substantial amount of text. A copy that is not "Transparent" is called "Opaque".

Examples of suitable formats for Transparent copies include plain ASCII without markup, Texinfo input format, LaTeX input format, SGML or XML using a publicly available DTD, and standard-conforming simple HTML, PostScript or PDF designed for human modification. Examples of transparent image formats include PNG, XCF and JPG. Opaque formats include proprietary formats that can be read and edited only by proprietary word processors, SGML or XML for which the DTD and/or processing tools are not generally available, and the machine-generated HTML, PostScript or PDF produced by some word processors for output purposes only.

The "Title Page" means, for a printed book, the title page itself, plus such following pages as are needed to hold, legibly, the material this License requires to appear in the title page. For works in formats which do not have any title page as such, "Title Page" means the text near the most prominent appearance of the work's title, preceding the beginning of the body of the text.

A section "Entitled XYZ" means a named subunit of the Document whose title either is precisely XYZ or contains XYZ in parentheses following text that translates XYZ in another language. (Here XYZ stands for a specific section name mentioned below, such as "Acknowledgements", "Dedications", "Endorsements", or "History".) To "Preserve the Title" of such a section when you modify the Document means that it remains a section "Entitled XYZ" according to this definition.

The Document may include Warranty Disclaimers next to the notice which states that this License applies to the Document. These Warranty Disclaimers are considered to be included by reference in this License, but only as regards disclaiming warranties: any other implication that these Warranty Disclaimers may have is void and has no effect on the meaning of this License.

2. VERBATIM COPYING

You may copy and distribute the Document in any medium, either commercially or noncommercially, provided that this License, the copyright notices, and the license notice saying this License applies to the Document are reproduced in all copies, and that you add no other conditions whatsoever to those of this License. You may not use technical measures to obstruct or control the reading or further copying of the copies you make or distribute. However, you may accept compensation in exchange for copies. If you distribute a large enough number of copies you must also follow the conditions in section 3.

You may also lend copies, under the same conditions stated above, and you may publicly display copies.

3. COPYING IN QUANTITY

If you publish printed copies (or copies in media that commonly have printed covers) of the Document, numbering more than 100, and the Document's license notice requires Cover Texts, you must enclose the copies in covers that carry, clearly and legibly, all these Cover Texts: Front-Cover Texts on the front cover, and Back-Cover Texts on the back cover. Both covers must also clearly and legibly identify you as the publisher of these copies. The front cover must present the full title with all words of the title equally prominent and visible. You may add other material on the covers in addition. Copying with changes limited to the covers, as long as they preserve the title of the Document and satisfy these conditions, can be treated as verbatim copying in other respects.

If the required texts for either cover are too voluminous to fit legibly, you should put the first ones listed (as many as fit reasonably) on the actual cover, and continue the rest onto adjacent pages.

If you publish or distribute Opaque copies of the Document numbering more than 100, you must either include a machine-readable Transparent copy along with each Opaque copy, or state in or with each Opaque copy a computer-network location from which the general network-using public has access to download using public-standard network protocols a complete Transparent copy of the Document, free of added material. If you use the latter option, you must take reasonably prudent steps, when you begin distribution of Opaque copies in quantity, to ensure that this Transparent copy will remain thus accessible at the stated location until at least one year after the last time you distribute an Opaque copy (directly or through your agents or retailers) of that edition to the public.

It is requested, but not required, that you contact the authors of the Document well before redistributing any large number of copies, to give them a chance to provide you with an updated version of the Document.

4. MODIFICATIONS

You may copy and distribute a Modified Version of the Document under the conditions of sections 2 and 3 above, provided that you release the Modified Version under precisely this License, with the Modified Version filling the role of the Document, thus licensing distribution and modification of the Modified Version to whoever possesses a copy of it. In addition, you must do these things in the Modified Version:

- **A.** Use in the Title Page (and on the covers, if any) a title distinct from that of the Document, and from those of previous versions (which should, if there were any, be listed in the History section of the Document). You may use the same title as a previous version if the original publisher of that version gives permission.
- **B.** List on the Title Page, as authors, one or more persons or entities responsible for authorship of the modifications in the Modified Version, together with at least five of the principal authors of the Document (all of its principal authors, if it has fewer than five), unless they release you from this requirement.
- **C.** State on the Title page the name of the publisher of the Modified Version, as the publisher.
- **D.** Preserve all the copyright notices of the Document.
- **E.** Add an appropriate copyright notice for your modifications adjacent to the other copyright notices.
- **F.** Include, immediately after the copyright notices, a license notice giving the public permission to use the Modified Version under the terms of this License, in the form shown in the Addendum below.
- **G.** Preserve in that license notice the full lists of Invariant Sections and required Cover Texts given in the Document's license notice.
- **H.** Include an unaltered copy of this License.
- **I.** Preserve the section Entitled "History", Preserve its Title, and add to it an item stating at least the title, year, new authors, and publisher of the Modified Version as given on the Title Page. If there is no section Entitled "History" in the Document, create one stating the title, year, authors, and publisher of the Document as given on its Title Page, then add an item describing the Modified Version as stated in the previous sentence.
- **J.** Preserve the network location, if any, given in the Document for public access to a Transparent copy of the Document, and likewise the network locations given in the Document for previous versions it was based on. These may be placed in the "History" section. You may omit a network location for a work that

was published at least four years before the Document itself, or if the original publisher of the version it refers to gives permission.

- **K.** For any section Entitled "Acknowledgements" or "Dedications", Preserve the Title of the section, and preserve in the section all the substance and tone of each of the contributor acknowledgements and/or dedications given therein.
- **L.** Preserve all the Invariant Sections of the Document, unaltered in their text and in their titles. Section numbers or the equivalent are not considered part of the section titles.
- **M.** Delete any section Entitled "Endorsements". Such a section may not be included in the Modified Version.
- **N.** Do not retitle any existing section to be Entitled "Endorsements" or to conflict in title with any Invariant Section.
- **O.** Preserve any Warranty Disclaimers.

If the Modified Version includes new front-matter sections or appendices that qualify as Secondary Sections and contain no material copied from the Document, you may at your option designate some or all of these sections as invariant. To do this, add their titles to the list of Invariant Sections in the Modified Version's license notice. These titles must be distinct from any other section titles.

You may add a section Entitled "Endorsements", provided it contains nothing but endorsements of your Modified Version by various parties--for example, statements of peer review or that the text has been approved by an organization as the authoritative definition of a standard.

You may add a passage of up to five words as a Front-Cover Text, and a passage of up to 25 words as a Back-Cover Text, to the end of the list of Cover Texts in the Modified Version. Only one passage of Front-Cover Text and one of Back-Cover Text may be added by (or through arrangements made by) any one entity. If the Document already includes a cover text for the same cover, previously added by you or by arrangement made by the same entity you are acting on behalf of, you may not add another; but you may replace the old one, on explicit permission from the previous publisher that added the old one.

The author(s) and publisher(s) of the Document do not by this License give permission to use their names for publicity for or to assert or imply endorsement of any Modified Version.

5. COMBINING DOCUMENTS

You may combine the Document with other documents released under this License, under the terms defined in section 4 above for modified versions, provided that you include in the combination all of the Invariant Sections of all of the original documents, unmodified, and list them all as Invariant Sections of your combined work in its license notice, and that you preserve all their Warranty Disclaimers.

The combined work need only contain one copy of this License, and multiple identical Invariant Sections may be replaced with a single copy. If there are multiple Invariant Sections with the same name but different contents, make the title of each such section unique by adding at the end of it, in parentheses, the name of the original author or publisher of that section if known, or else a unique number. Make the same adjustment to the section titles in the list of Invariant Sections in the license notice of the combined work.

In the combination, you must combine any sections Entitled "History" in the various original documents, forming one section Entitled "History"; likewise combine any sections Entitled "Acknowledgements", and any sections Entitled "Dedications". You must delete all sections Entitled "Endorsements."

6. COLLECTIONS OF DOCUMENTS

You may make a collection consisting of the Document and other documents released under this License, and replace the individual copies of this License in the various documents with a single copy that is included in the collection, provided that you follow the rules of this License for verbatim copying of each of the documents in all other respects.

You may extract a single document from such a collection, and distribute it individually under this License, provided you insert a copy of this License into the extracted document, and follow this License in all other respects regarding verbatim copying of that document.

7. AGGREGATION WITH INDEPENDENT WORKS

A compilation of the Document or its derivatives with other separate and independent documents or works, in or on a volume of a storage or distribution medium, is called an "aggregate" if the copyright resulting from the compilation is not used to limit the legal rights of the compilation's users beyond what the individual works permit. When the Document is included in an aggregate, this License does not apply to the other works in the aggregate which are not themselves derivative works of the Document.

If the Cover Text requirement of section 3 is applicable to these copies of the Document, then if the Document is less than one half of the entire aggregate, the Document's Cover Texts may be placed on covers that bracket the Document within the aggregate, or the electronic equivalent of covers if the Document is in electronic form. Otherwise they must appear on printed covers that bracket the whole aggregate.

8. TRANSLATION

Translation is considered a kind of modification, so you may distribute translations of the Document under the terms of section 4. Replacing Invariant Sections with translations requires special permission from their copyright holders, but you may include translations of some or all Invariant Sections in addition to the original versions of these Invariant Sections. You may include a translation of this License, and all the license notices in the Document, and any Warranty Disclaimers, provided that you also include the original English version of this License and the original versions of those notices and disclaimers. In case of a disagreement between the translation and the original version of this License or a notice or disclaimer, the original version will prevail.

If a section in the Document is Entitled "Acknowledgements", "Dedications", or "History", the requirement (section 4) to Preserve its Title (section 1) will typically require changing the actual title.

9. TERMINATION

You may not copy, modify, sublicense, or distribute the Document except as expressly provided for under this License. Any other attempt to copy, modify, sublicense or distribute the Document is void, and will automatically terminate your rights under this License. However, parties who have received copies, or rights, from you under this License will not have their licenses terminated so long as such parties remain in full compliance.

10. FUTURE REVISIONS OF THIS LICENSE

The Free Software Foundation may publish new, revised versions of the GNU Free Documentation License from time to time. Such new versions will be similar in spirit to the present version, but may differ in detail to address new problems or concerns. See http://www.gnu.org/copyleft/.

Each version of the License is given a distinguishing version number. If the Document specifies that a particular numbered version of this License "or any later version" applies to it, you have the option of following the terms and conditions either of that specified version or of any later version that has been published (not as a draft) by the

Free Software Foundation. If the Document does not specify a version number of this License, you may choose any version ever published (not as a draft) by the Free Software Foundation.

How to use this License for your documents

To use this License in a document you have written, include a copy of the License in the document and put the following copyright and license notices just after the title page:

> Copyright (c) YEAR YOUR NAME.
>
> Permission is granted to copy, distribute and/or modify this document
>
> under the terms of the GNU Free Documentation License, Version 1.2
>
> or any later version published by the Free Software Foundation;
>
> with no Invariant Sections, no Front-Cover Texts, and no Back-Cover Texts.
>
> A copy of the license is included in the section entitled "GNU
>
> Free Documentation License".

If you have Invariant Sections, Front-Cover Texts and Back-Cover Texts, replace the "with...Texts." line with this:

> with the Invariant Sections being LIST THEIR TITLES, with the
>
> Front-Cover Texts being LIST, and with the Back-Cover Texts being LIST.

If you have Invariant Sections without Cover Texts, or some other combination of the three, merge those two alternatives to suit the situation.

If your document contains nontrivial examples of program code, we recommend releasing these examples in parallel under your choice of free software license, such as the GNU General Public License, to permit their use in free software.

Appendix 2 – Authors who granted permission for inclusion here

Cecil Adams/Ed Zotti
Les Albert
Alan Allport
Guy Almes
Robert Alston
Eric Alterman
Piers Anthony
Dr. Robert Anthony
Laura M Antoniou
Rebekka Armstrong
Tom Armstrong
Mark Atwood
Amy Austin
Bernard Avishai
Lee Ayrton
Bill Baldwin
Scott Barnes
Randall Bart
Jerry Bauer
Bruce Baum
Peter S. Beagle
Richard Beal and Robert Sward.
Pete Becker
William J. Bennett
Annie M Benson-Lennaman
David Berlind
Charles Bishop
William B. Blakemore
Derek Bok
Elayne Boosler
James H. Boren
Nathaniel Borenstein
Bo Bradham
Gloria Brame
Mike Brandt
Joe Bob Brigg
Peter Brimelow
Peter Eng
Estron
Barry Farber
David Brin
Rosa Brooks
Fredric Brown
Jan Harold Brunvand
Richard Lee Byers
Huey Callison
Dana W. Carpender
Jonathan Carroll
Mike Causey
S. Checker
Bob Church
Paul Ciszek
Peter Coffee
Bill Conlin
Stephen Coonts
Bernard Cornwell & Susannah Kells
Tommy Craggs
Karen J. Cravens
crayfish@mail.com
Robert Crowe
Dale Dauten
L. Sprague de Camp
Stephen Dedman
David Denslow
Steve Devaux
Bill Diamond
Paul C. Dickie
Charles Wm. Dimmick
John Dodge
Glenn Dowdy
David Drake
R.H. Draney
Freeman Dyson
Dover Beach
Nicholas Eberstadt
Neal Eckhardt
John Eisenberg
Kim
Eben King
Stephen King

Mary Featherston
Mike Fester
Alan Follett
Ed Frank
John L. Freiler
David Friedmann
James Alan Gardner
Bill Gawne
Bob Geary
Dr. Darren S. A. George
David Gerrold
Kathryn Ghent
Hank Gillette
Michael Glaser
Mike Godwin
Lee Gomes
Robert Goodman
Laura Goodwin
Greg Goss
GrapeApe@AOL.com
groo
Lt. Col Dave Grossman
Ronald F. Guilmette
M C Hamster
Donna Haraway
Richard Hershberger
Hiawatha aka Dr H
Bob Hiebert, Jr.
Lizz Holmans
John Hopkin
ibm@svpal.org
Christopher Jahn
Jeannie
Martin Johnson
Andrea Jones
Alan Kay
Merle Kessler
Bob Kravitz
Larry Kubicz
Drew Lawson
Patricia Voichahoske Lehman
Tom Lehrer
Barbara Lewis
Brad Linaweaver
James Linn
Lisa Ann
Eric Lundquist
Viet Tam Luu
Pattie Maes
Tom Magliozzi
Jack Mayberry
Sanford M. Manley
Barbara Mikkelson
David Mikkelson, (Snopes)
Don Middendorf
Mitchell Moss
Chuck Muth
Joseph Nebus
Maggie Newman
nostradamus@nostradamus.net
Kevin S. O'Neill
Tom M. Oliver
Scott Ostler
Clarence Page
John Palmer
Mike Palmer
Troy Patterson
Jackie Patti
Gordon W Paynter
A. Padgett Peterson
Philip the Foole
Leonard Pitts
Jerry Pournelle

Terry Pratchett
Brian Proffit
Gloria Quinn
Kevin D. Quitt
Lee Rudolph
Rusty the Bookman
Luke Salisbury
Maggie Scarf
Mike Schilling
JoAnne Schmitz
Paul Seabury and Angelo Codevilla
Steve Sebelius
Mary Shafer
Roger C. Shank
Gary Shelton
Joe Shimkus
Leo G Simonetta
Simon Slavin
Leslie Small
Gary D. Solis
S.P. Somtow
spectrum@magenta.com
Mike Sphar
Norman Spinrad
Mark Stalzer
Ervin Staub
Gloria Steinem
Mike Stone
Lon Stowell
S. Andrew Swann
Andrew Tannenbaum
Linda Terrell
Tracy Thompson
David H. Thornley
Paul Tomplin
Edward Tufte
Bill Turlock
TyMeDwn1st
Veronique chez sheep
Elaine Viets
Kurt Vonnegut Jr.
Don Wade
David Wall (Darkon)
Bob Ward
Peter Ward
Andrew Warinner
John Warren, Ph.D.
Laurence Watkins
Charles V. Willie
Tim Wright
Stephan Zielinski

Appendix 3 – On the vagaries of trying to quote people

While assembling this collection of quotations was mostly fun, there were moments of drudgery and disappointment.

When I finally prepared to edit the book down to usable form, I had nearly 1700 sources. While some of those sources are long dead and their work is in the public domain, many were still with us or their material was still under copyright. I began a year-long effort to obtain permissions from literally hundreds of people.

Some, like Sir Terry Pratchett and Dr. Jerry Pournelle responded quickly and many provided words of encouragement. Appendix 2 listed those people who explicitly gave permission to be quoted. Such correspondence was enjoyable and more icing on the cake, but not all was so easy...

Some people or their agents refused permission to include their remarks in this work. Really, though, very few actually refused permission. In fact, only nine people or their agents actually said, "No." While the loss of most of the material did no great damage to the manuscript, I really wish I had been allowed to include the material from Dr. Isaac Asimov and Mohammed Ali. In one case, Newsweek magazine somehow overlooked my inability to pay royalties and demanded $445 for the right to quote 18 words. That material, too, is not to be found herein.

Eight people were quick to point out that they did not actually utter the snippet which was attributed to them or that they were quoting someone else. These folks were usually quite helpful in pointing me in the right direction. Some of this material was re-attributed, some met Mr. Blue Pencil.

In four cases, people gave me permission to quote them, but I chose to omit their material after all.

Many folks just didn't bother to respond. I have enough excised material from folks in this category to fill another book. For example, two efforts to reach Harlan Ellison elicited no response. Rather than waste my limited time trying to get a response, I chose to omit his five lines of text. People at the Washington Post and ESPN did not respond. Likewise, their material has been omitted. Agents were notably bad for not responding. Probably one in six bothered to answer and a third of those refused permission. In all, 180 people didn't respond and I removed their material.

The GFDL gave me a little leeway to quote people. If material has been published (normally on the web) under the GFDL, it is possible to use that material. In other cases, people have been so widely quoted without any effort to stop such quotations that the copyright has been diluted.

Still, in every case, I have been careful to keep within the de minimis* rules as applied to copyright law. In no case have I quoted a substantial portion of any author's work and I have been careful that such quotations are not done in such way as to harm the author. In some cases, I have added comments to make clear what the author intended (i.e. the quotation from David Brin).

* For example, the total number of words from Robert A. Heinlein is 118. In the context of the number of words contained in 50 published books by Mr. Heinlein (millions of words?), this is an insignificant number of words and is unlikely to dilute the value of his written work or otherwise injure the interests of the Heinlein Estate. At the same time, 118 words is an insignificant portion (0.14%) of this 83,000-word book. To paraphrase Justice Story: So little was used that the value of the original is not diminished nor have the labors of the original author substantially or to an injurious extent been appropriated.

Here endeth the lesson.

LaVergne, TN USA
28 September 2010
198859LV00003B/1/P